Described as a career crimi[nal] [...] [...]story in the underworld spanning over 50 years. Very few people have such a detailed understanding of how the violent and brutal criminal world operates and the real lives that criminals live. Born in New Zealand, James operated at the highest levels across New Zealand, Australia, England and the United States. Acknowledged by the 1983 Stewart Royal Commission as second-in-charge of the Mr Asia Drug Syndicate, he was sentenced in 1986 to 25 years' imprisonment for his involvement. Over the years he has often been approached by the media for the real Mr Asia story. A private, articulate and intelligent man, James now chooses to live a quieter life in Sydney, Australia.

MR ASIA

LAST MAN STANDING

MR ASIA
LAST MAN STANDING

JAMES 'DIAMOND JIM' SHEPHERD

MACMILLAN
Pan Macmillan Australia

First published 2010 in Macmillan by Pan Macmillan Australia Pty Limited
1 Market Street, Sydney

National Library of Australia
Cataloguing-in-Publication data:

Shepherd, James, 1941–
Mr Asia: the last man standing: inside Australia's most notorious
drug syndicate/James Shepherd.

ISBN: 978 1 4050 4020 4 (pbk.)

Shepherd, James, 1941–
Drug abuse and crime – Australasia
Drug traffic – Australasia

363.45092

Typeset in 11.5/15.5pt Sabon by Midland Typesetters, Australia
Printed by McPherson's Printing Group

Papers used by Pan Macmillan Australia Pty Ltd are natural, recyclable products made
from wood grown in sustainable forests. The manufacturing processes conform to the
environmental regulations of the country of origin.

ACKNOWLEDGEMENTS

Over the years there have been many people who have helped me survive the turbulent life I have lived. Some were family, some were people who loved me and some were friends. I would therefore like to acknowledge some of those people here.

I would like to thank my elder sister Marion, my elder brother Ron, my younger sister Faye and all my nephews and nieces for their love and support. I want you all to know that your brother and uncle is finally home from the sea.

To Glenda Hughes for your friendship and gentle persistence that was the catalyst for me eventually agreeing to write this book.

Many thanks to writer Ian David for taking the time to pass on invaluable advice and encouragement to someone trying to write a book for the very first time.

To Cec McQuillan, Tim Anderson, John O'Hara, Duncan McFarlane, Ray Miller and big-hearted Steve Moorehouse, my thanks for your friendship.

Over the years I have been represented by some dedicated and brilliant legal people. Among them were Bill O'Brien, Peter Ash and David Patch. We may not have won our High Court appeal, David, but I appreciate the long hours you and Greg James QC spent working on my case. Those sentiments go to you as well, Peter, I will never forget all the many years you tirelessly and diligently represented me on legal matters. From Croke & Associates I would like to acknowledge all the work done on my behalf by Michael Croke, Kiki Kyriakou and Maree Carey. From Chambers, the most compassionate barrister I know, April Francis, and her brilliant colleague Steven Odgers SC. For his legal advice on this book, I would also like to thank Greg Jones SC. I am forever indebted to you all.

To my agent Rick Raftos I say many thanks to you for your encouragement, advice and integrity. You have made a difficult process easy for me.

From my publisher Pan Macmillan Australia, I would like to first thank Tom Gilliatt for believing I had a story worth publishing; and secondly, my editor Joel Naoum for helping me through the demanding task of editing this book.

And finally, this book is dedicated to Cheryl, a very special lady.

FOREWORD

What you don't know won't hurt you. It's on a need to know basis and you don't need to know.

As a young police officer in Wellington, New Zealand, in the 1970s, these were my usual responses to questions about crime. I was naive enough to believe the dreadful cliché: 'What the eye doesn't see, the mind doesn't grieve.'

Thirty-nine years of life experience later, I realise that this approach enables criminally focused individuals and groups to succeed. As the first major international drug ring from New Zealand and Australia, the Mr Asia syndicate took full advantage of the secret society of corrupt police officers that existed in the seventies.

As a serving police officer in December 1978, I was directly involved in the arrest of two members of the Mr Asia syndicate (Allison Dine and Wendy Shrimpton) in Wellington. Because of this involvement with the syndicate and my later work both in the media and as a criminologist, it has always been my goal to seek the truth about this organisation. Despite 30 years having passed since the arrest of Terrence Clark, the head of the syndicate, I have been amazed at the sustained and ongoing public and media interest in this criminal group.

One important lesson I learned during my time in the police and working in the media is that very seldom does the reporting of crime by the media reveal the true reality or context of crimes that have been committed. The reporter will always be influenced by their own values and the desire for ratings and the storyteller will often relate what they think the reporter wants to hear. This results in an understated or overstated and sometimes completely incorrect version of what happened.

It is not often that you come across a prominent member of the criminal world who has sufficient self-awareness and understanding to be able to analyse the motivations behind their actions, or whose self-awareness is strong enough for their recall not to be self-serving. When I first visited James Shepherd, the man acknowledged as second-in-charge of the Mr Asia syndicate, at Parklea Maximum Security Prison in 1987, I was astonished by his insight and understanding of the downstream consequences of his actions.

In the cold, sterile environment of the Parklea Prison visitors' room, we were surrounded by many prison inmates whose lives and families had been destroyed by drugs. A fitness fanatic and a member of the old school of criminals, James has never been afflicted by drug addiction and during his time in the Mr Asia syndicate did not comprehend the full impact of his actions.

It was his regret and acknowledgement of the part he had played in the devastation of other people's lives that made me ask him if he would ever be willing to document what really happened during his time in the Mr Asia syndicate. What I was asking him for was the truth about the Mr Asia syndicate and its members. Without the truth, from those who really know, research about criminals, their motivations and the context in which they offend will always be flawed.

FOREWORD

When James finally agreed to collaborate on a book about the Mr Asia syndicate it was intended that the book be written as a reported story. But it soon became obvious that in order to maintain the integrity of this very significant piece of history it was important that James wrote the story himself. This was a tough ask as it required him to confront his demons and address many parts of his life that he had filed away in the hope that he would never again have to face up to the reality of what he had done.

James was well aware of the risks he faced both personally and publicly if he wrote his own story. And it is a brave step he has taken by doing so. James Shepherd should have been a successful contributor to society. He has all of the skills and understanding to have achieved in any field he wanted. Instead of choosing to make a positive contribution to society, James chose a life of crime. He knows he can never correct the damage he has done and he genuinely hopes that others will learn from his mistakes and not follow in his footsteps.

I would like to thank James for maintaining the integrity of our first conversation in the Parklea Prison visitors' room and writing a true account of the realities of a life of crime. His insight and understanding of criminal behaviour will benefit those who work in the area of crime prevention.

James Shepherd's story is one that we can all learn from. It is the raw account of a life that he regrets.

Glenda Hughes, 2009

Glenda served as a police officer in New Zealand for eighteen years, and has a degree in criminology and sociology.

INTRODUCTION

This is a book I never intended to write because of the realisation that if I, or anyone else, wrote an honest, factual book about the Mr Asia drug syndicate, it would evoke in me uncomfortable memories of a period of my life that I am not proud of. I first started to seriously think about writing this book after a meeting I had in Sydney in May 2004 with John Keir, a television producer from New Zealand. A trusted friend of mine, Glenda Hughes, a well-known business and media personality from Wellington, had arranged the meeting to discuss whether I was willing to appear in a two-hour documentary about the Mr Asia drug syndicate that John Keir was producing for TVNZ. As John Keir explained during our meeting, in six months time it would be 25 years since Terrence Clark – the acknowledged head of the Mr Asia syndicate – and other members of the syndicate were arrested in London and charged with murder and drug trafficking, thus effectively bringing to an end the Mr Asia drug empire.

It was John Keir's view that as the syndicate was initiated and controlled by New Zealanders, he felt it represented a huge part of

New Zealand's criminal history and was a story that had never been accurately or properly told. It was his personal belief that the public should be told the true story about the syndicate. As all the other senior members of the syndicate were now dead, he thought that someone like myself, who had been involved at the highest level, would be able to help him with his project. Despite John Keir's genuine desire to produce an authentic documentary about the Mr Asia syndicate, I declined his financial offer to be interviewed or involved. This was not the first time I had been approached to tell the real story about the Mr Asia syndicate but, after speaking with John Keir that Friday evening, I came to the realisation that no matter how valid his personal integrity was or how good his intentions were, without my personal involvement there was no way he or anyone else could make an accurate documentary.

My change of heart about writing this book has been influenced by the continued public interest in the Mr Asia syndicate, despite the fact that 30 years have elapsed since the head of the syndicate, Terry Clark, was arrested in London on 31 October 1979. The *Underbelly* television series shown on Channel 9 in Australia which centred on Terry Clark and the Mr Asia syndicate, once again highlighted this continuing public interest. After watching that *Underbelly* television series, I am now of the firm belief that the public should be told the real truth about what actually happened inside the Mr Asia syndicate between 1976 and 1979.

The three *Underbelly* television series, whether by design or not, have glamorised criminals and criminal behaviour. Because of that disquieting fact, I have also written this book to tell people that criminals and the crimes they commit are not glamorous and should not be portrayed as such. All the people who were associated with the Mr Asia syndicate between 1976 and 1979 – and that includes me – were nasty, vicious, immoral and evil. We made a living off other people's addictions and misery: there is nothing glamorous about that.

I want this book to be a warning to others. Do not make the same mistakes I have made over a lifetime of violence and crime. Do not think for one instant that a life of crime is glamorous and exciting. It is not. It is a life of degradation, dishonesty, misery, violence and loss of liberty. A life of distress and disgrace for your family and loved ones. I now deeply regret the shame I brought on my family throughout my long criminal career. For anyone who might be inclined towards a life of crime, please accept this counsel from someone who has been a criminal for most of his life and learnt these lessons the hard way. No amount of money is worth the heartache, anguish and pain brought on your family and loved ones by becoming a convicted criminal; and no amount of money is worth spending even one day of life behind bars. It has taken me a lifetime of regret to realise that.

With Terrence Clark; Robert 'Aussie Bob' Trimbole; Martin Johnstone (the original Mr Asia) and Choo Cheng Kui 'Chinese Jack Choo' now all dead, I am the only surviving member of the leadership able to give an accurate and truthful account of what really happened inside the Mr Asia drug syndicate between 1976 to 1979. In early 1981, the Royal Commission into Drug Trafficking in Australia was initiated by Prime Minister Malcolm Fraser. The Royal Commission was headed by Justice DG Stewart, it centred predominantly on the Mr Asia drug syndicate and ran for nearly two years, from 25 June 1981 to 25 February 1983. During that time the Stewart Royal Commission interviewed hundreds of people and travelled worldwide. When the commission's report was finally tabled in the Australian Parliament on 25 February 1983, it contained the most detailed account ever of the Mr Asia drug syndicate.

However, even Justice Stewart had to rely on what I call 'coloured' evidence provided by people motivated by self-interest, or whom I considered insignificant within the syndicate. I refused to appear before this Royal Commission, but others cooperated and received immunity. Like good Catholics they went and confessed their sins – and the sins of others – in return for absolution. Many of those who traded their sins for their testimony and freedom had played important roles and profited from their involvement in the syndicate. The result of all those indemnified witnesses, all that money, all that legal and investigative work, was the conviction of two senior people involved in the syndicate in Australia, myself and Chinese Jack Choo.

Despite having a lengthy criminal record in New Zealand dating back to March 1958 when I was just sixteen years old, most of my convictions were for minor crimes such as car conversion, burglary, break and enter and such. Certainly, none of my convictions involved murder, drug importation, drug dealing, money laundering, bribery or dealing with corrupt police, which were some of the charges laid against myself and other members of the Mr Asia drug syndicate. Following my arrest in San Francisco in 1984, I unsuccessfully fought extradition to Australia for sixteen months. Despite having legal avenues of appeal still open to me, on 24 July 1985 I was forcefully extradited to Australia, where I stood trial in early 1986 for my involvement in the Mr Asia syndicate.

After a trial lasting just over two months, in April 1986 a jury rejected my plea of not guilty and I was convicted of conspiracy to import heroin into Australia between 1 January 1976 and 1 January 1980. My pleas of innocence fell on the hard-line attitude and unsympathetic ears of old-fashioned, no-nonsense Justice McInerney. So it came about that on a cold and wet June morning in 1986 at the old NSW Supreme Court in Darlinghurst, Sydney, I had the unwanted distinction of being the first person in Australia to be sentenced to 25 years' hard labour – with no parole – on a drug related charge. Fortunately for me, remissions were still available in New South Wales in 1986, so after a period of fourteen years and nine months after my arrest in San Francisco, I was released from prison on 6 December 1998, having paid my dues to society in full.

Over those many years I was in prison – predominantly in maximum security – I came to realise what an evil and insidious drug heroin is. I saw thousands of young inmates come through the prison system suffering from heroin addiction. It very forcibly brought home to me that I had been part of the machine that fed the addictions of these unfortunate souls. None of us, no matter how much we desire it, can take back or change what we have done, but for me, if it were possible, despite all the money I made, my involvement in the Mr Asia drug syndicate is something I would change in a heartbeat. To this day I bitterly regret my two-year association in the syndicate and that is not only because of the lengthy prison sentence I received.

Between 1976 and 1979, when the Mr Asia syndicate was flourishing, I witnessed human behaviour of the worst possible kind from both men and women – betrayal, treachery, deceit, disloyalty, greed and violence – behaviour I do not absolve myself from. During those years I was also made aware by other members of the syndicate of the murders committed by Clark and others. Because I knew many of those people who were murdered, to this day I still have nightmares about what happened to them. I wake up some nights and see their bodies walking towards me. Not even the oblivion of sleep can suppress my memories.

So after much soul searching I have decided to exorcise a few demons, dispel a few myths and detail for the first time ever, the real story behind the rise and fall of the Mr Asia drug syndicate. It is a story of violent men, betrayal, murder, corruption, bribery and greed. It is not a story I am proud of, yet it is a story I need to tell, otherwise the complete and accurate story of the syndicate will die with me. How the syndicate evolved is not a pleasant story but then again stories about murderous drug dealers never are.

1

GOULBURN PRISON

On 25 July 1986, I observed my forty-fifth birthday in the depressing surrounds of Goulburn Maximum Security Prison. This antiquated, run-down, filthy relic of a prison is located 198 kilometres south of Sydney in the town of Goulburn. This small country town straddles the Hume Highway, which runs straight through to Melbourne some 680 kilometres further south.

During the early 1800s Goulburn was a garrison town, a centre for police patrols searching out the highwaymen frequenting the area. A major stockade for convicts was based there and became a principal penal establishment well known for the harsh treatment given to convicts. The stockade housed about two hundred convicts who slept on bare boards, had one blanket each and ten men were confined to a cell. This history helps explain the prison's tough and brutal origins.

Built along the design lines of an 18th century American penitentiary, Goulburn Prison was already over a century old when I arrived there a few weeks before my 45th birthday. To give some indication of its antiquity, Australia's most celebrated bushranger, Ned Kelly, was once an inmate there. The prison has a fearsome reputation and I can say without any fear of contradiction that it was, in 1986 and remains to this very day, the most violent, dangerous prison in Australia. Murders, suicides, stabbings, bashings and gang-related warfare are a way of life. During the year I was confined there, two inmates were murdered in their cells.

Unlike other prisons, Goulburn does not have a big exercise yard like those seen in most American prison films. Instead there is a series of small exercise yards, some 30 metres long by twenty metres wide behind each cellblock. All these small yards have razor wire running around the top of dank, moss-encrusted walls, minimal seating, and usually a lone, filthy toilet. Unless someone has had the misfortune to spend time in a prison, it is hard to convey or explain the sense of foreboding you feel in a hostile, dangerous environment like Goulburn Prison. It is almost as if the legions of men who have been executed, murdered or died there have imbued the prison with their rage, misery and despair at ending their lives inside its walls.

During the course of the fifteen years I spent in the NSW prison system, I was moved around all the maximum security prisons – Long Bay, Parklea, Parramatta, Lithgow and Bathurst – but none of them came close to the harsh, draconian atmosphere of Goulburn Prison. It is certainly not a place for the faint or weak hearted and definitely not the place anyone would want to serve a 25 year prison sentence, which was the predicament facing me on that icy cold July morning. I clearly remember that morning, even today, some 23 years later as if it were yesterday. It's funny how some memories stay vivid in your mind while others fade away. The memory of that July morning has stayed fresh in my mind and more than likely was the genesis for writing this book.

To commemorate my birthday on that bleak, wintry morning and to get out of the depressing cell where I spent a minimum twenty hours locked in every day, I had decided to go for a brisk walk in one of the small exercise yards behind B Wing, where my cell was located. Because it was so cold there was no one else willing or perhaps foolish enough to be out exercising. To help keep out the cold I was wearing a singlet, white T-shirt, prison issue green sweater, heavy green parka, long johns, two pairs of track pants, long football socks and a pair of running shoes. Despite being so well rugged up, I could not generate any warmth in my body. I guess it was a combination of the prospect of the long prison sentence and the grim surroundings of the prison that made me feel cold, depressed and forlorn, and just when I felt it could not get any worse, it started to snow! As the snowflakes fell on me, I remember looking skywards and thinking, What the fuck am I doing here?

The last time I had lived in Australia, in early 1979, I was leasing a luxury apartment overlooking Sydney Harbour in one of that city's most exclusive suburbs, Darling Point. The lawn below my apartment ran to the harbour's edge, where there was a private jetty for the sole use of myself and the other apartment owners. At that time I had also acquired, through debt, a share in a top class restaurant called Tati's located in the inner-city suburb of Darlinghurst owned and run by a dapper, suave, Argentinian restaurateur by the name of Robert Fionna. A lovely man with impeccable manners, Robert's weakness was a penchant for backing losing racehorses, which is how I came to acquire a share in his restaurant. The food served at Tati's was of the highest quality. During my travels around the world I have eaten in many fine restaurants and Robert's food more than held its own in comparison. Besides the food at Tati's, beautiful and accommodating women were the order of the day as was Dom Perignon champagne, gambling at the races and bundles of cash to pay for all these pleasures.

The memories of those happier times seemed a lifetime away as the snow fell on my head that morning. The harsh reality of my situation was almost overwhelming. I was in a prison full of dangerous, miserable and despairing men, living in a grimy, barren, three-metre by two-metre cell with cardboard instead of glass to stop the elements from blowing through the window, the food was barely edible and my life was in constant danger.

How had it come to this? How had I allowed myself to become involved with a murderous outfit like the Mr Asia syndicate? A syndicate the likes of which this country had never seen before, or for that matter since. How had I allowed myself to get involved with Terry Clark, New Zealand's biggest serial killer and the acknowledged head of the syndicate?

Greed is a terrible weakness and, like many poor souls before me, it led to my downfall as well. It took the bleak confines of Goulburn Prison and a 25 year sentence for me to finally start examining my life and the circumstances that led to me becoming involved in the syndicate.

Perhaps before starting my story about the rise and fall of the Mr Asia drug syndicate, I should fill in the details about myself, my early life, my criminal background and prison experiences in New Zealand that brought me to the attention of Terry Clark and led to him offering me a lucrative position as the syndicate's 'Banker' – the man in charge of safeguarding his ill-gotten drug money and laundering it all overseas. Looking back on it now, I realise my involvement with Clark also gave him what he craved – credibility within the criminal community.

2

MY STORY

My full name is James William Shepherd, as I write this I am 67 years of age. Since I was sixteen, when I received my first conviction and prison sentence in March 1958 for robbery with violence, I have constantly been at war with the police, drug enforcement agencies, the judiciary, other criminals and society in general. Over the course of my criminal career I have known or met nearly every major criminal in New Zealand and New South Wales. Notorious criminals from the sixties and seventies who I knew well in New Zealand included George Wilder, John Gillies, Ron Jorgenson, Len Evans, Jon Sadaraka, Paddy McNally, Bruce McPhee, Phillip Weston, Peter Fulcher, Slim Horton, Les Green, Ian Saxon, Trevor Nash, Errol Hincksman and Darryl Sorby. Over the last 35 years in New South Wales I have known or met – both inside and outside prison – Arthur 'Neddy' Smith, Graham 'Abo' Henry, Jim 'Jockey' Smith, Tom Domican, Dave Kelleher, Bobby Chapman, Arthur Loveday, George Savas, Dr Nick Paltos, Bruce

'Snapper' Cornwall, Roy Thurgar, George Freeman, Lenny McPherson, Stan Smith and Robert 'Aussie Bob' Trimbole.

Many of those men and all my contemporaries from the Mr Asia syndicate – Terry Clark, Martin Johnstone, Robert Trimbole and Jack Choo – are now dead. It is more by good luck than good management that I am still alive. I have survived two serious attempts on my life, three major car accidents – one where the car I was in rolled six times down a steep embankment, I know because I counted each roll – bullets from police and other criminals whistling past my ears, some of the most violent prisons in New Zealand and Australia, as well as many other incidents that could have resulted in my death.

My torturous journey through life began in New Zealand where my humble origins never designated me as a potential international drug dealer. On 25 July 1941 I was born into a poor family in Auckland. Despite what the Stewart Royal Commission into Drug Trafficking and quite a few media publications have stated, I was not born in Picton, a small town located in the South Island of New Zealand. Indeed, my mother told me before she died that I came kicking and screaming into this world around 7pm at St Helen's Maternity Hospital, which used to be situated opposite the main fire station in Pitt Street, a street running through the heart of Auckland, New Zealand's largest city; my original birth certificate has since confirmed this fact. During the Second World War, however, my mother and father lived for a while in Picton where Dad was in charge of building the first government development housing programs in New Zealand. My younger brother Brian was born while we were living there, which is more than likely why I am always mistakenly reported as being born in Picton.

My mother's Maori name was Kataraina – Catherine or Rena. She was a strong, outgoing and fun-loving woman who enjoyed a drink, and had little formal education but a wide circle of friends. A proud, full-blooded Maori, she had my birth registered with the then Maori Affairs Department, which identified me as a Maori. In those less enlightened times, anyone with a white father and Maori mother, or vice versa, had to be registered as either white or Maori. My mother was very proud of her ancestry, which is why my birth was registered with the Maori Affairs Department.

My mother's maiden name was Rutene and she belonged to connected branches of the Ngatihine/Te Rarawa/Auhpouri, all sub-tribes of the mighty Ngapuhi tribe, long regarded as the most ferocious, warlike tribe in New Zealand. The sub-tribe my mother belonged to, the Ngatihine, were the last Maori tribe in New Zealand to stop fighting the English troops prior to the signing of the Treaty of Waitangi that ended the Maori wars. High on the slopes of Mount Ruapekapeka, some 210 kilometres north of Auckland, the ramparts from where my ancestors fought the English to a standstill are still visible. Local people swear some nights they can hear the cries of the dying, sounds of muskets firing, the war chants of Maori warriors echoing across the mountain. The mountain has a strange aura about it, not unlike the aura surrounding the Ngapuhi tribe. Stories abound of the murderous rampages of the Ngapuhi during the 1800s in New Zealand. Suffice to say, the deaths of thousands upon thousands of Maoris from other tribes scattered throughout New Zealand can be directly attributed to marauding Ngapuhi war parties during the 1800s. My mother's lineage is ancient, and through her ancestors I am connected to a history steeped in tradition and marked by many great Maori warriors. Although I was born in the city and have lived in cities all my life, I still feel the blood of my ancestors coursing through my veins. There has always been an aggressive, warlike streak in my nature and I have no doubt it comes from my Maori ancestry.

My father by contrast was a quiet, introverted, gentle man, a builder and carpenter by trade. He had survived the horror of the First World War when he enlisted in the army at the young age of seventeen. My father's name was James St Andrew William Shepherd. A white New Zealander or Pakeha, he was born and bred in the Waikato region, a tranquil part of the North Island, about 160 kilometres south of Auckland. His family were farmers who also owned a butcher shop in the area that sold meat sourced from the farm.

His ancestry in New Zealand can be traced back to the 1850s when the first Shepherd arrived from Edinburgh, Scotland, as a remittance man. I believe he was the original black sheep of the Shepherd clan, and was sent out to the colonies in disgrace. After arriving in New Zealand he lived in Dunedin, a cold and miserable city located on the east coast of the South Island, where he eventually married the daughter of a Norwegian sea captain. My grandfather on my paternal side was James William Shepherd, as was my father. On my father's side of the family we are sixth generation New Zealanders, while on my mother's side it is believed that we are 40th generation New Zealanders. I am not proud to say that at the time of my involvement in the Mr Asia syndicate, I was the only member of my immediate family, Maori or Pakeha, to have ever been in trouble with the law.

A year after the end of the Second World War, in 1946, I can remember standing outside what was then termed a 'house of ill repute' in Vincent Street, just down the road from St Helen's where I was born and just a few houses from where we lived at that time, waiting for American servicemen to emerge from the brothel in the hope they would give myself and other kids candy or chewing gum. Like most New Zealanders, during the war we faced shortages of everything: meat, sugar, flour, butter, milk. It was not until a few years after the end of the war that food supplies became more readily available. That is, of course, if you had the money to buy food with. We could never afford luxury items like butter when I was a child and I can remember going to school with a couple of slices of bread smeared with dripping, the fat we used to fry our food in. To compound the indignity and highlight how poor we were, my few slices of bread would be wrapped in old newspapers. But there were many children at Napier Street Primary School like me.

Today in Auckland, Freeman's Bay is a trendy place to live. The area is populated with stylish townhouses, luxury apartments and fashionable hotels favoured by upwardly mobile types with money to spend. By contrast in the late 1940s and into the 1950s Freeman's Bay was where you lived if you were poor. All the houses were run down and of very poor quality. Back then it was made up of life's downtrodden battlers, waterside workers, garbage men, labourers, ex-servicemen down on their luck, the unemployed, winos and derelicts.

Our family – my mother, father, younger brother Brian and my younger sister Faye – lived in a run-down house in Morton Street that we shared with two other families. I would like to blame poverty or the disadvantaged area of Auckland I grew up in for my eventual criminal record, but I cannot. During the course of the years I spent in New Zealand's prison system, I only once came across another individual who grew up in Freeman's Bay who had also been convicted of a serious crime; an interesting sociological fact that would no doubt intrigue any criminologist attempting to correlate poverty with crime. I guess my penchant for luxury living later in life can be attributed to my impoverished childhood. Wearing imported handmade Italian shoes was probably a subconscious response to all those days I walked to school, rain, hail or shine in bare feet.

One unusual aspect of living in Freeman's Bay in the 1950s was the fact there was not much theft from households. Despite being poor, none of the kids I ran around with ever stole money. We did, however, make forays into more affluent suburbs where we raided orchards for fruit. And I have to admit that while doing an early morning paper route in downtown Auckland, I used to take a bottle of milk for myself most mornings, as well as a cake or two from the boxes left outside the large department stores. My first acts of dishonesty, but certainly not my last.

Although I excelled at sports, I was an indifferent school student. After leaving primary school I attended Seddon Memorial Technical College, which in 1956 was located opposite Albert Park in the heart of Auckland. Seddon Tech specialised in teaching trades such as carpentry, welding, engineering and motor mechanics. I played rugby and cricket at college but my main sport was rugby league and I represented Auckland Schoolboys in 1956. As neither my heart nor interest was in schoolwork, in 1957 at the age of sixteen I left my school days behind me.

My story after leaving college is no different from hundreds of other lads. Unemployed, I fell in with the wrong crowd, gave up a promising football career and started to drink far too heavily for my age. One fateful night in February 1958 while out drinking with two friends, I beat up a man for no reason at all and then, to compound my stupidity, I robbed him. Don't ask me why but that stupid, drunken moment was to cost me dearly and shape my future life.

Within two weeks I was a remand prisoner in Mt Eden Prison, New Zealand's toughest adult prison. Although only a short distance from the centre of Auckland, the prison was built alongside a stone quarry where the inmates used to crack rocks with sledgehammers. Despite being only sixteen and a first offender, the serious nature of the charge I was facing; robbery with violence, plus a few burglaries thrown in for good measure, meant no mercy would be afforded me: and none was. Three years borstal training at Invercargill Borstal was the sentence. Little did I realise at that early stage of my life, that years of prison lay ahead of me – years of violence, gang wars, murder and treachery; years of degradation in the prison systems of Australia, the United States and New Zealand; and years of misery for my family and loved ones. If only we could turn back the clock.

Although my mother and father had been separated for many years at the time of my arrest, it nevertheless affected them both deeply. My mother was distraught with concern for my wellbeing, my father overwhelmed by the shame I had brought upon the family name. As none of my father's successful brothers or sisters had ever offered to help him or our family when we needed help, what his family thought did not concern me. But it did distress my father more than I imagined and a few months after my transfer to Invercargill Borstal, he died, a lonely and broken-hearted man. In those days there was no such thing as compassionate leave to attend funerals. Not that it would have mattered anyway, because by the time the letter from my mother reached me at Invercargill Borstal which is located 1600 kilometres from Auckland at the bottom of New Zealand's South Island (next stop Antarctica), my father had already been laid to rest as was his right at Waikumete War Memorial Cemetery in Auckland.

Looking back on my father's death all these years later, I now realise his death impacted on me more traumatically than I ever cared to admit. I blamed myself for his death, as no doubt did his family. Perhaps a psychiatrist or psychologist would identify his death as the catalyst for my subsequent criminal behaviour, but I tend to think a rogue gene pushed me towards a life of crime and my own folly kept me there. Why do I think that? Because no one else in my family at that time even remotely looked like getting into trouble with the law. My brother Brian, who was a few years younger than me, was a highly respected captain of a fishing trawler who never had any trouble with the law. Equally my younger sister Faye had a successful career in politics. Obviously having a brother hell-bent on destroying himself affected their lives but neither of them, or for that matter my mother while she was still alive, ever stopped loving me. Despite my family's love, from March 1958 my life became one of never-ending conflict with the police and judiciary.

3

PRISON DAYS

Apart from Martin Johnstone, nearly all the male members of the Mr Asia syndicate – myself, Terry Clark, Errol Hincksman, Peter Fulcher, Greg Ollard, Wayne Shrimpton, Darryl Sorby, Patrick Norton-Bennett, Brian Agnew, even Douglas Wilson who was later murdered – served time in NZ prisons. Obviously the correctional system operating in New Zealand during the sixties and seventies did neither myself nor any of the above mentioned much good.

With so much time on our hands – we didn't have televisions or radios back then and very limited decent reading material – most of the time was spent day-dreaming or talking with our fellow crims. We would talk about the successful crimes we intended to commit, the large amounts of money we would make, the beautiful women we were going to bed, the luxury cars we were going to own, the stylish apartments in the best part of town we intended to live in and myriad other things we were going to succeed at. Bullshit is one commodity there is no shortage of in prison. An old crim once told me many years ago when I first entered the prison system: 'Son, in here, believe nothing of what you hear and half of what you see and you will not go far wrong.' That wise old crim was spot on. If I had a dollar for every lie I have heard in prison, I would be an extremely wealthy man today.

The sad truth is that only a handful of criminals out of the tens of thousands who commit crimes actually make any money out of it. For the rest it is a constant struggle for survival, a life of pain and misery for themselves and their loved ones, and a life of dreams never realised. For a few years, myself and other members of the Mr Asia syndicate were able to live out our wildest dreams with huge amounts of money, beautiful women, luxury cars, stylish apartments, the finest clothes, classy restaurants, nightclubs, vintage champagne – we enjoyed all of it. Such grand living comes at a high price, however – for me, that price started in Invercargill Borstal.

In March 1958 Invercargill Borstal was a harsh, merciless prison for young offenders aged between sixteen and 21 years. The treatment handed out to all inmates, particularly new arrivals, was brutal. On arrival an older, bigger inmate immediately challenged you to a fight. If perchance you won your first fight, then another even bigger inmate was lining up to fight you, and so it would go until you got your arse kicked. My co-accused who was sent to the borstal with me was a tall, gangly seventeen year old named Graham 'Blonde Mac' McKay. Although only slightly built, my lifelong friend had the heart of a lion and never stopped fighting for the first six months we were there. Fortunately for both of us there were a few guys there we knew from Auckland who could handle themselves, and more importantly, helped us survive our first six months at Invercargill. As common sense and the age gap would indicate, a sixteen-year-old inmate stood no chance physically against a fully mature, much stronger 20 or 21 year old. At sixteen I was short, I still am today, but like a lot of short men, feisty and naturally fit, with a stocky build and the ability to give as good as I got in a fight.

It would be no exaggeration to say that life for young inmates at Invercargill was hell. Besides having to deal with the standover tactics of older and tougher inmates, we were constantly being harassed and threatened by thug prison officers who were not adverse to beating up inmates who were on their own in solitary confinement. I was never 'touched up' by any of these mongrel guards but I know plenty who were beaten by them. Where the sadistic prison officers came into their own was on work details. In summer it was not so bad but in winter they would have us scrubbing the long, cold concrete corridors on our hands and knees with a small scrubbing brush, our white moleskin pants soaking wet, our knees skinned raw from the constant shuffling. Out on the borstal's farmland they would have gangs of inmates waist deep in ice-covered drains, chipping away at ice-encrusted banks with a spade. On other winter days they would take work gangs of inmates down to Invercargill Harbour where they would have us standing in the freezing seawater stacking large rocks around the foreshore.

Rehabilitation was not a word in anyone's vocabulary in 1958. Punishment was the name of the game and no one did it better than Invercargill Borstal, which still rates as one of the tougher prisons I have had the misfortune to be in. Despite the harsh conditions and the many fights, the friendships forged in the adversity that was Invercargill Borstal followed me out onto the streets and through other NZ prisons. Graduating from Invercargill Borstal was my first step along the dead-end street called crime. My life after borstal became a revolving door of petty crime, prison, release, more crime, prison, release – I was no sooner out than I was back in again. It was almost as if I was continuously punishing myself for my father's death by my senseless crimes and equally senseless punishment. What a waste.

Like a lot of men who have spent time in boys' homes, borstals or prisons, I began to solely identify and associate with people I had met inside. They became my family, people I was familiar with, people who had experienced the same hardships as me, people who belonged to the same club as me. To have served time in prison was a passport into a world where committing crime is the common denominator.

The criminal world is not unlike the business world, you start at the bottom and work your way up. It is a world where you have to earn respect; a world where murder and violence is accepted as part of the business. At the top only the most violent survive, which does not put me in a good light, but that is just how it is in the criminal hierarchy. Reputations have to be made. During the 1960s that is what I did, both inside and outside prison: I acquired a reputation.

Out of prison my crimes became more serious. From burglaries, car conversions, breaking and entering and other minor charges, I graduated to safe-breaking and armed robberies. In those days everyone wanted to be a safe-cracker and I was no exception, as that was the pinnacle of NZ crime. A sad commentary I guess on the calibre of criminals in New Zealand at that time. For me, knowledge gleaned from seasoned, top-class cracksmen like Ron Tattley and Jack West while they were inside, and from a few personal experiences with explosives outside, allowed me to become an expert safe-cracker.

My proficiency with explosives took an interesting turn in 1963 while I was serving a term of imprisonment in Mt Eden Prison. A couple of inmates I knew came up to me in the wing where I was working as a sweeper and asked for my help with an extremely confidential matter involving explosives. I naturally thought they wanted to tap into my knowledge as a safe-cracker so I took them into an empty cell where I could expand in private on my limited knowledge of explosives. But knowledge was not what they wanted. After telling me what a stand-up guy I was and swearing me to secrecy, they showed me what they needed my expertise for. From a pocket inside his grey prison coat, one of the crims produced two sticks of gelignite, a length of cordite fuse and a percussion detonator. Well to say I was shocked would be an understatement but I hid it well and continued talking to the two inmates as though being in an empty cell with two crims carrying explosives inside Mt Eden Prison was an everyday occurrence. Outwardly I appeared calm but inwardly I was shaking. For those not familiar with explosives, gelignite is used for blasting rocks in quarries, also by farmers when getting rid of large tree stumps. The cordite fuse is fitted into the detonator and the opening is then crimped against the fuse so that it will not drop out. Then the detonator is pushed into the top of the gelignite, the fuse is lit with a match and hey presto . . . *kaboom!*

As my two fellow crims knew nothing about explosives, they asked me if I would prep the gelignite for them. You did not have to be Einstein to figure out what they were up to, but I did not ask and they did not tell me. I just felt flattered that these two notorious crims had enlisted me to help in such a risky, dangerous venture, so I did what they requested. After explaining to them that once they lit the fuse they would have about 30 seconds to detonation, I bid them good luck. Exactly four days later in an exercise yard in the high security section of Mt Eden Prison, a group of desperate long term prisoners blasted a hole in the outside wall and then streamed through the opening, climbed a steep embankment and, amid a hail of bullets, ran along an adjacent railway track to freedom. After hearing the explosion and the sound of gunshots, I was pleased that I had wished those two crims good luck. That night locked away in my cell, I silently toasted those escapees and had a quiet chuckle to myself. If my memory serves me well, it took six months to recapture them all. Needless to say, after the successful breakout my reputation started to grow, albeit slowly.

4

MAXIMUM SECURITY

Anyone who has served time in a prison, particularly a maximum security prison, will confirm that inside those festering cages of deprivation the law of the jungle prevails. While intelligence is respected, brute force and violence rule. The weak, the young, the cowardly, the mentally ill and the non-violent are all cannon fodder inside prison. It is extremely rare to find a prison inmate with the reputation and physical strength to back it up, willing to protect vulnerable inmates.

With the dog-eat-dog mentality that exists in maximum security prisons, nearly all inmates will turn away or ignore a defenceless inmate being stabbed, beaten or robbed. I am ashamed to admit I have done it myself on numerous occasions – far too many. The reasons you behave in such a reprehensible way are manifold. One, inside prison you do not get involved in situations that are none of your business as it could very easily get you killed. Two, the inmate being attacked could be an informer, a child molester, he could have insulted someone, he may have done something to some other inmate's family or loved ones, he may have owed money – a very common motive – for drug purchases; there are myriad reasons why and none of them are any business of yours. In maximum security especially, you learn to suppress your feelings, you learn to suppress your humanity; you become what you thought you wanted to be – a cold, unfeeling, hard man. I only have myself to blame, I invented the person I became.

A fight I had in early 1965 while I was serving a sentence for burglary in Mt Eden Prison really helped foster my burgeoning reputation among the criminal hierarchy. At that time Mt Eden was New Zealand's main maximum security prison. It housed the majority of that country's long term prisoners and was a very tough place indeed. Because the inmates – mainly Maoris – used to work cracking rocks in the prison quarry with sledgehammers, there were many well-built, extremely fit men. Some of these men were huge. Back in those early days every prison had a kingpin, the toughest man in the jail. In Mt Eden it was a huge Maori named Richard McDonald. Maori Mac stood just over six feet tall, weighed in around 115 kilos, and as the result of countless past battles had a face only a mother could love. Unusual for a Maori back then, Maori Mac was an intelligent crim who had built a ferocious reputation for himself inside prison. Whatever it took to win a fight – fists, boots, knees, head butts, grabbing a man's testicles, ripping an eye out or ear off – Maori Mac was your man. His reputation was such that no one would fight him, which is where I came in.

At that time in early 1965 I was 24 years old, 63 kilos ringing wet and short enough to be a jockey. My job in the prison was working as a sweeper in the north wing where all the long term prisoners were housed. Being a sweeper in a wing entailed sweeping and mopping the wing area, handing out rations – milk, butter and so on – and dishing up food at meal times. As he was serving a fourteen year sentence at the time, Maori Mac was housed in the wing where I worked. Putting the daily bread ration of a small loaf of bread into each inmate's cell was my responsibility. One Saturday morning Maori Mac came up to me while I was preparing the bread for distribution and complained loudly to me about the size of his bread ration. Not wanting to antagonise the toughest man in the jail, I politely told him he was getting the largest ration in the wing, but my explanation fell on deaf ears. His tirade against me grew louder: I was an arsehole, my mother was a whore, he would break every bone in my body. On and on he went while I just stood there mute.

Finally I had the temerity to say, 'I will fix it up,' but it was not enough to pacify him. With a murderous look in his eye, he reached over to grab my shirt, no doubt intending to give me a slap around the ears. To this day I don't know what possessed me, perhaps it was my Maori heritage, because at that time in my life I was nowhere near as proficient with my fists as I became in later years. Whatever the reason, before Maori Mac could grab me, I launched myself at him and punched him six times before he realised he was under attack. For a small man I have always had a powerful punch but against such a large opponent, my punches were not that effective. In those days there were not that many shivs – knives – around like there are today and the prison guards let you fight until someone dropped. Despite the disparity in size and weight between us, the guards on duty were no doubt somewhat fearful of Maori Mac and refused to intervene.

Although it seemed much longer, for the next five minutes we fought up and down the wing. My superior speed was negated by the fact I was wearing a pair of boots, which did not give me good traction on the recently mopped and still wet floor. Every time Maori Mac hit me I would stagger back four or five paces, shake my head to clear it, then wait for him to come charging at me again. *Bam, bam, bam*! I would hit him three or four times, then *pow*, one big hit from him and I was lurching back four or five paces again. After five minutes of sustained attack, my eyes and nose were streaming blood and, despite my superior fitness, I could feel myself tiring badly and I was nearly done for. Although still on my feet, a stiff breeze would have blown me over as I could barely hold my hands up. Perhaps it was all the blood pumping out of me, perhaps it was his sense of fair play, but whatever the reason an old senior officer named Kavenaugh stepped in and saved the day for me. Bloody, but still upright and unbowed, I was taken to Auckland Public Hospital to have my eyes stitched up, the cuts courtesy of a heavy ring Maori Mac wore.

Every Saturday at the prison there used to be a basketball competition. Despite being short I was a handy basketballer and played for a team called the Beagle Boys. So this Saturday when they brought me back from the hospital with my eyes stitched up and my face badly bruised, I made a point of going out onto the basketball court to play a full game with my team. This resolute action so soon after my battle with Maori Mac did not go unnoticed by my fellow inmates. One of the smallest men in the prison had not only fought Maori Mac but was still on his feet when the fight was stopped. And furthermore, he was out playing a game of basketball a few hours later.

That fight was the end of the reign of Maori Mac as the kingpin in Mt Eden Prison. The fear and mystique around him were well and truly gone after our fight. In fact he was never the same man again. Guys who had been too terrified to even look at Maori Mac suddenly wanted to challenge him. This is what happens to ageing fighters in prison, young up-and-comers build their reputations on these once hard men. In his prime Maori Mac would have chopped me up and spat out the pieces in two minutes flat. Even though he was only in his forties, that was an old man I fought. But because I fought him when no one else would, respect for me increased tenfold. I never told anyone I was on the point of collapse when the fight was stopped – far from it, I used to tell everyone I was just getting my second wind when old Kavenaugh intervened. A little white lie never hurt anyone and I did not want to spoil my moment by revealing how spent I was. Despite open hostility between us there were no repercussions after the fight. Perhaps it was embarrassment; perhaps my punches had more effect than I thought, but for whatever reason, Maori Mac never challenged me a second time and I certainly did not ask for a rematch.

A few months later in July 1965, after a failed armed escape attempt from Mt Eden Prison that resulted in the gutting and destruction of the jail, all the inmates were transferred to other prisons throughout New Zealand. I ended up in Waikeria, a youth institution situated some 190 kilometres south of Auckland, which in the space of a few weeks was reinforced with steel, barbed wire and armed guards so that it could hold most of the long term prisoners from Mt Eden. My nemesis Maori Mac ended up there as well. I will not expand on the gory details but one morning I ran into his cell, caught him in bed and using a couple of steel razor handles as knuckle dusters, evened the ledger for my cut eyes and swollen face.

The irony of all my prison conflicts with Maori Mac was the fact that several years later while playing rugby league for a club in Auckland, Maori Mac was one of the football coaches there. In fact, I played one game for the team he coached before I was promoted to the senior team. Neither one of us acknowledged all the violence that had gone between us. Life can be strange sometimes, can it not?

5

THE RIOT

Although it happened over 40 years ago, on 20 July 1965, the attempted armed escape from Mt Eden Prison by two remand prisoners left an indelible imprint on my mind and dramatically shaped my life. If I live to be a hundred, I will never experience or take part in anything remotely similar to what happened that destructive July night. While serving my 25 year sentence at Parklea Prison in Sydney, I was unfortunate enough to be there when a full scale riot erupted in late September 1990 and the prison was destroyed in an orgy of mindless destruction. I distinctly remember it because it occurred on the date that the rugby league grand final was played that year: Penrith and Canberra if I remember correctly. Anyway the riot started during the half-time break, and all these years later I am still pissed about it as I never got to see the second half of that game. The riot lasted just over six hours, but during that time the prison was destroyed as a functioning institution. While it lasted it was one hell of a riot, but nowhere near as destructive as that 1965 Mt Eden outbreak. While it had nothing to do with drug dealing, the attempted outbreak at Mt Eden was pivotal in my life because after the subsequent attempted break-out and riot was quelled, I was identified as one of the ringleaders. That denouncement was to cost me over three years in solitary confinement and further enhance my reputation as a so-called hard man.

Earlier I mentioned that during my years in the NZ prison system I only met one other person from Freeman's Bay where I grew up who was also in prison for a serious crime. That individual was a man named Jon Sadaraka (aka John Sadler), whom I had known since childhood as we attended the same primary school. My younger brother Brian was a classmate of Jon's, which is why I reluctantly agreed to offer whatever assistance I could when he broached his escape plan to me. I say reluctantly because I never thought his desperate plan had any chance of success, but loyalty to a fellow 'Bay' boy made me a concerned observer as Jon and his partner in crime – a chappie named Phillip Western – put their plan into action.

Both the men involved in this doomed escape attempt would go on to become extremely dangerous and notorious criminals. In the early 1980s in Sydney, Jon was convicted of murdering his sister's husband over a domestic dispute that escalated out of control. During his fourteen years in the NSW prison system, Jon was known as John Sadler. During his incarceration there he was regarded not only by prison staff but also by the other fearful inmates as one of the toughest men in the system. I was told by a friend of mine who was in Parramatta Prison with him in the early 1980s of an incident that highlighted how tough Jon was. During an argument with a fellow prisoner in the exercise yard, the guy pulled a shiv out and stabbed Jon in the stomach. Calmly Jon reached down and pulled the shiv out of his side, then licked his blood off the blade and said to the other crim: 'You'll have to do better than that son.' He then proceeded to flog the crim who'd had the audacity to stab him.

When I was extradited from the United States in July 1985, I learnt personally how fearful prison staff and other crims were of Jon. While in the remand section of Long Bay Prison in Sydney awaiting trial for my involvement in the Mr Asia syndicate, Jon used his considerable influence to get a special escort from the prison he was in at that time to come visit me. To say I was flabbergasted would be putting it mildly when my old friend from Freeman's Bay walked into the visiting room of the remand prison. Sadly, after doing fourteen years of very hard time in the NSW prison system, Jon was deported back to New Zealand where in the mid-1990s he was convicted of another murder only six months after his release and sentenced to twenty years imprisonment in Auckland. Very sad – very sad indeed.

At the time of the escape attempt, Phillip Western was on remand for an armed bank robbery, a rare crime back in the 1960s, particularly in New Zealand. To add further intrigue to his crime, Western and his co-accused brother David were both students at Auckland University. A double rarity in New Zealand at that time: intelligent criminals. If I remember correctly, both the Western brothers were convicted of that bank robbery and sentenced to six or eight years' jail. After his release Phillip Western (aka Phillip McMillan), moved to Australia, where in the 1970s he became a very active bank robber all over New South Wales. He was shot dead in a gun battle with detectives from the NSW Armed Robbery Squad in a house at Avoca Beach, a small town located on the Central Coast. The notorious and disgraced former NSW detective Roger Rogerson was among the police officers who shot him. I was told by a reliable source that McMillan/Western was still breathing when police found him lying on the floor in the bathroom of the house where the shootout occurred. They then made sure there would be no more bank robberies committed by him. Perhaps what I was told was just an urban myth, but it is amazing how many of these urban myths end up being true. Whatever the reality, one thing I am sure about is this: after Terry Clark, I would have to rate Phillip Western, because of his intelligence and readiness to use violence, as one of the most dangerous men ever to come out of

New Zealand. Back in July 1965, however, all that murder and death still awaited both of them.

To help facilitate his escape attempt, Jon had smuggled into the prison a ten shot .22 automatic pistol. When he handed it to me for safekeeping, I remember thinking, What the fuck is going on in this prison? First I have a couple of crims asking me to prime two sticks of gelignite which they then used for a break-out; then for a short period of time I had in my possession a sawn-off shotgun which three inmates used in another unsuccessful break-out; now here I was with an automatic .22 pistol in my possession. The ongoing escape attempts and drama never seemed to end.

On the fateful day of their escape attempt from the remand wing, Jon asked me to give him back his gun as he was going that evening. Despite my pleas that it was madness and not to attempt such a foolhardy escape, my friend was determined and not to be deterred. So it came to pass that not long after midnight that July evening, using a handmade cell key which they acquired from another inmate, both he and Phillip Western were able to open the cell door of the four-man cell they shared. Once out of their cell they laid in wait for the late shift officer to do his rounds. That was the plan anyway, but like a lot of plans, this one went wrong from the first blow they struck.

I say first blow advisedly because what happened next caught both men by total surprise. After hitting an old prison officer named Sammy Lyons over the head with a broom, they both watched in amazement and horror as, with blood gushing from his severe wound, old Lyons bolted down the remand wing screaming his lungs out. I clearly heard his screams in the adjacent north wing. The central control centre located at the entrance to the north wing was the hub of the prison, from which senior prison officers directed day-to-day activities. Enclosed by a semicircle of bars, the control centre was accessible from the north wing, the east wing running off its middle, and the south wing, which was directly opposite the north wing on the other side of the centre. The prison's west wing used to run off the south wing.

After hitting Lyons over the head and watching him bolt away down the wing, blood pumping out of his severe wound – Officer Lyons never fully recovered from that blow – both Sadaraka and Western took off after him. Because neither man reacted quickly enough, Lyons was able to run into the north wing and alert officers in the control centre that something was seriously wrong. I have to say that what Lyons so bravely did that night helped avert a full scale breakout. With the element of surprise well and truly gone, the two men could only watch in dismay as the officers on duty in the control centre hit the escape siren. More in frustration than intent, Jon loosed off a couple of shots at the control centre. I heard the sound of the bullets ricocheting down the wing from my cell. Most of the officers on duty managed to get out through the front office entrance but a few were not so lucky and were taken hostage by Sadaraka and Western.

The echoes of the gunshots had barely died away when the first police cars started surrounding the prison. Using a small piece of mirror strategically placed outside my cell window on the second tier of the north wing, I was able to observe all the police activity on the outside of the prison walls. By the minute more police cars were arriving, so the escape attempt was over before it had even begun, but not what was to follow.

Desperate men do desperate things and neither Sadaraka nor Western were ready to give up so easily. With the prison officer hostages leading the way, they accessed the segregation–punishment section located beneath the east wing. At that time this section housed New Zealand's most dangerous and desperate prisoners. Included among them were John Gillies, who was serving a life sentence for a machine-gun double murder, he was also one of the inmates who used a sawn-off shotgun for a previous escape; George Wilder, a legendary escape artist serving 24 years for numerous escapes; and Lenny Evans, serving sixteen years, who had also been involved in the shotgun escape with Gillies and Wilder. Using cell keys taken from the prison officers, all these men and anyone else in the segregation section were released from their cells by Sadaraka and Western.

After releasing the men, Sadaraka, Western and this motley band of desperadoes then proceeded to try and find a way out of the prison – to no avail. Armed police had by this time every conceivable exit covered. Perhaps it was frustration at seeing their vision of escape foiled or perhaps it was someone who hated religion, but whatever the reason, one of the men set fire to the drapes in the prison chapel, which was located directly above the control centre. Being full of old, tinder dry, wooden pews, the chapel soon went up like a bonfire on Guy Fawkes Night. The smell of smoke that began swirling about the north wing became increasingly ominous.

About an hour after the escape attempt started there was a loud bang on my cell door and someone called my name. Looking out through the glass spyhole in the middle of the cell door I was shocked to see Jon Sadaraka standing there, gun in his right hand, surrounded by other wild-eyed inmates who were wearing their captive prison officers' hats as well as the officers' shoes. The fearful, dishevelled prison officers were standing alongside them in their bare feet. I knew the officer standing closest to my door as a fair, decent man and he pleaded with me: 'Jim, get them to give themselves up!' His plea fell on deaf ears as none of the men were ready to surrender and he was told unceremoniously to 'Shut the fuck up!' When my friend Jon asked me if I wanted to be let out of my cell I categorically said no, as it was obvious to me that someone was going to pay a heavy price for all the mayhem occurring and I did not want that someone to be me. However, my refusal to leave my cell ultimately did me no good, as by approaching me, Jon identified me as either part of his escape team or at the very least, someone who was familiar with his plan. Well I guess they were correct in that assumption. There is no doubt in my mind that Jon's approach to me on that destructive night was the catalyst that in the aftermath of the prison riot led to me spending years in segregation and solitary confinement.

It must have been ten or fifteen minutes after Jon left my cell door when I began to realise that the smoke-filled air was getting harder to breathe. Dying of asphyxiation in my cell was not an option for me so I sent a message to Jon to come and let me out. About five minutes later my door opened and I walked out to a scene I will never forget. The prison chapel was an inferno, the bone-dry wooden pews were exploding as they burnt, huge flames from the blaze were erupting out the chapel entrance, and the heavy, dark smoke was rapidly filling the prison wings. Below my cell on the first level a group of rabid prisoners surrounding the hostage prison officers were shouting, 'Burn, burn, burn.' No one was thinking about the hundreds of prisoners still locked in their cells as they shouted burn, burn, burn.

However, a group that included Jon Sadaraka, Phillip Western, Len Evans, George Wilder and myself, hastily convened together to work out what our next move should be. Both Len Evans and I voiced our concern about all the inmates still locked in their cells. I remember commenting on the possibility of the whole prison catching fire and the danger this would present to all the inmates unable to get out of their cells. Phillip Western's voice was dismissive as he pointed his finger at the stone walls and said: 'The whole prison is built from quarry stone, it will never burn!' How wrong he was. Although the prison was indeed built of stone, the rafters in every wing were not – they were made of highly inflammable wood. Consequently, the fire in the chapel ignited the wooden rafters in the ceilings of each wing and one after the other they caught fire.

It soon became obvious to all of us that we would have to do something about all the men locked in their cells or else there would be a disaster with many men dying of smoke inhalation. So Len Evans, George Wilder and myself, using cell keys taken from the captive prison officers, took it upon ourselves to start unlocking every cell in the prison. It took over 30 minutes for the three of us to get everyone out. None of us ever got any credit for what we did that fateful night. On the contrary, we were seen as helping foment a riot by releasing those prisoners; we were definitely not perceived as men who had saved lives. I have since read reports that said several courageous prison officers risked their lives by coming back into the prison to ensure no prisoners were still in their cells. All I can say is that I never observed any of them moving around the wings at any time during the riot. For any prison officer to have come back into that maelstrom of fire, smoke and madness would have taken courage of the highest order. If they did, then I acknowledge their courage.

After everyone was released from their cells around 3am there was total chaos in the prison. With the rafters above each wing burning, smoke from all the fires billowing into the wing, prisoners yelling and screaming everywhere, in the eerie half-light it looked like something out of a Fellini movie. Particularly when you consider the confused, frightened and in many cases terrified prisoners huddled together in various groups wondering what the fuck was going on.

A group of courageous firemen who had come into the control centre through the front entrance to try and battle the many fires burning throughout the prison were subjected to a continuous bombardment of milk bottles and other objects thrown at them by prisoners. Fearing for their personal safety they retreated back out the front entrance, thus leaving us in total control of the prison. In all the confusion and pandemonium, the captive prison officers managed to slip away in the dark and make good their escape. Ironically, theirs was the only successful escape that night.

After the firemen moved out, it was every man for himself. Old scores were being settled everywhere in the prison as with no prison officers around it was 'get square' time. At the time of the riot I had a six inch razor-sharp shiv for my own personal protection. With my shiv wrapped in a towel in my right hand and a long iron bar in my left hand, I set out amid the smoke and confusion to look for some of my enemies. The two men I was looking for – Maori Mac being one of them – must have realised that retribution could come for them at any moment in the darkness, not only from me but also from their many other enemies, so he and quite a few other inmates ran up the front entrance by the control centre and surrendered themselves to the police.

Alongside the north and east wings there used to be a big exercise yard that could be accessed from either one of those wings. The problem for us was the fact that the gates that led out to the exercise yard not only had chains and padlocks to fortify them but recently installed security locks that we did not have keys for. By about 3am the situation inside the wings was getting desperate as the dense smoke was making it increasingly difficult to breathe. Despite managing to break off the padlocks on the gates to the exercise yard, we could not open them because of the security locks. Those security locks certainly did their job, until one of the men reminded us about this big, heavy roller that was normally used to roll the grass surface where they played bowls in the exercise yard. That roller turned out to be just what the doctor ordered and no doubt helped save many lives. With half a dozen men pushing the heavy roller we repeatedly rammed the east wing security gate until it exploded outwards. There were at least ten armed police officers in the gun tower overlooking the exercise yard, so no one was keen to test them out. It was at least three minutes before one fearless prisoner boldly ventured outside and walked down the steps into the yard. When no shots were fired at him, a trickle of prisoners soon became a stream as everybody got out of the burning prison as quickly as they could.

With gangs of prisoners running rampant through the wings, every cell in the prison was destroyed or vandalised in an orgy of destruction. Terrible things happened that night. Prisoners being bashed and beaten were the least of them. A group of depraved inmates accessed the segregated area of the remand wing where they raped many of the young remand prisoners being held there. In some of the large eight-man association cells sex orgies involving numerous men were going on. I am embarrassed to say many of those men were friends of mine. Despite having spent a considerable amount of my life in prisons, I have never indulged in homosexual activity while imprisoned. Homosexuality was never an option for me, I guess I just liked women too much. However, because of the unnatural environment that prison inmates live in, I have never held it against any of my friends who engaged in such activities. It was always a personal decision with me. Anyway, during the riot I walked into one of the association cells, where despite the roof above them being ablaze and smoke billowing everywhere, every bunk in that cell had men in it involved in homosexual acts. I remember this particular event for two reasons. The first was an old, straight, safe-cracker friend of mine (Ron Tattley), sitting on a chair in the middle of the cell smoking his pipe while trying to remain oblivious to all the sexual activity going on around him. When I asked him what the fuck was going on, he just replied: 'Safer in here than out there, Jim.' Just as he uttered those words one of the guys in the cell called out: 'Has anyone got any butter?'

That was it for me. I walked out of the cell and joined my friend Jon Sadaraka in the smoke-filled east wing. As I stood outside that cell with my boyhood friend, him with an out-of-control look in his eyes and a gun in his right hand, me with a blade in my right hand and a iron bar in my left hand, in the dim, flickering light, with smoke and flames swirling all around us, I thought that this is what it must have been like when Sodom and Gomorrah were destroyed – utter chaos, depravity and madness.

In the chill early light of the next morning, the prison looked decidedly the worse for wear. Fires were still smouldering and burning in the roofs, large sections of the corrugated roofing had blown off during the night and fallen into the yard. In the yard itself, the shivering, bedraggled inmates with blankets wrapped around their shoulders for warmth were huddled in groups everywhere. They all looked stunned at what they had just been through.

Because the police and prison staff knew there was an armed inmate somewhere inside the prison, they were hesitant to move against us and quell the riot. So for two days we were left to our own devices inside the blackened ruins of Mt Eden Prison. During that time I cannot remember sleeping one wink, adrenaline plus a combination of excitement and anxiety kept me wide awake and alert. No doubt most of the other inmates would have undergone the same emotions as me.

Our food problem was solved when a group of inmates ripped the heavy mesh enclosing the kitchen window off the wall. A small and thin inmate was then able to slip between the iron bars and access food supplies in the prison kitchen. Anything edible was handed out through the bars: meat supplies from the freezer, tinned food, butter, bread, dried goods, everything but the kitchen sink came out. A large bonfire was started in the middle of the yard using wood taken from all parts of the prison. The heavy mesh ripped off the kitchen windows was used as a large improvised barbecue to cook on. Three or four men were delegated as cooks and did a proficient job. Once the food was cooked the men were surprisingly well behaved. There was no mad scramble for food, no standover tactics were used against the weaker inmates, all the men lined up and waited patiently until they were given some food. Prison inmates are creatures of habit because they are used to getting fed at regulated times, so the novelty of feeding ourselves was welcomed by everyone.

Situated under the east wing stairs was a small alcove which we turned into a makeshift bunker for hard-core inmates. Included among the hard core were Jon Sadaraka, Phillip Western, John Gillies, George Wilder, Len Evans, Danny Rauhihi – a good friend of mine – and myself. It had become apparent to all of us that first morning that no one was going to escape as there was literally a wall of armed soldiers, police and prison officers surrounding the prison. Even my old friend Jon Sadaraka and Phillip Western, two really desperate men, had accepted the fact that every conceivable exit was blanketed by police. All that remained was how long we could hold out before surrendering. That evening we ate the last of our food and made ourselves as comfortable as we could for another night out in the open.

The following morning the decision to surrender was taken out of our hands. The government had brought in army and naval troops to reinforce the police and help the prison administration retake control of the prison. On an illegal transistor radio one of the men had, we were able to pick up short-wave messages being relayed between sections of the armed forces outside the prison. When the order to 'fix bayonets' was heard, we immediately convened an emergency meeting in the bunker where it was unanimously agreed that to fight on with only one pistol against the armed might gathered outside the prison would be suicidal. So an emissary – I cannot recall who it was – walked up to the control centre and told them we were ready to surrender. As I recollect, Jon Sadaraka threw the pistol into a flooded section of the north wing where it was later retrieved by the police.

One by one with our hands raised above our heads, we marched out through the control centre. Those deemed not ringleaders were escorted out to the holding yards at the back of the prison. Jon Sadaraka and Phillip Western were immediately handcuffed and taken away by detectives. Among those deemed to be ringleaders were Gillies, Evans, Wilder, Ron Jorgenson, Frank Matich, Bruce McPhee and myself. With none of the cells in the prison habitable, everyone spent a cold and miserable night in the back yards, while the prison authorities desperately tried to work out where they could send everyone. Within a week, all the inmates from Mt Eden Prison were relocated to other prisons throughout New Zealand. All long term prisoners and those regarded as troublemakers were moved to Waikeria, a youth prison, some 200-odd kilometres south of Auckland.

6

THE AFTERMATH

That riot changed the face of New Zealand crime forever, because the government of the day and the public had had enough of rampant prisoners and their escape attempts. A sawn-off shotgun had been used in one attempt, gelignite in another, now prisoners armed with a pistol had not only attempted to break out of but had destroyed the prison in the process. Drastic measures were called for by the public and the government responded accordingly.

After two days of misery out in the back yards with no shelter and minimal food, the bulk of us were transferred by heavily armed escorts to Waikeria Prison. To accommodate the sudden influx of long-term prisoners, Waikeria Prison was rapidly turned into a steel fortress, while a brand new maximum security prison was being built at Paremoremo on the outskirts of Auckland. It took four years for that prison to be built, so for the duration of that time all the men at Waikeria were locked in their cells or in small steel cages located behind the cell blocks.

There were two levels to the wing we were housed in. All the cells had steel plates welded over the windows and armed guards patrolling outside the windows. The first ten cells in our wing had a steel cage built around them and extra padlocks put on the doors. Into these cells went Jon Sadaraka, Phillip Western, John Gillies, George Wilder, Len Evans, Ron Jorgenson, Bruce McPhee and Frank Matich. I cannot remember who the other two men were. I was pleasantly surprised to escape being housed with those deemed extremely dangerous. Now you would have thought with all the security we were now being subjected to that nothing untoward could have happened. Well like me, you would have been very mistaken, for as I said earlier, desperate men do desperate things.

While reading an old book off the library trolley, John Gillies read about this character who made a home-made bomb out of soap. That story line got John thinking about how he could do something similar. Rather ingeniously, he fashioned a pseudo bomb using red carbolic soap, paper wrapping, copper wire and an old battery taken out of a transistor radio. What he did was put the soap inside the brown paper wrapping, stick two wires into it and hey presto, a home-made bomb with a battery to set it off. I believe John Gillies was the only man who could have pulled off what transpired over the next two hours.

At that point of time in his life, in my opinion, and I might add in many others including prison staff, John Gillies was a dangerous, psychopathic killer. He was serving a term of life imprisonment for the machine-gun murder of two men at a house in Bassett Road, in Remuera, an affluent suburb in Auckland. He had not long before the Mt Eden riot put a shotgun to the head of a senior prison officer – if my memory serves me correctly, it was senior officer Kavenaugh, the same officer who intervened when I was fighting big Maori Mac – and marched him and another officer at gunpoint right out through the control centre and the front gate to gain a short-lived freedom. I say short lived because with George Wilder and Lenny Evans along-side him, just inside the prison gates Gillies commandeered the prison truck used to shuttle metal from the prison quarry to a nearby crusher.

Using the truck as a battering ram they smashed through the gates at the front of the prison, but unfortunately for them, a wooden splinter from the boom gate punctured the front wheel of the truck, and the three of them were soon cornered in a house nearby. After a four hour standoff they were coaxed by lawyer Kevin Ryan to surrender peacefully. But not before drinking a bottle of whisky which was part of the inducement used to get them to surrender.

The point I am trying to make is that for the bomb hoax to succeed, the prison inmate holding the dummy bomb had to be a man who the prison officers not only believed was extremely dangerous but also a man who would be prepared to blow himself up. John Gillies fitted that psychological profile to a tee. On the designated night in late 1965, Dirk – John Gillies' nickname – called out that he was desperately ill and needed to see a doctor. So around 7pm a doctor accompanied by four prison officers opened his cell door. All of us housed at Waikeria during that period had no beds or bunks in our cells, we all slept on straw mattresses on the floor. When they entered his cell, Dirk was on his mattress covered by grey, prison-issue blankets. As soon as the unfortunate doctor asked him rather innocuously: 'What seems to be the problem, Gillies?' You can imagine the doctor's horror as Dirk stood up from his mattress holding what looked like a home-made bomb and stated to all of them that unless they did what he ordered, they would all be blown to bits. According to Dirk when he was telling me later about what occurred that evening, the shocked, hapless doctor fainted on the spot and the prison officers immediately begged him not to blow them up. Even a cursory glance at his so-called bomb should have been enough to expose his hoax, but fear can blind even sensible men and that is what happened that night. After taking their keys and batons off them, Dirk had them kneel with their hands on their heads in the corridor outside the cells where the other high-security prisoners were being held. Two other officers who had come into the wing to see what was going on were unceremoniously told to join the other four officers and put their hands on their heads as well.

By this stage blind panic had well and truly set in among the terrified prison officers. Some were crying, some were praying, some were pleading they had wives and kids, so not to blow them up. Their panic-stricken pleas only emboldened Dirk and he contemptuously slapped a couple of officers around the head and admonished them by saying: 'They should die like men.' While all this was going on outside their cells, Sadaraka, Western, Wilder, Evans and others were shouting out: 'Blow the fuckers up, Dirk. We're safe behind these reinforced doors.' Talk about a sideshow!

The only obstacle to Dirk getting the other inmates out was the new padlocks that had been recently installed on their cells. While he was able to open two locks on the cell doors, Dirk needed an iron bar to prise off the padlocks as each door had different padlocks, so an officer was delegated to go off and find an iron bar. Death awaited those officers left behind if he did not follow instructions and return with this iron bar. When he returned a short time later, he had no iron bar but instead a message from the superintendent – who had been informed by this stage as to what was transpiring in the security wing – that they were prepared to release Gillies on his own but the other maximum security, high-risk prisoners were non-negotiable. A reliable prison officer source told me later that they had a sharpshooter outside ready to shoot Gillies as soon as he stepped out the door if he had accepted the superintendent's offer. Being the stand-up guy he was though, Dirk told the officer to inform the superintendent that he was not leaving without the others, and unless he sent the officer back with an iron bar, he was going to blow everyone up, including himself.

After two hours of terrorising his hostages, Dirk had become careless. While talking to Sadaraka, Evans, Wilder and a few of the other guys, he had put his dud bomb on the ground beside him as he discussed what his next move should be. The officer he had sent off to find an iron bar had noticed this careless behaviour and to his credit, the officer saw an opportunity to act. When he returned some fifteen minutes later he had no iron bar but told Gillies one would be delivered in ten minutes' time. As he anticipated, Dirk walked over to one of the cells to tell George Wilder what was happening. Dirk made two fatal errors that evening: the first was his carelessness in putting his sorry excuse for a bomb on the floor beside himself as he spoke to his buddies; and the second was he did not search the officer when he returned from his efforts to find an iron bar. Unbeknown to Dirk, the officer had a heavy baton concealed under his coat. As soon as he saw Gillies put his home-made bomb on the ground while he spoke to George Wilder, the officer pulled his concealed baton out, walked up behind Gillies and hit him a powerful blow to the head. *Thwack!* I heard the blow from my cell some 30 metres away. 'You bastard,' was all Gillies could say before he slumped to the ground. Letting out primeval cries of relief at being saved and shouts of pure animal rage, the prison officers who had been subjected to hours of terror now vented their anger on the semiconscious Gillies. How he survived that flogging is beyond me. Like a pack of demented animals they fell on him. They kicked him, hit him with batons, all that pent-up anger at the indignities they had endured, the cowardice some of them had shown, was now unleashed on Gillies. They battered him to within an inch of his life. The boys in the adjacent cells who heard the feral screams of 'Kill him' emanating from Dirk's cell were sure he was dead.

Over the past 50 years I have met many men who had balls, many men who have committed outlandish and daring crimes – and I include myself in that group – but I have never to this day seen anyone come close to what John Gillies did that evening in 1965 with his pseudo bomb. That took nerve of the highest order. I remember spending years in segregation during the 1960s with John Gillies and I came to respect the man. On more than one occasion I saw prison officers dragging his unconscious body past my cell in solitary. They do not make them like John Gillies anymore. Despite having 120 stitches put in his head, I was astounded a few days later to watch Dirk stagger out, his head swathed in bandages and his body black and blue, to the steel cages we exercised in, for his daily exercise of one hour. He was, believe me, one tough motherfucker.

7

THE SECURITY BLOCK

The abortive escape attempt by Gillies only hastened the building of an escape-proof security wing at Mt Eden Prison. The undamaged women's section of the prison was gutted and thus the security block was born. For those deemed the most dangerous prisoners in New Zealand, their prison accommodations were about to get a whole lot tougher. This dreadful abomination, euphemistically called the security block, would be their home for nearly three years. No expense had been spared to make this prison within a prison escape-proof. It served that purpose well, but a new breed of tough and violent criminals, myself included, was about to be spawned from this punishment block.

Despite having been involved in nearly all the escape plots from Mt Eden Prison between 1963 and 1965, as well as being involved in the July 1965 prison riot that gutted and destroyed the prison, and certainly deserving of a place there, I nevertheless did not think I would end up in the dreaded security block. My reason for thinking along these lines was the fact that I was not housed in the high security section of the wing at Waikeria Prison with the other so-called most dangerous prisoners. I mistakenly thought I had kept under the radar.

Therefore I was completely taken by surprise around the middle of March 1966 when my cell door was opened at about 5am one morning and I was confronted by at least ten prison officers as well as a few police officers. I was told to strip naked and then marched naked from my cell the 40 metres or so to the wing exit. All my personal possessions were left behind – not a letter, photo, or even a toothbrush left with me, just my naked self. At the end of the wing, George Wilder, John Gillies, Jon Sadaraka, Len Evans, Ron Jorgenson and myself were examined separately by a doctor to make sure we had nothing concealed up our rectums. After being dressed in brand new boiler suits and heavily shackled, the six of us were then placed on a reinforced, armoured bus. In a sealed-off section at the front of the bus were five armed prison officers and in a sealed off section at the back of the bus another five armed prison officers. The bus, accompanied by four car loads of armed police as well as traffic police to clear the roads for us was then driven non-stop to Mt Eden Prison.

During the course of my life I have had many embarrassing things happen to me, but none of them came close to what occurred that day we were transferred to the security block. On arrival at Mt Eden Prison the bus was driven through the gates and parked just inside. Each of us was then unshackled separately and ordered to strip naked on the bus, and we were then made to walk naked between police officers standing shoulder to shoulder – I do not exaggerate here – the 30 metres to the entrance of the security block. What made it so surreal was the fact they were all wearing black raincoats. It was a very cold morning as I recollect and all our appendages were decidedly shrunken. If this arrival procedure was meant to demean and humiliate us, it certainly worked. Once inside the security block we were examined by another doctor, including another rectum search, just to make absolutely sure we had nothing concealed on us, then marched naked to our designated cells. Because of the security measures put in place on our arrival, during the three years it was operational, no one even remotely looked like escaping from the block while it was open. It served that purpose exceptionally well.

The security block was virtually an underground steel and concrete bunker. With twelve escape-proof cells, it was designed to break men physically and mentally. Something it succeeded at all too well. Guantánamo Bay in Cuba would have had nothing on this place; it was ahead of its time. I realise now that we were subjected, unknowingly, to what is now considered torture. For example, we were housed in cells four by three metres. These cells had doors that were opened manually but all the other gates in the block were electronically opened from a control centre. The officers manning this control centre had specific instructions never to open any gates without authorisation, not even if their fellow officers' lives were being threatened. Security was so tight we were checked every 30 minutes. As a consequence those electric gates would religiously clang open every 30 minutes, day in day out, as the officers came around for their cell checks. During the night a pale blue light shone continuously so the officers could see into our cells. Sleep deprivation, continuous noise 24 hours a day, the blue lights on all night, plus our harsh, and solitary confinement conditions would be construed as torture today. To give some balance to the extreme conditions we were held in, however, I guess it is only fair to say that none of us being housed there could be called choirboys. We were, in fact, the most dangerous prisoners in New Zealand at that time.

The security block had been planned so that the inmates housed there had minimal living conditions. Each cell had a steel frame bolted to the wall and floor that served as a bed. A thin canvas mattress, a low pillow, two blankets and no linen was all we were allowed. There was a steel table with a flat steel sheet welded onto it that served as a seat. The table was also bolted to the floor. The only other item in the cell not bolted to the floor was a small plastic toilet pot for us to use during the long hours we were confined in our cells. There were no toilets in the cells in those days. Our clothing consisted of one pair of white moleskin pants, no belts allowed, one grey shirt, one singlet, one pair of underpants, one pair of brown plastic sandals, no shoes allowed and one towel. At 4pm every afternoon we had to hand our clothes out through a small slot in the middle of our doors, these clothes were then stored in a bag outside our cells and returned to us at 8am the following morning.

While two-thirds of the door was solid steel, the top and bottom was heavy mesh so that the officers could see into our cells at all times. Also at the bottom of our doors was a small, padlocked opening used to slide our meals through to us – very similar to the way they feed the lions at the zoo. No prison inmates were allowed within ten metres of the entrance to the security block and only one of us at any given time was allowed out into the corridor area outside our cells. When we were, there had to be a minimum six officers present, four of them carrying batons in case of trouble. We used to get this escort every morning as we walked down to the ablutions block at the end of the wing to empty our toilet pots. There were six cells on each side of the block so as we walked down to the ablutions area, we were able to say hello to those guys on our side of the wing we were still talking to.

A sad effect of the harsh conditions we were subjected to in the security block was the fracturing of many friendships. We all entered the block as friends, but due to the psychological breakdowns of quite a few men while we were there, many of us left the block mortal enemies and that is allowing for the fact that we never saw the other six guys opposite us. Prison officers handled all our food so cigarette butts, pubic hair, glass, cockroaches and other unmentionables in our food were the order of the day. I remember eating a salad one day and on feeling a crunching as I chewed my food, I looked down at my plate of salad and observed half a praying mantis lying there. It tasted a little like peanut butter as I recollect. Because of the fact some officers were contaminating the food, inspecting your food became a necessary precaution before every meal time while we were in the block.

For the first six months the security block was open, the only people we saw were prison officers, not even the prison chaplain or the Catholic priest were allowed to visit us. Society and the government of the day could rest easy, for New Zealand's so-called most dangerous prisoners our isolation was complete and there would be no witnesses to whatever punishment they deemed fit to hand us.

8

LIFE IN THE BLOCK

Despite the harsh and brutal punishment that was inflicted on me during the time I spent in the block, I still managed to take a few positives out of that psychologically damaging experience. Those positives would, in time, make me a more proficient and determined criminal. Up to that stage of my life the crimes I had committed were trivial, one or two safe-cracking jobs but not much of any note or value. The long hours spent looking at the walls of my cell contemplating my future and thinking about my past crimes instilled in me the belief that if I wanted to be a successful criminal I had better change my modus operandi and get serious about making a living from crime.

From the vantage point of looking back to that fateful decision some 40 years ago, I now realise that despite making me millions of dollars that decision would also cost me another twenty years of misery in prison. I now deeply regret that I did not harness that steely, determined drive and pursue an honest life as a businessman, postman or labourer – anything but life as a criminal. Hindsight is a wonderful thing, is it not? In my cell in the security block in 1966, however, all that money and misery still awaited me.

The first positive I took out of my time spent in the security block was my decision to improve my neglected education. To help alleviate the long hours in my cell and to help stop my brain from stagnating, I applied to the authorities to do a Form Five correspondence course in geography. A request from one of the so-called most dangerous men in New Zealand to do a correspondence course must have raised a few eyebrows among the hierarchy but to my surprise they said yes. Unlike today where inmates can complete university degrees while serving their sentences, back in the 1960s, it was hard to get toilet paper let alone permission to do an education course. Nevertheless, doing that geography course helped me to keep my brain functioning, because being imprisoned in such harsh, repressive conditions meant intellectual stimulation was in short supply. Punishment was the name of the game in the security block. So even though it was only a low level course, that simple Form Five course gave me not only a tenuous intellectual lifeline to hold on to, but just as importantly, helped me pass the time in my cell. I passed that course comfortably and was then allowed to do Form Five courses in history and bookkeeping, which I also passed comfortably. By 1969 when we were moved to the maximum security prison at Albany, some 50 kilometres from Auckland, my educational rebirth was well under way.

The second positive to come out of my time spent in the security block was my development as a street fighter. Although I had managed to last the distance with Maori Mac at Mt Eden Prison just before the riot in July 1965, my fighting skills were instinctive, not taught. I never had any formal training as a fighter. That all changed when an inmate named Paddy McNally arrived at the block a few days after me. When his family queried his placement in the block as he had never caused any trouble, they were given the dubious excuse that as he was regarded as the leader of all the Pakeha inmates, he had to be kept segregated. They used the same excuse on my family, except in my case I was regarded as the leader of all the Maori inmates and therefore had to be kept segregated from them. Still sounds flimsy all these years later.

To say Paddy was a character would be an understatement. A gregarious, outgoing man, Paddy had such an infectious personality he would be smiling at you as he robbed you playing a game of cards or two-up. Paddy came under that well-worn cliché, a likeable rogue. Before he fell foul of the law, many astute boxing experts regarded Paddy as the most naturally gifted boxer of his generation in New Zealand. All the McNally clan who originally came from Dunedin on New Zealand's South Island, could fight. Even his big sister May could knock you out with a punch. His eldest brother Joe, also a professional fighter in the 1960s, held the NZ lightweight title for a time. Despite the fact that he hated training and seldom did enough, Paddy still managed to win the NZ welterweight championship.

There is a legendary tale about Paddy McNally that is well worth retelling here to illustrate what a character he was. In the early 1960s, Paddy took a bout at short notice to fight a seasoned pro named Sam Leuii who held the welterweight title at that time. I cannot recollect where the fight was held but Paddy arrived for the fight half drunk and with no boxing shorts, boxing boots, protective cup or even a mouth guard. So from a friend in the crowd he borrowed a well-worn pair of khaki shorts, another friend supplied an old pair of sandshoes, while someone else gave him an ill-fitting mouth guard. He went without a protective shield for his testicles. Then with two drunken friends acting as his seconds, Paddy staggered into the ring. Despite spewing twice during the fight, to everyone's amazement he not only lasted ten rounds but also won the fight on points! Besides being a skilled boxer in the ring, Paddy was just as adept at street fighting. In street fights he fought some of the toughest men in New Zealand. His arrival in the security block was the start of my fistic education.

Every afternoon in groups of three we were allowed about 90 minutes' exercise in the six metre by six metre yards adjacent to our cells. Despite being only five metres from our cells to the exercise yards, getting there was an experience in itself. At least six prison officers would arrive outside your cell door and ask if you wanted to go to the exercise yard. If you replied yes, an officer would call out your cell number and another officer at the end of the wing would take note before they unlocked your cell. You would then take two paces forward and they would manually open a steel-grilled gate in front of you. You would then walk into a small enclosure and they would lock the gate behind you. An officer locked inside a concrete bunker adjacent to the enclosure would then slide the steel-grilled gate in front of you open so you could step into another small enclosure. Once the gate behind you was secured the officer would then slide open the last steel-grilled gate which let you walk into a steel and concrete six by six metre exercise yard. With mesh and steel bars overhead and an officer standing above you watching your every move, including when you used the toilet, the exercise periods were very closely monitored. Those daily breaks were a welcome respite from our daily cell confinements, however. Just being able to talk and interact with someone else during the exercise periods helped me keep my sanity.

Once you were in the exercise yard the same procedure would be repeated with two other inmates. At that time my two exercise companions were Paddy McNally and my old schoolboy friend Jon Sadaraka. Usually Paddy would warm us up by doing press-ups, stomach strengthening exercises and skipping. After the warm-up exercises, Paddy would have Jon and I punching a long seat cushion we doubled over to use as a rudimentary punching pad. While punching this seat cushion, Paddy would be telling Jon and I where we were going wrong with our punches. He taught us how to punch with either hand as well as all the basic punches. He showed us how to throw a hard straight left-hand punch, how to jab with the left hand, how to throw a lethal left hook. Body punches, left and right rips to the body, uppercuts, how to shorten our right-hand punches so they travelled no more than 30 centimetres. He improved our footwork, taught us how to balance ourselves when throwing a punch and how to use our body weight and leverage to get maximum power when punching.

After our daily clinic was over Paddy would wrap a towel around each of his hands and then press each hand into a grey, woollen, prison-issue sock that either Jon or I would be holding. The end result was a rock hard, home-made boxing glove. Jon or I would repeat the procedure ourselves and then Paddy would spar Jon and I for five three-minute rounds each. Because of his superior boxing skills, Paddy would let Jon and I throw as many punches at him as we liked. Even if we tagged him with a hard punch, which we both did occasionally, he would not get angry and try to retaliate. He was a patient teacher but every so often he would let loose a right or left rip to the body that would leave us gasping for air. Those punches hurt.

Besides boxing skills Paddy showed us a wide variety of his street-fighting talents. We were shown how to use our knees, elbows and head when street fighting. How to punch to the throat, kick or punch directly at an opponent's testicles as well as the old 'walnut grip', grabbing someone's testicles. A particular favourite of his was the 'Liverpool kiss,' a street-fighting technique made famous by count-less Liverpool-bred merchant seamen. This distinct form of attack entails you grabbing your opponent's clothing, pulling him forcefully towards you and then hitting him in the face with your forehead as often and as hard as you can. Liverpool seamen have been known to hit an opponent six times before he hits the ground.

Once our sparring sessions were over we would take turns to wash the sweat and occasional blood off ourselves under the cold water tap in the exercise yard. Very invigorating in winter but necessary as we only used to get two showers a week. By the time he was moved out of the security block, Paddy McNally had moulded me into a super-fit, proficient, boxer/street fighter capable of fighting well above my weight and size – a legacy that has stood me in good stead over the many intervening years of numerous street and prison battles.

To further highlight what a character Paddy was, in 1980, he was shot during a dispute with other criminals in Sydney. While lying in his hospital bed recovering from his bullet wounds Paddy was questioned by Sydney detectives about who shot him. When one of the detectives asked him if he had seen who shot him, Paddy replied: 'Yes.'

'Could you give me a description please,' the detective asked.

'Yes, I can,' Paddy replied. 'He was a large man with a long white beard and he was wearing a red suit.'

'Did he say anything?' the detective asked.

'Yes, he did,' Paddy replied.

'And what did he say?' the detective inquired.

Keeping a straight face Paddy replied: 'Ho, ho, ho.'

That is a true story.

Sadly, a few years later, Paddy was murdered in an underworld feud in Sydney. Wherever your spirit is now Paddy, know I will always remember you. You were one of a kind.

9

LAST RITES AT THE BLOCK

In early 1968, those of us unfortunate enough to still be held in the security block were told that our new home, a maximum security prison at Albany, a small, quiet, hamlet some 50 kilometres from Auckland, was nearing completion and we would be among its first residents. It was touted to be the most advanced maximum security prison in the southern hemisphere and for its time I guess it was. For prison inmates it had two amenities that were unheard of in those days but are regarded as normal today: toilets in each cell and a water basin with a tap. For prisoners used to slopping out their toilet pots every morning, toilets were an unheard of luxury.

During the years the security block was operational – 1966 to 1969 – there was only one man who had access to the block that all the prisoners housed there respected and spoke to. That man's name was Leo Downey and he was a Catholic priest. Every week without fail he would come into the block, stop at each cell and offer kind words of encouragement to each one of us. In such draconian prison conditions, a kind word is like gold. Even today, over 40 years later, I can recall his compassionate, kindly face as he unlatched the slot in my door, looked in and said: 'How are you today, Jim?' What an honourable and decent man he was. A man devoted entirely to the Church and serving those less fortunate than himself. I have never been a religious man but seeing someone like Father Leo Downey offering kind words of encouragement to villains like us, while at the same time doing selfless work in the community, gave me a respect for religion I otherwise would not have had.

I particularly remember two observations Father Downey made to me during my time in the block that are worth mentioning here. The first observation happened just months before we were moved to the new prison at Albany. Father Downey had stopped by my cell for his weekly visit and found me sitting at my steel table waiting for my evening meal. On my table I had placed a white tea towel on which I had put my plastic knife and fork as well as my plastic cup, and if memory serves me correctly an apple I had saved from lunch that day. Anyway, there I was sitting on my cold steel seat at my steel welded table when Father Downey unlocked my door latch to say hello. After observing me sitting at my table waiting for my meal, he made an interesting comment to me. He said: 'You know Jim, I have just learnt something today.' When I asked what that was, he replied: 'After all the time you men have spent in here, you are the only one still eating at his table. All the others are either eating on their beds or on the floor.'

That observation really surprised me as I had naturally assumed everyone in the block behaved like me. I did not realise my behaviour was the exception, not the rule.

The other observation he made just days before we were moved to the new prison was, sadly, wrong. Father Downey had come up to my cell to wish me well and shake my hand before we left. As he shook my hand he made a surprising statement. He observed that of all the men who had the misfortune to be incarcerated in the security block since its inception, only myself and Ron Jorgenson were leaving in the same physical and mental state as when we had arrived three years earlier. Although I did not acknowledge it at the time, I now know I too was psychologically damaged by the time I spent in the security block. That place stayed in my psyche for many years.

Like the majority of the men who were housed there, I developed a cold-blooded, ruthless attitude towards crime. I do not think in the long history of NZ crime that there has ever been a group of men who went on to commit more violent and serious crime than those men who were imprisoned in the Mt Eden security block between 1966 and 1968. That security block was the beginning of crime as we know it in New Zealand today. Cruel and brutal prison conditions breed cruel and brutal men.

What my time in the security block taught me is this: treat a man like an animal and he will behave accordingly. The psychological damage inflicted on men who have been caged in punishment blocks never leaves them. I am certain men who served time in Grafton Prison in New South Wales; in H block in Pentridge Prison, Victoria; or in Katingal Prison inside Long Bay in Sydney would agree with my assessment. All these years later I can still remember every detail of the brutality inflicted on me inside that security block. I do not offer that punishment as an excuse for my subsequent behaviour, because at the end of the day we are all responsible for our own actions, I only make the observation that the inhumane and degrading treatment meted out to me and others like me makes it very easy to become involved in, or stand by while terrible crimes against others are committed. It certainly made it easy for me to ignore what was going on around me while I was involved with the Mr Asia syndicate.

I am saddened when I think about many of the men who had the misfortune to be incarcerated in that terrible place with me, men who did not fare well in their later lives. Of the twenty or so men who served time in the block, nearly one third had to be transferred to mental asylums for treatment and in later years many met an unhappy end. Of the alumni I have already mentioned Paddy McNally was murdered in Sydney's Kings Cross in the early 1980s; Mike Davidson was shot dead in Auckland in the 1970s; Ron Jorgenson is still missing believed murdered in the South Island; Merv Rich missing believed murdered in an underworld feud in Auckland; Phillip Western was shot dead in a gun battle with NSW detectives near Sydney; Jon Sadaraka was convicted of one murder in Sydney and another murder in Auckland after his release from an Australian prison; Mike Sneller was convicted of murder; Wayne Carstairs was convicted of murder; John Gillies was re-sentenced to life for shooting a man in the head in Auckland; Len Evans served ten years for shooting police in Sydney; Peter Fulcher, fourteen years for drug trafficking for the Mr Asia syndicate, Auckland; and of course myself, 25 years for drug importation, Sydney. These are just the men who I am aware of, what happened to the others I do not know. I believe a few guys made it through, I hope there were others.

Looking back at my life, it is a sad reality that at that time, being included as one of the twelve most dangerous, recalcitrant prisoners in New Zealand at the age of 26, meant it had only taken me ten years since my first conviction as a sixteen year old to attain what I regarded as my arrival as a tough guy. I am embarrassed now to say that at that point in time I revelled at being classed as a dangerous criminal. I remember thinking at the time, How tough am I? That sentiment should have been, How stupid am I? With the amount of time I have spent in prison, I am the living, breathing embodiment of the maxim 'Crime does not pay'!

10

FAREWELL TO THE BLOCK AND THE MOUSE

The day before we were moved to Paremoremo prison in Albany on the outskirts of Auckland, disaster struck a little mouse who used to make nightly visits to our section of the security block and whom we had adopted as a pet. The mouse first appeared about six months before our departure from the block. How he got into that concrete fortress is still a mystery but one night there he was. I think it was John Gillies who called out one night: 'Hey guys there's a mouse in the corridor.' A mouse in the corridor! Like the five other guys on my side of the block I got down on my haunches and looked out through the mesh at the bottom of my door into the corridor and sure enough, there was a little grey mouse clearly visible in the pale blue light, darting along the corridor. The first night he appeared he only stayed a few minutes before he darted off but during his brief visit he had the six of us transfixed. After he left – I am assuming the mouse was a he – there was a flurry of questions. Where had he come from? How did he get in here? What type of mouse was he? Would we see him again? Was the mouse an omen? I reckon we must have spent the next hour telling mouse and rat stories to each other. For men whose lives had been subjected to solitary confinement and mind-numbing days of regimented sameness, that little mouse was a breath of fresh air.

The next night the six of us must have spent about four hours sitting on our haunches peering out through the mesh on the bottom of our doors, waiting to see if the mouse put in a reappearance. All we got for our efforts were sore arses. But two nights later one of the boys called out that 'Mickey Mouse' was back. And lo and behold, there he was, scurrying to and fro along the corridor. The way he moved along the corridor, it was almost as if he deliberately stopped outside each of our cells to let us have a look at him before moving on to the next cell. In anticipation of his reappearance we had all saved some bread which we proceeded to push out through the mesh into the corridor. But the mouse did not eat one morsel. It would have been four or five nights later that he finally accepted some of the bread we offered him. After that he used to come visit us at least four times a week and did not hesitate to accept our offerings of bread and the occasional bits of cheese we gave him. The cheese they used to give us in those days was so bad that one of our running jokes was, 'This cheese is so bad a rat would not eat it!' Well like a lot of disparaging comments prisoners make, that comment was definitely debunked by the mouse – he loved our cheese.

The inmate who grew closest to that mouse was the same man who had machine-gunned two men to death and tried to escape from Mt Eden Prison using a shotgun, as well as trying to escape from Waikeria Prison using a pseudo bomb. A man noted for his psychopathic tendencies befriending a mouse! Anyway for John Gillies, whatever reason, Dirk would sit by his door every night waiting for that mouse to show up. Without fail, every time the mouse put in an appearance, Dirk would cheerfully call out: 'Mickey Mouse is here, boys.' That little mouse kept Dirk captivated as it would invariably make a beeline to his cell and eat the bread and little bits of cheese Dirk saved for him and placed outside his door. I have to say that little mouse supplied all of us with a lot of joy and kept us amused with his antics on many a night. The carefree way Mickey the Mouse darted up and down our corridor mesmerised us. Who would have thought a little harmless grey mouse, could get six paranoid neurotic sociopaths like us to find common ground every time he put in an appearance. I guess in adversity even enemies can find common ground – that is what that mouse did for us, he became a neutral focal point for the six of us.

Besides visits from the mouse there was another way we tried to amuse ourselves. There was a Dutch prison officer named Harry who did the night shift in the block. I cannot recall what his last name was but he was a nasty bit of work. I do not know what it is about Dutch prison officers but it has been my experience that they make particularly nasty screws. When people immigrated to New Zealand in the 1960s, particularly those who were assisted immigrants, they had to work for their first two years in some branch of the NZ government. As a consequence many male immigrants chose the prison services, which is no doubt how big Harry became a screw. I say 'big' advisedly, as the man was about six feet six inches tall. Whatever his height, he was one big motherfucker.

That saying 'Small things amuse small minds' would have fitted many of us in the security block to a tee. One of the mindless games we used to play involved the big Dutchman. As I have said earlier, prison officers used to come around and check us out every half hour. So some nights when big Harry was doing his rounds, by common agreement, the six of us would stand silently at our doors and watch him. As he approached our doors from the right, we would just look at him silently as he walked past our doors to the end of the wing. As he walked back we would all look at him from left to right as he passed. Not a word was said, but as soon as he got to the electric gate at the end of our wing, we would all yell out abuse at him. 'You dog,' 'you mongrel', and the old standby, 'you motherfucker', were just a few of our insults. As big Harry came charging back down the wing, we would all dive back onto our beds and be lying there feigning innocence as he stood at our doors frothing at the mouth. He would become so angry that his English would falter, at which point one of us would say: 'Speak English man so we can understand you.' And that would make him even more inarticulate. Very childish I know, but as I said at the top of this paragraph, small things amuse small minds. However, big Harry evened the score with us the night before we were moved.

No doubt over the previous months, big Harry had observed us feeding the mouse. From our comments to one another he would have become aware how attached we had become to that little mouse so the mongrel just bided his time until we were ready to leave. The night before we were due to go, Mickey the Mouse came in for one, fateful, last meal. So that neither the mouse nor we would hear his approach, on his last cell check the Dutchman had left the electric gate at the end of the wing unlocked. This allowed him to tiptoe up to our side of the block and pounce on poor, unsuspecting, overfed, Mickey the Mouse. A year earlier, Mickey the Mouse would have eluded the big Dutchman easily. But all that cheese and bread we had fed him had slowed him down. 'Got you!' he screamed as he jumped on the mouse. Poor old Mickey never had a chance. One terrified squeak and he was gone. The big Dutchman was beside himself with glee at killing something that meant so much to all of us. His small mind would have been right at home with us. Unfortunately our little friend paid a heavy price for all the abuse and childish games we had inflicted on the big Dutchman.

Well to say there was pandemonium and anger after Mickey's demise would be putting it mildly. There is no doubt that had we been able to get out of our cells, despite his size, we would have pulled the big Dutchman apart, limb by limb. Killing the mouse enraged us all, but John Gillies was incandescent with rage. That little mouse over the last six months had become his revered and much-loved pet. There is no doubt in my mind had he been able to he would have killed that Dutchman in a heartbeat. I can still hear him screaming out at the Dutchman: 'You fucking murderer!' I have often reflected on the irony of Dirk's impassioned outrage. Here was a man who had machine-gunned two men to death, calling someone a 'fucking murderer' for killing a mouse! I guess if we were brutally honest with ourselves we would have accepted that it was our continual insults and hostility towards him that drove big Harry to kill our much-loved mouse. The old causes and effects theory proven true once again.

Our departure from that cruel, inhumane, concrete tomb called the security block the next morning helped to alleviate some of our anger over the death of the mouse. For those of us who had been there when the block opened and were there when it closed, leaving it was a cause for celebration. We had survived, but at what cost? Not only to ourselves but to society in general, because a number of the men who left that security block in shackles would go on to become extremely violent criminals. That security block certainly succeeded in containing the men held there, which in the overall scheme of things was what is was meant to do. But when its effectiveness is compared with the death, violence and criminality perpetrated on others by the men who were held there, you have to question the value to the public of such places. Although its a bit late for me to be moralising, that place did no one any good, neither us, nor the government of the day.

I did a little jig, though, as I walked out the door to board the armoured bus that was taking us to our new home at Paremoremo. Life for us was about to get a whole lot better.

11

THE PAREMOREMO HILTON

After the conditions we had been used to at the security block at Mt Eden, our new home was like a Hilton hotel. We could not believe it: a toilet in our cell and running water! Prisoners today have no idea how tough prison used to be in the sixties. Not only that but looking out through the bars of the cell, we could see trees and green grass in the distance. There were thick concrete walls opposite our cells but through the bars on the windows we could see the surrounding countryside. For guys like us who had seen nothing but concrete and steel for three years, such views were priceless.

The prison was based around a long corridor that ran for about 150 metres. Along the corridor there were three wings running off to the right. The three blocks were named A block, B block and C block. At the end of the corridor on the left was D block, which housed the so-called intractable inmates; we were its first customers. There was only a skeleton crew at the prison when we arrived and it took about two months to bring everybody up from Waikeria and get the prison fully operational. That was in 1969, over 40 years ago. I believe the place is still powering along all these years later, although they have expanded it to include medium and minimum category prisons as well. The reason I mention the year is for the simple fact that 1969 was the year I became a serious criminal. Paremoremo Prison was where I completed my education and also where I learnt how to move money illegally around the world from a master criminal doing time there. The same gentleman was also instrumental in getting me to reassess my behaviour while in prison.

My first step in improving myself was to drop my surly disposition and threatening attitude towards the authorities. By that I mean my mindset towards prison officers, welfare officers, the superintendent, and anyone who was not an inmate. One thing the security block taught me was the undeniable fact that when you are isolated you are a sitting target for the prison authorities, you are really on your own, with no help from anyone. In solitary confinement you are no threat to anyone and the only person in danger of being hurt or damaged is yourself. While being in solitary and, as a consequence, being seen as a tough guy can enhance your reputation, after some serious contemplation I came to the conclusion that such behaviour was not smart. Therefore I decided my new rules of engagement in prison would be to keep my mouth shut, ask no one for anything, never deal drugs, mind my own business and stay out of jail politics. Those rules have stood the test of time and allowed me to survive my 25 year sentence in some of Australia's worst prisons.

Whenever I think of the time I spent at Paremoremo Prison I often think of that excellent British comedy series *Porridge* starring Ronnie Barker, where he played a conniving prisoner who was always outwitting the staff and getting up to mischief. Well, our Ronnie Barker was Ron Jorgenson. A big, solidly built man, Ron stood about six foot two inches, had receding hair and a gruff way of talking to people, but underneath that gruff exterior was a warm, likeable personality. In fact, I thought so much of Jorgy that about ten years later when his release from prison was being held up because of an unpaid $10,000 debt, I had the money sent over to New Zealand so that he could be released. The female lawyer who handled the transaction for me was a young Karen Soich, but as they say, that's another story altogether. Although convicted of the Basset Road murders in Auckland with John Gillies, unlike Dirk, Jorgy was not a raging psychopath. He was a frustrated entrepreneur and would have been right at home in the world we live in today if he was still alive. All I can say about the man is he was a good friend to me and I still think about him to this day. We had some fun together at that prison and got up to a lot of shenanigans.

After an initial settling-in period of about three months my friend Ron Jorgenson was given a job in the prison kitchen as the butcher, a highly sought after job because of access to all the meat rations. Because of my school studies I was moved from D block to A block. The system worked like this: if you were a troublemaker or someone who continually flouted the authorities then you ended up in the 'intractables' wing, D block. As your behaviour improved, you were then moved from D block to A block, which is what happened to me. My education courses deemed me an inmate trying to improve himself so I was moved to A block. After A block, B block was your next step along the way. By the time you reached C block you were classified as ready for a move to a medium or minimum security prison. That was how it was supposed to work anyway. Within a few months of his appointment as the prison butcher, Jorgy had me assigned to the kitchen detail as a trainee chef. The fun and games were about to begin.

My new jail rules did not preclude me from pursuing my plans to improve myself as a criminal, however. As I mentioned earlier, a master criminal I met in Paremoremo became my mentor and taught me a lot about life, lifestyles and, most importantly, how to move money between countries. That man was a swindler named Robert 'Skip' Gardiner. Skip was in his late forties when I met him. A heavy-set man, he was around five foot nine inches tall with a body tending towards fat, due no doubt to many years of luxurious living. Despite having receding hair, his body was very hirsute indeed, with hair all over his back and front. Although not a handsome man, Skip as you would expect from such a masterful criminal, had a forceful and charismatic personality. He was a well-educated, worldly and erudite individual. Gardiner was not his real name but he would never tell me his true one, only that it was one of many on his charge sheet. Skip was the first millionaire I ever met. His scam was cosmetics and he used to sell cosmetic franchises in an outfit he called: 'Leidrum Hartnell.' Quite a catchy name. The only problem with his franchises was that no one ever received any cosmetics. Anyway, he had run the same scam in England, South Africa, Canada, Australia and of course New Zealand. He was wanted all over the world for different scams. I had a look at his charge sheet one day and noted he was wanted for a $10 million bank scam in Mexico and another huge scam in Israel. What a fucking character he was. During the many years I spent in prisons all over the world I met quite a few inmates who were wealthy men, but none of them used his wealth in the prison system like Skip Gardiner did.

I had met Skip during a court appearance and for some reason he liked me. Maybe he recognised my potential or maybe he saw a little of himself in me, but whatever the reason, we became firm friends. Both Skip and his beautiful Swiss girlfriend Ursula could speak six languages and they used to give the prison officers fits in the visiting section as they constantly switched languages while talking to each other during her visits. Ursula was a beautiful woman, much younger than Skip, tall with a slim build and long, dark hair. She carried herself like a model, which, truth be known, she more than likely had been. She had the kind of skin European woman seem to have: soft, pale, delicate. Whenever I spoke to her in the visiting section she was always polite and very charming. She had class with a capital C that lady. During the two years Skip spent inside, she lived in a luxury penthouse in Auckland. Every Saturday she would get a taxi out to Paremoremo Prison, keep the taxi waiting two hours while she visited

Skip, and then it would take her back to her apartment in the city. Every Saturday she would also bring out all the latest bestseller books for us and any magazines we wanted. In return, Ron Jorgenson and I protected Skip from the many jail predators waiting for an opportunity to shake him down.

During the course of the time I knew Skip I came to realise what an extremely intelligent man he was. One thing that really irked him though, was the fact that a tiny little country like New Zealand had been able to effect his arrest while he had been able to elude law enforcement agencies in countries all around the world. It was through Skip I learnt about eating fine food; what wines to match with meals when out dining; the importance of appearance and choosing what clothes to wear; where to get handmade shoes, tailored suits and shirts; to always live in affluent areas; to associate with people who were not criminals; having the best financial people handle your money; to always keep a top-flight lawyer on a retainer; the importance of good manners, speech and diction; how to interact with and treat people; to make sure I always kept abreast of world and current affairs; to keep improving my education; learning other languages; and most importantly, how to hide any future illegal earnings overseas. Skip showed me there was another world I could aspire to, another level I could go up to – all I needed were brains and balls. I always knew I had the balls, it was the brains I had to work on.

Although I had no money at that time in my life, I used to say to Skip: 'One day I'll have a lot of money. When that day arrives, how will I get it from A to B?' Very patiently he would sit down with me and explain the intricacies of banking and how to go about moving money between countries. Unlike today where money movements are tightly regulated and anything over $10,000 has to be reported by banks, in the sixties and seventies it was open slather. Skip explained to me how to set up financial structures in overseas countries using false identities. How to use the banks to transfer money, how to buy shares or gold that could be converted overseas, how to have accounts so that when the money arrived at one overseas bank account it was immediately moved on to a bank account in another country. For example, if I went to Bank X in Sydney and had it transfer X amount of dollars to my account in Singapore, on arrival in Singapore that money would be immediately transferred to an account held by me in Hong Kong. The reason for moving it to Hong Kong was that back then you did not pay tax on any monies not earned in that country: that is, you could bring money into Hong Kong tax-free. Your money could sit there, either in a bank like the Bank of Red China which did not allow anyone, and that included law enforcement agencies, access to your accounts, or in an account with a discreet accountant there. Skip also explained to me how I could then bring that money back into the country legally and lend it to myself using dummy companies. When I started moving money for Terry Clark and the Mr Asia syndicate, I was able to put everything Skip Gardiner had taught me into practice, and I have to say, it all worked exactly as he said it would.

Besides getting all our required reading material, Ursula was also in charge of seeing Skip's weekly requests of luxury food items was met. To this end Skip was paying two prison officers a weekly wage to bring in contraband food and liquor for us. All the contraband was kept in the officers' personal lockers outside the prison so there was no way we could be caught with any of it. But no matter how careful you are in prison, shit happens and on a few occasions that is what happened to Ron and I in the kitchen. The times we were caught were funny and illustrate why I thought of Ron Jorgenson as our Ronnie Barker.

The first incident involved caviar. At that point of time in my life I had never eaten caviar, mainly because it was out of reach of my financial pocket. Caviar was something I had read about in magazines and that was as far as it went with me. In the years since I have been able to afford the luxury of eating caviar at restaurants all over the world, but I have to say I never acquired a taste for it. I guess it was the simple thrill of eating such expensive contraband inside a maximum security prison with Skip that had me licking my lips and saying it was 'fucking fantastic' as I tried it for the first time. By contrast, Skip really loved caviar and literally spent thousands of dollars having bottles of the stuff brought in. Sometimes Ron Jorgenson would keep some of the caviar in a little fridge he had in the butcher's shop. One afternoon while I was sitting in the butcher's shop with Ron just shooting the breeze and telling a few lies, one of the officers who worked in the kitchen came into the shop. If I remember correctly his first name was Wally: elderly, overweight, just looking to collect his pay check and go home to his family every night, he was a decent sort of an officer.

Anyway, on this particular day he decided to look in the fridge and spotted the bottle of caviar. 'Hello, hello,' said Wally, 'what do we have here? If I'm not mistaken this is caviar.' Evidently Wally had actually eaten some caviar years ago and that is why his suspicions had been aroused.

Jorgy immediately got up from his chair and exclaimed: 'Caviar, Wally? Where the hell would I get caviar from?'

Despite Jorgy's protestations Wally was still sceptical and said: 'If this is not caviar, what is it?'

Jorgy did not hesitate for one moment: 'That's not caviar, Wally, those are miniature Japanese blackcurrants my mother sent me for Christmas!'

'Well I'll be,' Wally said, 'it sure looks like caviar to me.' And with that he walked out of the butcher's shop. Needless to say, we didn't keep the caviar in that fridge again.

The next time we ran into a problem it was over Chinese noodles. Besides being a proficient butcher, Jorgy was also an accomplished cook and was always preparing excellent meals for himself, Skip and I to eat. On this particular day he had made us a Chinese dish using noodles that had been smuggled into the prison. Usually when we were eating food not available in the prison we would have another inmate keeping lookout for us while we ate our food. However, an urgent call of nature meant our lookout had to dash off to the toilet, which allowed the prison superintendent, a no-nonsense man named

Norm Buckley, to walk in on us unannounced. 'Hello men,' he said, 'what is that you are eating? It looks good.'

'Just a little something I made from leftovers, sir,' Jorgy replied.

Being an observant type, Buckley spotted the noodles. 'Are those noodles you men are eating? We don't get noodles here, where did these noodles come from?' a suddenly suspicious Buckley asked.

Quick as a flash Jorgy replied: 'These are home-made noodles sir.'

'Home-made noodles. How do you make those?' an incredulous Buckley replied. I thought right then, We are fucked here! But not my old mate Jorgy, he was a real quick-witted man and he replied immediately.

'It's a simple procedure, sir, and I'll show you how it's done.' With that he raced off to the bakery next door and came back with some bread dough. He put the bread dough in the meat mincer, turned the handle and out came long pieces of dough. Jorgy turned to the superintendent and said: 'I then bake the pieces in the oven and there you have it, sir, home-made noodles!'

With an admiring look at Jorgy the superintendent replied: 'Ingenious Jorgenson, ingenious,' and with that he left the butcher's shop. We both had a chuckle after he walked out, another close shave averted.

The next time the superintendent caught Jorgy and I unawares was due to our own laxness. The security block seemed a lifetime away to both of us and we had become fat and slipshod due to all the luxury food items we had become accustomed to eating courtesy of Skip. At that time our alcohol of choice was vodka, mainly because of its lack of smell and the fact that it looked like water. In the butcher's shop which we used as a de facto office there was a large chopping block and on many an afternoon Jorgy and I would sit around it and pontificate to one another about what we intended to do in the future, all the money we intended to make and how successful we would be after we were released. On this particular day Superintendent Buckley walked in on us while we were both sitting at the large chopping block. The problem for us, though, was the fact we were both blind drunk. We had been drinking a mixture of vodka and Raro orange juice all afternoon and could barely stand up.

'How are you men?' Buckley asked.

'Fine, sir,' we both replied. The vodka mix we had been drinking was in a large stainless steel bowl, which was sitting in the middle of the chopping block.

'What's that you boys are drinking?' Buckley asked.

'Raro orange juice, sir,' Jorgy replied and with that he reached out, poured some of the mixture into a mug and offered it to the superintendent.

If I had not been so drunk I would have fallen off my chair at Jorgy's audacious move. But to my heart-felt relief Buckley declined the proffered drink. 'No thanks boys, I'll leave it all to both of you,' and with that he walked out the door. I was just thankful he did not ask us to stand up because I know I would not have been able to do so.

Our most daring escapade at Paremoremo Prison involved a gun, or to be more precise, parts of a gun. By now it should be obvious why I held Skip Gardiner in such high esteem. The life lessons he taught me during our many walks around the prison yard have stood me in good stead over the intervening years, just like my boxing lessons from Paddy McNally have. I'll always remember him saying: 'Money is just paper Jim, never forget that, and always remember, you cannot take it with you.' I also remember asking him one day: 'How do you get sensible people to part with their hard-earned cash?' All these years later I can still recall his answer like it was just yesterday: 'Jim, you only ever get the greedy ones.' Whenever I see people on one of the current affairs programs nowadays complaining about being robbed of their hard-earned cash by some fraudster or fraudulent scheme, I always think back to those words. To this day Skip is still one of the most intelligent criminals I have ever met, and I've certainly met a few over the last 50 years. How he organised to get himself extra remission was just another example of that distorted intelligence.

One day while we were walking around the yard, Skip said to me: 'What do you think would happen Jim if someone got a gun in here?'

'It would not do them much good,' I replied, 'because the prison officers have implicit instructions to never open any gates, even if their fellow officers' lives are being threatened.'

'It would be highly embarrassing for the government and prison authorities though, would it not?' was Skip's next enigmatic comment. I looked at him when he said that and thought to myself, Just what are you up to my friend?

Knowing how much I loathed screws in those days, Skip did not let me in on his scheme until it was successfully concluded. He then told me what had transpired. Through an informant he had word leaked to the authorities that there was a gun in the prison and it was going to be used in a mass jail break-out. With the abortive armed break-out from Mt Eden Prison just a few years in the past, such information had to be taken seriously. Consequently, the prison was searched from top to bottom looking for the gun, with no success. The authorities were frantic and inducements were offered to anyone who could help locate the weapon. That is when helpful inmate Gardiner stepped forward and offered his services. He was only prepared to risk his neck, however, if there was a definite reward of extra remission. On being assured there was, Skip said he would consult with two of the prison's most influential inmates – that is, Ron Jorgenson and I – and see what he could do. What he had done was this. Unbeknown to one of the prison officers who was bringing in contraband for him, concealed in the large cheeses he had ordered that week were the parts of a gun. After breaking the cheese open and taking out the parts, Skip assembled the gun and then delivered it to an astonished and grateful superintendent. I believe he got six months off his sentence and Ron and I got an honourable mention in dispatches. Not a word ever leaked out about that gun and I'm sure the authorities are denying it to this very day. I often wonder what happened to Skip Gardiner. After he was released he was extradited to Australia to stand trial on fraud charges. I believe he skipped bail while awaiting trial and I have not heard from him since. Certainly one of the most fascinating and engaging men I have met in my life and definitely a larger than life character. I hope you made it to that island we talked about, old friend, and lived to a ripe old age.

My last year at Paremoremo was spent productively. Because I was deemed a bad influence on the hardworking butcher, my devious friend Jorgy, I was sacked from my cushy job in the kitchen. So to further my education I applied to become a full-time student and study for my university entrance exams. In New Zealand it is the exam students have to successfully complete if they want to go on to university. Because of my success in passing all my previous exams, albeit easy ones, I was given permission by the authorities to become a full-time student. My subjects were English, geography, book-keeping and history. Determined to pass I spent all my spare time studying. While my buddies were playing cards and other games to pass the time, aimlessly away, I had my head down beavering away in the classroom. A very interesting development from my studies was the fact that I found I had to lower my vocabulary when I spoke to my fellow inmates. Because of my studies my thought processes were well ahead of theirs, so I found myself in the unusual position of having to talk down to guys I had known for years. It really reinforced in me how deceptively easy it is for a man's brain to stagnate in prison without intellectual stimulation. All my hard work paid off in ways that I had not imagined when I first started studying for my University Entrance. Although my pass mark was nothing to boast about, at least I passed and that gave me a great deal of personal satisfaction. I believe, although I could be wrong, that I was the first inmate, certainly in a maximum security prison in New Zealand, to pass the university entrance exam. Nowadays inmates regularly complete university degrees while in prison, but back then in the late 1960s, education was not high on the authorities' agenda, so my accomplishment was a big deal.

Despite my horrendous prison record while serving my sentence, in recognition of my successful educational studies the parole board granted me an early release. I guess they felt that to induce other inmates to follow a similar path to me they had to show there were rewards for such endeavours. So no doubt somewhat reluctantly and against their better judgement, they gave me an early release in 1971. The new improved me was about to be let loose on the unsuspecting public. For the next thirteen years I would make millions of dollars and live the life I had often dreamed of.

12

OUT ON THE STREETS

Like most ex-inmates I found it hard to re-establish myself outside. For a short period I played rugby league football for an old established Auckland team, City-Newton. Despite my increasing years – I was 31 at the time – I had kept superbly fit and therefore more than able to hold my own in the brutal way the game was played back then. Despite my love of the game, however, getting my head busted open every weekend for a 100 bucks a match was not an attractive option for me. So reluctantly, after playing the game I loved for a few years, I retired. But my main reason was that the illegal bookmaking activities I was involved in at that time had to take precedence. There was much more money to be made on a Saturday accepting bets rather than getting battered playing league.

An interesting highlight to my days as a league player was how I acquired my nickname of 'Diamond Jim'. The obvious assumption is that I got the name because I used to wear a diamond ring, but that was not the case. In fact when I was given that colourful nickname I didn't even own a diamond ring. The nickname was started by a well-known Auckland identity named Laurie Burleigh who used to drink at the City-Newton clubrooms. Laurie was a lovely man but he had the type of rugged face that only a mother could love. In fact his nickname was 'Lee' as in the American actor Lee Marvin to whom he bore an uncanny resemblance. Most Saturdays after finishing our game the players and supporters would return to the City-Newton clubrooms for a drink. Usually Laurie, who was a good friend of mine, would be sitting by the front door quietly nursing a beer. In those days I knew quite a few ladies and would usually have an attractive female with me when I went to the clubrooms for a drink. On seeing me enter the clubrooms with an attractive lady, Laurie would good-naturedly call out: 'Diamond Jim strikes again!' And that is how I acquired the sobriquet 'Diamond Jim'. The nickname has stayed with me for all these years. Personally, I hate it but it has stuck to me like glue.

About three years after Laurie Burleigh gave me the name, I accepted it was here to stay and got myself a diamond ring to go with my nickname. Although 2.5 carats it was not a good quality diamond, nevertheless I thought it gave me the appearance of a successful man about town. I now realise that such an ostentatious show of afflu-ence is not a smart move at all. It has never ceased to amaze me the number of successful criminals who flaunt their prosperity by driving expensive cars, wearing large gold necklaces, gold bracelets, diamond rings, emerald rings, expensive jewellery of all descriptions, even fur coats. I will not even start on about the expensive jewellery some of their wives, girlfriends and mistresses wear. If you are an active criminal who wears expensive jewellery and has a female companion bedecked with jewels, you may as well carry around a neon sign that says: 'Successful criminal here!' because that is how the police view such outward displays of flagrant showiness by criminals. Discretion is always the better part of valour when you are trying to beat the forces of law and order. The police do not like having success flaunted at them. But then again, who does?

I will not go in to what all my criminal activity was during the 1970s in New Zealand. Although the police were not able to convict me of any serious crime during that decade, they have a fair idea of what I was involved in. The NZ police at that time were hardworking and dedicated, and unlike their Australian counterparts, strictly honest. So for me to elude them for a number of years was due more to good luck than anything else. I have never had a problem with honest police; they do a very necessary job protecting the public. And I have to say, when I think of the many murderous, homicidal psychopaths and other violent madmen I have encountered over the last 50 years, both inside and outside prison, average Joe Public should be very thankful they have a police force to protect them. No, it is the crooked cop on the take, the cops who plant evidence and verbal you in court by saying you confessed to them, who I despise. During the seventies and eighties the Australian police were masters of this type of behaviour. In fairness to the current police force, however, I should preface those comments by saying that those days are well and truly over. When I first arrived in Australia in the early 1970s, it was hard to find – although no doubt there were – an honest cop. Today it is the exact opposite: it is hard to find a dishonest cop. With the economic climate like it is today though, I would suggest that law enforcement agencies be very vigilant. Police officers, like the rest of us, are struggling to make ends meet. If ever the time was ripe for corrupt police to make a comeback, that time is now. I know for sure and certain that affluent drug dealers will be zeroing in on anyone they think is susceptible to a bribe, because that is just the nature of the beast. That is how drug dealers and criminals have operated since time immemorial.

Before I came over to Australia though, my main source of early income was illegal bookmaking. I was actually convicted in Wellington on a bookmaking charge and fined $200. Despite paying that fine many years ago, I have been told that there is a warrant for an unpaid fine out against me. I guess I'll have to pay that fine for a second time, whenever I venture back to New Zealand again.

Nevertheless, bookmaking was good to me. I got involved in book-making through a very dear and respected friend of mine, a gentleman named Barry McFarlane, who lived in Wellington. At that time, Barry was one of the biggest illegal bookmakers in New Zealand. If you were a bookmaker anywhere in New Zealand and had more money bet on a horse than you were willing to risk, you just called Barry and laid the bet off with him. If the bet won you would collect your cash the following Thursday, or pay the money you owed for the losing bet the same day. Through Barry's connections I was given a pub at Taita, a suburb about 25 kilometres out of Wellington, to set up shop as a bookmaker. The pub was the favoured watering hole of all the Maoris who worked at the local meatworks. On Saturdays the joint was always packed with Maoris eager to have a bet. It used to get so busy I had to have two guys helping me.

On my first day of business, the locals were very wary of me, until a Maori named rather fortuitously, Lucky, backed a rank outsider with me that paid about $30. If I remember correctly, he had $20 each way on it, which meant I had to pay him about $700. Up to that point I had taken a measly $80 in bets and was having to pay out $700, but with a smile I paid Lucky his winnings. 'There's plenty more where that came from,' I told the happy, satisfied Lucky, as he counted his cash. There is no doubt the smiling Lucky went off and told all his buddies about the new accommodating bookie in the front bar with loads of cash, because before you could say Jack Robinson, I was inundated with eager punters, all of them wanting to relieve me of my cash. Fortunately for me, like most punters, they were hopeless, and soon my pockets were overflowing with cash. That pub was a little goldmine. I never had a losing day there, ever. I used to pull between $3000 and $5000 there every week. A lot of money back then, even today for that matter. It used to be so good that by the time the sixth race on an eight race card rolled around, I would be so far in front with my winnings that I would ring off all my remaining bets to my friend Barry so that I could go home winning big, no matter what happened in the last two races.

It did not take long for me to build up a considerable bankroll, and despite my best attempts to spend it as quickly as it came in by wining and dining ladies as well as nightclubbing in Wellington and Auckland, there was still large amounts of cash lying around my apartment. One of the many problems associated with being a successful criminal is the fact that you cannot go and put your illegally earned cash in a bank account. Although I used to have bank accounts in Auckland and Wellington, I only ever kept minimal cash in them. Obviously if you are unemployed or working in a menial job, you cannot have thousands of dollars in your accounts. So what was I to do with all my hard-earned illegal cash? My problem was solved in a very unusual way.

At least twice a week I used to go to a gym in downtown Wellington to work out. It was an up-market type of gym frequented by a wide range of businessmen. While in prison, I never fell into the foolish habit of many of my friends of getting jail tattoos on my fingers, hands, arms, face or legs. So when I stood naked under the shower at the gym, my body free of any incriminating jail tattoos, I looked just like the men around me, another businessman enjoying a good workout. Sometimes I used to go for a run before my workout and one day a gentleman at the gym on seeing me come back from my run, enquired if I had run far. 'Just a few miles,' I told him. The chappie, whom I will call Dave, then informed me about a group of enthusiastic runners who met at the gym twice a week before travelling by car up to some of the hilly areas located around Wellington, where they ran around various paths and tracks. I was invited to join them and I jumped at the opportunity. The hilly tracks and paths the group used to run were tortuous. I thought I was in reasonable shape, but on my first few runs I was trailing by at least 50 metres behind these super-fit runners. It took at least two months of punishing running before I was able to keep up with these human mountain goats.

After running with the group for six months and enjoying the occasional drink with the guys after our workouts, I learnt one of the runners, whom I will call Robert, owned a finance company. Robert was very brusque in his manner but he was a very smart businessman, and like a lot of successful businessmen, was always on the lookout for a deal. One afternoon while having a drink with Robert I broached the subject of money. Was there any way I could quietly invest some money I had available, was my tentative query. 'How much are we talking about?' he inquired. On informing him that I had a lot of illicit, residual money available, Robert told me to come see him at his office the following day. When I went to see him, he explained to me how I could increase my wealth with him if I was interested. Besides making legitimate loans, he also had a private loan portfolio where he charged exorbitant rates for making loans to people whom could not get a loan anywhere else. 'Desperates,' he called them. Robert then explained to me that if I was prepared to leave my money with him for two years and let it roll over continuously, my wealth could increase fourfold, if not more.

One of the advantages of being a criminal prepared to use violence is the fact that if people owe you money and refuse to pay, you do not need to worry about taking that individual to court to get your money back. No one wanted to owe money to guys like I was back then, as it could prove very detrimental to their health. So because of that in-built belief, I did not have any hesitation in handing over a large amount of cash to Robert to invest for me. In fact, any money I earned over the next two years – illegally of course – went to Robert to be invested in my portfolio. Once a month I would visit Robert and he would show me my portfolio, just so that I could see whom we were lending money to. There were many times while walking the streets of Wellington – I never owned a car back then – that someone who had borrowed money from Robert to purchase the expensive car he was driving, would drive by me. There goes five grand I would say to myself as the car went by. Investing my money with Robert was one of the best decisions I ever made in my life, because over the years my money quadrupled. Thanks to Robert, I was well on the way to my first million.

13

DRUGS IN THE EARLY YEARS

I have deliberately condensed the period of my life before I became involved with the Mr Asia syndicate because the crimes I committed during those years have got little to do with the subject of this book. What I have tried to do to this point, is convey a sense of me as an individual, to give some insight into why Terry Clark would want me to come over to Australia and work with him. Although only 35, I already had a big reputation among New Zealand criminals and I am only stating a cold, hard fact – and not boasting – when I say that guys like I was back then did not grow on trees. And for anybody affronted about me admitting to committing other crimes before I got involved with the Mr Asia syndicate, the 25 year sentence I received for my involvement in the syndicate certainly helped square the ledger in that regard.

Because I have been around drugs since 1964, when I used to acquire grass and buddha sticks for musician friends of mine in Auckland, I think I can reasonably say that no one in New Zealand or Australia has had a greater involvement in handling drugs at the highest level than me. It's not a fact I am proud of, but it's not one I can hide from either. To watch at close range the evolution of the drug trade in New Zealand and Australia has been a disquieting yet compelling experience. Like the mythical Topsy, the drug trade has just got bigger and bigger.

I remember back in the 1960s in New Zealand it was very difficult to get drugs of any description, there just did not appear to be a market for them. Every so often you would see a small influx of grass or hashish, but heroin, cocaine or speed was virtually unheard of. Most of the grass, hashish or LSD available was brought in by independent, small-time importers. I knew many of these pioneering drug entrepreneurs, so I was able to acquire grass or hashish for friends of mine whenever it was available. A friend of mine said to me back then: 'New Zealand is not big enough to sustain a large drug market.' How wrong that statement turned out to be would be evident in the early 1970s when buddha sticks became more readily available.

Although I used to get grass and hashish for friends, mainly musician friends, back in 1964, I never did it for a profit, just as a favour to them. Considering the risk involved that was rather foolish, but when you're young you think you're bullet-proof and risk doesn't enter into the equation. I can honestly say that I never looked at the financial side of dealing drugs until 1973, when I started to take a closer look at the drug trade. It came about because a friend of mine in Auckland put a proposition to me while we were having a drink at a bar one night. 'How would you like an all expenses paid trip to Wellington?' he asked me. I knew this guy to be a solid, reliable villain, so I asked him what the trip involved. 'I need someone to watch my back down in Wellington,' he said. 'I am taking a load of grass down there, and just need someone I can trust to accompany me. Besides all expenses, I'll give you $50 for every pound I sell. I expect to sell at least 60 pounds.' Because I liked the guy, the chance to earn a few bucks while enjoying an all expenses paid trip to Wellington sounded very appealing, so I said yes. A few days later we were ensconced in a

Wellington motel. I looked after the cash while my friend ran around disposing of his 60 pounds of grass. To my surprise, it was all gone in a day. That trip was a real eye opener for me. After he paid me $3000 for my efforts, my wee brain went into overdrive. If my friend could afford to pay me $3000 to just stand around, how much was he making?

From around 1973 to 1976 buddha sticks were readily available in New Zealand. Because of the potency of buddha sticks, if there was a choice between the cheaper home-grown weed or the more expensive imported buddha, the latter won out every time. Avid pot smokers are like amateur wine connoisseurs, always comparing the potency of any weed they get. They love giving pot exotic names like Thai Tripping Grass, Maui Wowee, Jamaican Gold, Mountain Mayhem, Black Lightning, and Hawaiian Magic. An exotic name usually helps an importer move his product quicker – it's a good sales pitch – so that is why they will always try to invent a catchy name.

In the beginning it was mainly guys like Marty Johnstone, guys who had never been in prison, who handled all the drugs coming into New Zealand, particularly the buddha sticks. Wherever massive amounts of illegal money can be made, however, it does not take long for hardcore criminals to recognise a lucrative, unlawful business opportunity and then devise ways to control that business – usually by resorting to violent means. It was in 1973 that I really started to become aware of the growing drug trade in New Zealand. In 1974, after his release from Wi Tako Prison, Terry Clark started his first tentative steps into the drug trade. With the upsurge of serious criminals taking an interest in the drug trade after 1974, it was inevitable that the likes of Martin Johnstone and other non-violent importers would have to form alliances with criminals who were ready to use violence against all comers. That is how Clark got his start with Johnstone.

The massive amounts of money available in dealing drugs are why many old-style criminals like me have gone into the drug trade. The pure economics is what makes drug dealing so appealing to hardened criminals. For example, if you are an armed robber it has to be a big bank before you or your accomplices can get away with at least $100,000. It usually takes three to pull off such a robbery, so you might end up with $30,000 each. Now take, for example, the same person acquiring, just for argument's sake, a kilo of cocaine at $150,000. Because he knows the distributor, usually another criminal, he gets that cocaine for a short period of time on credit. If the cocaine is good quality, he will off-load that kilo for $180,000 or $200,000. For going from A to B he has made up to $50,000. Obviously the risk factors are just as great, but it is far easier to just hand over a kilo of cocaine to someone in a quiet spot than run yelling and screaming into a bank wearing a balaclava and carrying a sawn-off shotgun.

In the Mr Asia syndicate there was myself, Terry Clark, Peter Fulcher, Errol Hincksman, Patrick Norton-Bennett, Brian Agnew and both Greg Ollard and Doug Wilson who were later murdered, who were all criminals who had done time in NZ prisons. In Australia there was the notorious Neddy Smith who was a hardened criminal, as well as others like Bobby Chapman and Dave Kelleher. All of these men were graduates of the Australian penal system. Criminals in both Australia and New Zealand at that time started to recognise the fact that there were massive amounts of money to be made in both importing and distributing drugs. The lure of easy money is what attracts hardcore criminals into the drug trade. I know that is what attracted me. Nowadays all the drug syndicates in Australia and New Zealand, be they Chinese, Vietnamese, Lebanese, Italian, Australian, Russian, Serbian, New Zealand Maori gangs, even outlaw motorcycle gangs, are mainly controlled by hardcore criminals who have done time in prison. There are exceptions to this rule, but not many. Anyone not violent or tough enough to fight off all challengers to his business will not last one minute against any of these syndicates.

Despite the crushing sentences they hand out to major drug dealers who have been convicted of drug importation or drug distribution, there is never a shortage of individuals who think they can beat the system.

Why does this happen? The simple answer is money – lots of money. Even in countries like China, Malaysia, Thailand, Singapore, Indonesia or Vietnam which carry the death penalty for even small amounts of drugs, there is no shortage of people prepared to risk their lives dealing in drugs. As long as there are huge amounts of money to be made, no sentence, be it 25 years in prison or even the death penalty, will deter people trying to succeed as drug dealers. Having said that, my advice to anyone contemplating a career as a drug importer or drug distributor is simply this: do not proceed any further with your plans. The drug enforcement agencies, even the police, are ten times more effective now than when we were running around Australia in the mid-1970s. It is much, much harder to be a successful criminal today. We had corrupt police protecting us for most of our time in Australia; criminals today do not have that luxury. Whoever made the statement 'Money is the root of all evil' certainly had drug dealers in mind when they said that.

I guess it is a fair comment to say that the Mr Asia syndicate was the first organised group to really recognise the huge amounts of money available in selling hard drugs in Australia. We were the fore-runners of all the drug groups that have since sprouted like bad weeds all over the country. Australian criminals in the sixties and seventies, despite many of them being violent and dangerous men, were mainly involved in standover rackets, armed robberies, illegal gambling, pros-titution, safe-breaking, fraud, arson and extortion. People reading this book may be surprised to learn that hardcore Australian criminals in the late sixties and early seventies took a very dim view of dealers selling hard drugs like heroin. Such people were regarded as being on the same level as pimps and hoons. In fact, I never told any of my Australian friends who were old-style criminals what I was doing in Sydney. They would have cut me dead had they known what I was doing. All my Australian friends thought I was involved in book-making and fixing races. Times change I guess, but that is how Aussie crims thought back then. Interestingly, during those years marijuana or hashish were not regarded with the same disdain as heroin and you could sell either of those drugs with impunity.

Although there were a few other outfits around selling smaller amounts of hard drugs besides us, only the Italians in Griffith, who were growing marijuana by the train-load, were actively selling drugs. They were a real smart group of men. Through my friendship with Bob Trimbole, I met some of the crew from Griffith and I found them to be good company. For guys regarded as illiterate peasants, they sure fooled a lot of people – they made millions selling marijuana. The fatal mistake the Griffith mob made was the killing of Donald Mackay. That brought their nefarious activities to a shuddering halt. Terry Clark suffered a similar fate; his arranging to have the Wilsons murdered was the beginning of the end for him and the Mr Asia syndicate. Both were particularly nasty crimes, committed by particularly nasty people. Nobody, and that includes me, who has dealt in or deals drugs are nice people. And as hard as that fact is to acknowledge, it is just the plain – unpalatable as it may be – truth.

14

THE REAL
MR ASIA

Now that I have given an account of my journey to getting involved with the Mr Asia syndicate, I thought I'd provide a sense of what the other major players were like and how it came about that all our lives intersected at that fateful juncture called the Mr Asia syndicate. The most significant person besides Terry Clark and Jack Choo in the organisation was Christopher Martin Johnstone. The money Clark made from handling the sale of over 450,000 Thai buddha sticks Johnstone had smuggled into New Zealand aboard the yacht *Brigadoon* in March 1976 gave Clark the financial independence he needed to buy hundreds of kilos of high grade heroin in Asia. Without Martin Johnstone there would have been no Mr Asia syndicate.

Although his full name was Christopher Martin Johnstone, everybody who knew him called him Martin or Marty. It has always been a prevalent misconception in New Zealand and Australia that Terry Clark was Mr Asia. He was not. That dubious distinction belonged to his fellow New Zealander, Martin Johnstone. There was a book written around 1976 by NZ journalist and author Pat Booth titled *Mr Asia*. The book was written to expose Martin Johnstone's – alleged at that time – drug activities between 1973 and 1976. During the years 1976–78 there were numerous articles about this elusive drug dealer called Mr Asia. During this period the *Auckland Star* newspaper compiled a lengthy dossier on Martin Johnstone. I have been reliably informed that because of legal advice, journalists working for the *Auckland Star* at that time were told they could not name Martin Johnstone as the notorious drug dealer they were writing about. So an enterprising editor came up with the mysterious pseudonym Mr Asia instead. In fact, one of the women Martin had befriended while living in Singapore, a Canadian lady named Monique van Putten, rather ingenuously told police: 'I only became aware of him being a drug dealer when I inadvertently came across some newspaper clippings from New Zealand that referred to Martin as being this big-time drug dealer named Mr Asia.' I have often wondered if she also told the police why she was rifling through Martin's personal belongings when she found those incriminating clippings? I think Miss Monique van Putten, like many others, was just covering her ample and well-perfumed arse. Like the majority of people involved in the syndicate, her involvement with one of the main players was minimal: she never took part in any major drug trafficking, she was just a bit player. Yeah, pigs might fly too!

The thing that really shocked me about Martin's death was, strangely, his age. He was only 29 when he was murdered. I had always assumed he was much older than that. I guess it was the beard he cultivated much of the time that made him appear older than he was. Perhaps that is why he grew a beard, to give himself an air of gravitas. When you are dealing with older drug dealers, particularly Asian drug dealers, you do not want to give the appearance of being a young man, someone still learning the business. From the time I first met him in 1974, Martin always carried himself like an older person.

I first met Martin in 1974 at a welcome home party for a gentleman called Jim M – I use the term gentleman loosely here, as Jim had just got out of prison – held at the Intercontinental Hotel in Auckland. As Jim was one of the new breed of well-educated, private school criminals running around Auckland at that time, to celebrate his release from prison his friends had hired the ballroom at the hotel for a welcome home party. I believe, although I never spoke to him there, that Terry Clark was also in attendance at that party. Through people I knew in the grass business, I had become aware of Martin Johnstone and his drug activities and wanted to take a look at him. Everyone was stoned and drunk and so I didn't get much of a chance to talk to him after a mutual friend introduced us. The next time I met Martin was a few months later at Oliver's Changing Times, a nightclub situated in downtown Auckland and frequented by most of that city's wannabe criminals. Martin was with another successful drug dealer of that time, George the Greek. They had about five ladies with them, which attracted a lot of attention and certainly caught my eye. As George was a guy I liked and respected, I stopped by their table to say hello. With a booth full of women and champagne on the table, Martin was enjoying all the attention and giving a good impression of being the nouveau riche drug dealer he had become. No business was discussed that night and I did not see Martin again until 1978 in Sydney, when the Mr Asia syndicate was well under way and flourishing.

Martin Johnstone was born in 1951 in a small, rural hospital in South Auckland, a farming area 80 kilometres from Auckland. A tall, slim and handsome man, Martin never had any trouble meeting attractive, compliant females, no matter what country he was in. Although he could be charming, Martin had a slightly arrogant air about him. Sudden wealth can do that sometimes. Always well dressed, he was a bit of a dandy. I was surprised to learn recently that he had attempted suicide several times when he was a young man, once by jumping into the water off the ferry that runs between downtown Auckland and Devonport on the North Shore. The Martin Johnstone I knew was always a smiling, gregarious man. I'm no psychiatrist, but his extroverted moods when I knew him taken in context with his earlier suicide attempts more than likely meant Martin was bipolar.

His honest, law-abiding parents were farmers before they moved to Auckland in the 1960s. They must have wondered in the years since – just as my family did – how did it all came to this. A quiet childhood, a good education, a comfortable upbringing, devoted parents, clean country air: where did his criminality come from? I never discussed his upbringing with Martin, so I cannot speculate on the motivation that led him to start dealing in drugs. I do know he was convicted as a young man on a couple of burglary charges as well as a drug posses-sion charge and given a period of probation. Such minor charges hardly serve as a springboard to the international stage as a major drug dealer, but that is what transpired.

My theory is this, and I do not think I am far wrong: Martin loved a joint, he loved smoking marijuana. When you are a habitual smoker of marijuana, or addicted to hard drugs such as heroin or cocaine, you can soon find yourself unable to afford your habit. 'How can I get money to pay for my supplies,' soon becomes the addict's mantra. Many addicts, particularly heroin addicts, commit crimes to feed their addiction. They commit burglaries, they steal, and some even prosti-tute themselves. Anything that will earn them the money needed to feed their addiction. Many addicts, whether their drug of choice is marijuana or a hard drug like heroin, become small-time drug dealers themselves. They become a salesperson for their dealer. The diluted garbage that a street heroin dealer sells to his clientele becomes even more diluted by them, but doing this allows the user to make a small profit on selling what is little more than milk powder. It is a little different with marijuana, as it is hard to tamper with grass, but the same principles apply. You buy your grass from X for a stipulated price, then on-sell to others for a slightly higher price. For someone applying the same methods to feed their habits, it is only then a small step to becoming a fully fledged drug dealer.

You originally start out selling to just your friends, but as time passes you find yourself acquiring customers who are not friends, customers who want more product. Your dealer's prices are exorbitant, so you go out looking for a wholesaler. When you are immersed in the drug culture, you soon become aware who the big players are. You find out who your dealer gets his drugs off. Then it is just a matter of making yourself known to that wholesaler, usually by friends who know him, and hey presto, you are suddenly someone able to access larger quantities of drugs, at a much cheaper price. I know for a fact that is how Martin got started. Between 1972 and 1973 he began moving small amounts of grass to trusted friends around Auckland, mainly local weed grown up north. The man who would later murder him, Andrew Maher, was his trusted accomplice back then, doing marijuana deliveries for him. It is from such innocuous beginnings that the Mr Asia syndicate evolved. It is an undeniable fact that, without Martin Johnstone's success importing and distributing buddha sticks in New Zealand in 1974–1976, the whole Mr Asia syndicate would not have happened. Ironically, it was his money that sowed the seeds for the network that was to become the Mr Asia syndicate and, ultimately, what killed him.

The one distinctive trait most marijuana smokers have is that they are usually laidback people. A few puffs of a marijuana joint and the world is a rosier place. I have found that people who deal in marijuana, or smoke marijuana, are rarely violent types. Obviously there are exceptions, Terry Clark springs to mind immediately, but on the whole, that is how I have found most of the people I know who deal in grass. Martin always struck me as being a non-violent person. Some people are just not cut out for violence and he was one of those people. I cannot recall one person being murdered back then over imported buddha sticks or marijuana. That is the difference between marijuana and heroin. Those people who deal in marijuana usually manage to live to an old age, whereas major heroin dealers either end up dead or serving long prison sentences. It's a shame Martin did not stay with the buddha sticks in New Zealand, because if he did, he would more than likely be alive today. In prison perhaps, but still alive.

For a man who liked to portray himself as a successful international businessman, Martin Johnstone was a very undisciplined person. He was always talking about multimillion dollar deals he was working on, grand schemes to operate a fishing fleet in South East Asia, as well as his attempts to develop mining concessions throughout Asia. Unfortunately, Martin did not possess the organisational skills needed to run a profitable business; he did not have the patience to look after the small details that can actually dictate whether a business deal can work or not. Both the *Brigadoon* importation of 450,000 buddha sticks into New Zealand in March 1976, and the *Konpira* importation of 400 kilos of heroin into Australia in March 1977, were nearly brought undone because of Martin's incompetence. His short life was littered with many failed business ventures. I can distinctly recall Clark telling me around May 1978 that Martin was using the syndicate's money to look for oil in Indonesia. According to Clark, Martin had some Indonesian generals on side and they were involved in his search for oil. When Clark told me this I laughed. I pointed out to him that if there was oil to be found in Indonesia, the big oil companies would have surely found it. Needless to say, Martin and his supposed associates never found oil; he did, however, lose a large amount of Clark and Jack Choo's ill-gotten gains. As I recollect, they were both extremely angry at the time, particularly Clark. There was no talk about killing him, but I'm sure the thought would have crossed Clark's mind. Unfortunately for him, Martin had a blasé attitude towards money that would eventually see him squander millions of dollars in unsuccessful business ventures. He mistakenly thought the good times and money would never end. Sadly for Martin, the good times and money did finally run out.

15

TERRENCE JOHN CLARK

Although Martin Johnstone was the man identified by NZ journalists in the mid-1970s as the original Mr Asia, there was absolutely no doubt that it was Clark who ran the drug group that would come to be known as the Mr Asia syndicate. A ruthless, cold, unfeeling psychopath, Clark was perfectly suited to the requirements needed to succeed in the violence-ridden world of heroin trafficking. He had both the capacity to organise large shipments of heroin into New Zealand, Australia, Britain and the United States, as well as the willingness to kill friend or foe to protect himself and his distribution networks. A willingness to kill is an advantageous mindset to have in the heroin trade. Heroin trafficking is a particularly nasty business and in such a violent and treacherous environment, Clark was in his element.

The question I have most often been asked about Terry Clark is, What type of person was he? I remember sitting in a legal room at the old Supreme Court at Darlinghurst in Sydney during my trial in April

1986, when my barrister asked me that question. My answer was the answer I give everyone. Terry Clark was not the type of person you would walk a metre in front of. In May 1979 I inadvertently ignored my own advice and nearly paid with my life. The man had no compunction about shooting friend or foe in the back.

I recently watched a documentary made and shown in New Zealand entitled, *Beyond the Darklands: Unveiling the Predators Among Us*. Evidently all the programs made were about New Zealand's worst killers and sexual predators. Terrence John Clark had the dubious honour of featuring in the fourth episode, the one I watched. It was clearly obvious that Clark had manifested psychopathic tendencies and behaviour at a very early age. I have always thought I was a bit of a rogue as a young lad, but after hearing some of Clark's childhood friends relate tales of his extreme behaviour when he was a boy, I was a choirboy by comparison. The most interesting fact to come out of the program for me was the confirmation of some of the details I was aware of.

According to the men who knew Clark when he was a schoolboy, he was a sadistic bully even at that young age. To join his gang, ten or eleven-year-old kids had to stand up against a wall while Clark fired projectiles, usually matchsticks, at them from an air rifle. As they got a little older, Clark's initiation ritual became even more violent and painful for those wishing to join his gang. He used to throw a dart – a rusty dart – at prospective members' stomachs. If they flinched or ducked away, they were denied membership. I know little country towns like Gisborne back in the fifties were devoid of any meaningful entertainment for young people, but that initiation ritual has got me scratching my head and wondering what the fuck those kids were thinking about, allowing Clark to throw a rusty dart at their stomachs. One of the men being interviewed told of another occasion where Clark got him and a couple of other kids to hold a young boy down who had upset him over some perceived slight. When Clark produced a knife and slashed the boy's foot, the man recounting the incident said: 'That was it for a few of us, we just got up and walked out, never to return. I realised at that very moment, that Terry Clark was an extremely nasty person and I did not want to be around someone like that.' Well, he certainly got that part right.

All the men interviewed mentioned how aggressive Clark was as a young boy. In any fight he had at school he was prepared to use anything to win. They all remembered him as wanting to be known as a tough guy, a trait that would stay with him throughout his life. His habit of carrying a knife around in his pocket as a young boy was an extremely unusual occurrence back in those days. Young people in the late fifties simply did not carry weapons. There used to be a lot of fights in the streets, but there were never any weapons involved. Clark's readiness to use a knife as a teenager to settle a dispute makes it easier to understand his willingness later in life to use guns to kill or threaten people.

Another one of the men being interviewed said he could recall a nasty incident involving Clark when he was sixteen. The man stated that one morning not long after Clark left school, his mother went into his bedroom to try and get him out of bed. Clark's response was to pick up a rifle and threaten to kill her. According to this guy, Clark kept his mother captive all day, threatening to kill her if she called out for anyone to come to her assistance. This is one story I hope is not true. I lost any respect I had for Clark many years ago, but that revelation about him threatening his mother all those years ago, well that just underlines what a nasty piece of work he was. The belated realisation that I worked for two years with a man who would treat his mother like that has deeply embarrassed me. Instincts honed by my close contact with murderers and psychopaths in the New Zealand prison system gave me a sense that there was a latent nasty streak lurking just below the surface with Clark, but to put a rifle to the head of your mother who loved you! That was definitely the action of a deranged person.

The common thread Clark, Johnstone and I had was our families. We all came from honest, law-abiding families, none of whom had ever had any trouble with the law. Martin Johnstone's family gave him a good upbringing; my family, despite the fact they were poor, loved me and did their best to give me a decent education; and the same applied to Clark. His father Leo and his mother Jesse were well respected in the local community. They were decent, loving parents to him, his brother Paddy and his sister Judith. His father was a quiet achiever, always trying to improve himself so that he could give his family a better lifestyle. A keen sportsman, his father was also an accomplished surf lifesaver. In fact, Leo Clark was one of the founders of the Midway Surf Club in Gisborne. His prowess and involvement as a surf-lifesaving official led to him being invited to be a judge at a few NZ surf-lifesaving championships. After working at the local meatworks, Leo brought the local Pie Cart, a well-known landmark in downtown Gisborne. The business was a great success and this allowed him to purchase a larger house at 428 Palmerston Road and relocate the family to this more affluent area. Besides acquiring the Pie Cart, Leo Clark also established the first driving school in Gisborne. It is easy to see where Clark got his drive from, but it's got me beat where the homicidal, psychopath came from. I had the pleasure of meeting Clark's sister Judith on a few occasions and found her to be a lovely lady. Unlike Terry, she had a delightful personality. I never met Paddy, but I have read reports that he excelled at school and was the complete opposite of Clark. Since I was a young man my family have stoically endured all the unwanted attention my criminality has caused, so I can totally sympathise with what Clark's poor family have had to endure. I am sure his family, Johnstone's family, and my family have at some stage wished they were not related to us.

Records show that Clark was first picked up in Auckland in 1962 for offences involving motor vehicles and given a period of probation. For a short time he worked as a welder's assistant and panel beater at a garage in Auckland. In 1963, while still on probation, Clark married Sally R. I will not use her full name because she does not deserve to have her marriage to one of New Zealand's worst serial killers revisited by me. I met Sally R for the first time in Los Angeles in August 1979, when she brought Clark's two children over from New

Zealand to see him. Clark and I were staying at the Beverly Hilton at that time. While they were in Los Angeles, I actually took his kids out to Disneyland at Anaheim, where we spent a lovely day. His kids loved Disneyland and so did I.

Before they were born, Clark scratched out a living from buying and selling stolen goods in Auckland. As I have explained earlier, in the 1960s safe-crackers in New Zealand were regarded as the top echelon in the criminal hierarchy. As he had no expertise with explosives, Clark started to dabble as a receiver of stolen goods to earn a little money on the side. In criminal parlance, a 'fence.' A fence is someone who buys stolen property from other criminals and then on-sells those stolen goods to known crooked shopkeepers, or to an even larger fence. In Clark's case this was the literal truth, as the biggest fence in Auckland during the 1960s was a criminal called 'Two Fats' Smith. A truly huge man, Two Fats was the number one receiver of stolen goods for many years. As I recollect, Two Fats did not live to get his old age pension; his ongoing weight problems killed him at an early age. He did, however, handle a lot of Clark's fledgling business as a receiver of stolen goods. That is, until Clark set him up.

Over the last 50 years I have been shocked by quite a few things that have occurred in my life – Brian Agnew, a friend of twenty years getting in the witness box against me in 1986 being one of them – but the revelation that Clark was a paid police informer during the 1960s left me absolutely stunned. The mere thought of having worked so closely with a paid informant sickened me. If I had not read the written reports and heard the detectives who controlled him at that time talk about their experiences with Clark, I would not have believed the allegations. A retired police officer – John Keatley – who arrested Clark back in the late 1960s stated on the television program: 'Once he started talking, we could not shut him up.' So much for Mister Tough Guy! I still find it incomprehensible that the homicidal psychopathic killer I knew could have once been a police informant. I first became aware of Clark's role as a police infor-mant in 1987 when I read a book called *Greed*, written by Sydney author Richard Hall, about the Mr Asia syndicate. Considering the author got most of his material about us from trial transcripts and all the different government inquiries that were held into the Mr Asia syndicate back in the early 1980s, he wrote a fairly detailed book. After reading what Richard Hall had to say about Clark, to allay my own doubts I had all his allegations about Clark checked out personally. To my disgust, any lingering doubts I had were well and truly dispelled. Clark had indeed been an informant. Life can certainly throw a few curve balls at you, and for me, this information about Clark was a real curve ball.

I can say without any fear of contradiction that had I been aware in 1976 of Clark's role as a police informer, there is no way I would have become involved with him. There are three classes of people most career criminals loathe: informants, paedophiles and police. Not necessarily in that order. Unlike many of my fellow criminals I have never hated the police, mainly because they are just doing their job. I respect that. But informants and paedophiles are another matter entirely. Since I first came into the NZ prison system as a sixteen-year-old, I have had the mantra 'informers are dogs' ingrained into my psyche. For a criminal, the worst and deadliest insult you can bestow on him is to call him a 'dog informer.' Over the years I have seen many men get murdered because they were informers. I have often wondered since I found out about Clark working for the police, whether all the murders he committed was his way of trying to erase his self-loathing at being a one-time informant. For someone who fancied himself a tough guy, knowing he had been a police informant would not have reinforced the image he had of himself, when he looked in the mirror. All the justification in the world about why he was doing it would not have been enough to erase his own perceived weakness for selling himself to the police. I don't care what any of the learned psychologists or psychiatrists have said about Clark not being emotionally affected by his role as a police informant. Selling his self-respect to the police, in my opinion, had to affect Clark's ego-driven self-image of himself as a really tough criminal.

The police officers who were his handlers back in the late 1960s all commented about his apparent enthusiasm when setting his fellow criminals up. One of the detectives – Clive Plunkett – who knew Clark then, said he was the type of person who would give up his mother to save himself. It is interesting to note that this ex-detective also maintained that they – the police – thought Clark was responsible for far more murders than he was credited with. From what police officers have stated, Clark used to dream up elaborate sting operations so that they could arrest other criminals. Evidently, after buying stolen property from fellow criminals, Clark would notify his handlers so they could then arrest them. It's got me beat how the guys he was doing business with never twigged to his modus operandi. I guess it just reinforces what I said earlier in this book, about New Zealand crims from that era being a little slow on the uptake. Despite all the treacherous undercover work he did for his handlers, none of them liked him. To a man they found him unstable and not to be trusted. One detective said he was always very wary and deeply suspicious whenever they met. I am uncertain how long Clark worked as an informant for the police in Auckland, but I have been told that by 1970, he had outworn his usefulness to them. There is an urban myth that in March 1971, the police set him up by arranging for him to do a burglary in Napier, a small town located in the middle of the North Island. They even made sure he had a couple of sticks of gelignite, just to ensure he got a longer sentence. I hope that urban myth was true, because it is always nice to know a hardworking informant's treachery was duly rewarded.

For the attempted Napier burglary, plus a couple of other offences, five years' imprisonment was the sentence. Wi Tako, a minimum security prison for first offenders, just a short drive north of Wellington was where he was sent to serve this sentence. Compared to the prisons I had been in since my first arrest, Wi Tako was a holiday camp. It was a pleasant, comfortable, easy-going place to serve a prison sentence. Between 1971 and 1974, while he was enjoying Her Majesty's accommodation, Clark would meet and befriend many of the men who would later become involved with him in the Mr Asia syndicate. It was there he met Greg Ollard, Errol Hincksman, Wayne Shrimpton and Dennis Williams. All these men would later work with him when he became a major heroin trafficker. No doubt Clark told them all: 'Stick with me boys, and I'll make you all rich!' Obviously that jailhouse promise did not pertain to Greg Ollard, whom Clark later murdered in September 1977.

During his time at Wi Tako Prison, Clark became known as the jail heavy. I will add a rider to that statement by saying that the majority of inmates serving time at that resort while he was incarcerated there would not have scared my sister. In Mt Eden, Paremoremo, Paparua or even Mt Crawford Prison in Wellington, Clark would have been cut down to size very quickly. Despite his willingness to use knives or iron bars in jailhouse confrontations, Clark at that time was not big enough or strong enough to have been able to handle some of the monsters that were running around the maximum security prisons in those days. Having said that, however, if all the prison tough guys were out on the street with Clark, I would have put my money on Clark to kill them first.

I remember having lunch with Errol Hincksman in Sydney late in 1978, where I asked him what Clark was like in prison. His reply has been confirmed by many other inmates who were at Wi Tako Prison with him between 1971 and 1974: Clark had an obsession with wanting to be the biggest criminal in New Zealand. I was surprised when Errol told me that during a visit to see him at Wi Tako, Clark's father had offered Terry $50,000 to help him set up a legitimate business after his release. Clark, who said he would make his own money, scornfully declined the offer. I often wonder what would have become of Clark had he accepted his father's generous offer. One thing's for sure, I would not be writing this book.

Before his release from Wi Tako in 1974, Clark got married in the prison chapel for a second time, to a long-time drug addict named Norma Fleet. I believe Errol Hincksman was his best man. I first met Norma in 1967, when she was involved with a good friend of mine,

Ray B. Norma was an attractive woman when I first met her, but heavy heroin use over a long period of time can slowly erode any woman's good looks. Norma was no exception to that sad fact. Besides heroin, Norma loved a drink and was always the life of the party wherever she went. The cynics have said Clark only married Norma so that he could get an entrée into New Zealand's heroin market. I tend to disagree with that theory, simply because after his release from Wi Tako, Clark gravitated towards the buddha sticks market and not directly into the heroin market, which is what would have happened if that theory was correct. Whatever his motive for marrying Norma, it is common knowledge in the NZ underworld that Clark gave her a 'hot shot' of heroin in 1975 which resulted in her death. For those readers who are unaware of what a hot shot is, I will explain it to you. Most heroin addicts who buy their drugs directly from street dealers, are sold very poor quality heroin. As a result, they get used to injecting very weak heroin into their veins. A hidden consequence of addicts injecting so much weak heroin over a long period of time is that their bodies cannot physiologically cope if they suddenly inject a much stronger dose. The outcome of injecting this stronger heroin usually results in a deadly overdose for the addict. Countless addicts have been murdered by someone administering a lethal hot shot to them. Accidental overdose is the usual coroner's finding. A very convenient outcome for anyone wishing to get rid of a troublesome addict or, as in Clark's case, a troublesome wife. I believe Norma was one of Clark's early murder victims. By my count, Clark either murdered, or had murdered, at least twelve people. Three of those twelve victims – Norma Fleet, Julie Theilman and Isabel Wilson – were women.

Many people have asked me over the years: 'Jim, how could you have become involved with such a psychopath?' Don't worry, that is a question I have asked myself on more than one occasion. Hindsight as they say, is a wonderful thing, and that is how I look at my involvement with Clark. I can honestly state, from the first time I met him in Auckland in 1975 until a few months before his arrest in London in November 1979, Clark always presented himself to me as a cool, intelligent, switched-on drug dealer. On only one occasion did he ever mention killing anyone and that was during a lunch I had with him at Eliza's restaurant in Double Bay, Sydney, around March 1978.

Rather an incongruous spot to be discussing murder, in those days Eliza's was a pretty trendy place to eat or have a drink at. The restaurant was always crowded with affluent customers and plenty of attractive women waiting to be noticed. The latter being the reason I liked going there. On this particular afternoon, Clark and I were seated in a secluded area of the restaurant enjoying a glass of wine after a nice meal, when Clark broached the subject of murder.

'How do you feel about killing, Jim?' he asked. Before I could answer, he threw in another rhetorical comment: 'If you are not prepared to kill Jim, you should not be in the drug business. I have already killed six people.' My first thought on hearing this startling confession was, Is this guy for real? My second thought was, If he is for real, what the fuck is he telling me for? It's none of my fucking business what he's done. I'm not a fucking priest!

Old-school criminals who I had modelled myself on back in the 1960s, used to operate on a need to know basis. To a man, all the major criminals I knew back then rarely spoke about what they had done. Clark must have mistaken my surprised silence for acquiescence, because he started to recount all the murders he had committed up to then. It is amazing the number of people Clark confessed to over the years about the murders he was responsible for, particularly to women. He seemed to have a morbid compulsion to tell others about the horrendous crimes he had committed. At the time I was very sceptical about his uninvited confession to killing six people: frankly, I did not believe him. But history has shown through evidence presented by numerous witnesses at trials and Royal Commissions, that my scepticism was definitely wrong. Clark almost certainly killed the number of people he told me he had.

I have a theory as to why Clark made his extraordinary confessions to me. Apart from Wayne S who helped Clark carry the bodies of Greg Ollard and Julie Theilman deeper into bushland after he murdered them, no one else knew about all the murders he had committed up till then. So an old-school criminal like me whom Clark knew as a man who had done hard time, and even more importantly for him, a man who knew how to keep his mouth shut, I would have been the ideal person for him to boast to about his murderous deeds. Clark must have been longing to tell someone, anyone, about all the murders he had committed. The man was very egotistical, and that is clearly evidenced by the amount of people he told in 1978–79, about what he had done.

Now that I know he did commit all those murders he told me about, I wonder why I ever doubted him. I can still see him sitting opposite me in that restaurant 30 years ago, a tight smile on his face as he started to tell me in a calm, unemotional voice, about all the poor souls he had murdered. He told me the first one was the most diffi-cult. The guy he shot was a drug dealer from Tauranga – though I'm not sure whether the guy was from there, or he killed the guy there. According to Clark, this guy had ripped one of his dealers off and had to go. I could detect the sudden animation in his voice as he told me how he took his first victim up to some nearby hills and shot him in the back of the head. He said after he shot him there was blood every-where but he did not die straight away. Because he was moaning as he lay on the ground, Clark said he shot the motherfucker four more times. I remember Clark's face was reflective as he told me how calm he felt afterwards looking down at the man's dead body.

The second guy he killed owed some people he knew in Auckland a lot of money, so according to Clark, he took this victim up to the Waitakeries, a large forested area just outside the city, on the pretext of helping to solve his monetary problems. He told me that when the prick saw his gun he begged for mercy, but he shot him once in the head and twice in the chest. He then went on to tell me that after shooting the second guy, the thing that really struck him was just how easy it was to kill someone. It has been my experience, having met numerous multiple killers in my lifetime – mainly in prison – that some men get a taste for killing and suffer no remorse or conscience after they have murdered someone. I would definitely place Clark in that horrific category. While he was unburdening himself to me, he never confessed to giving his second wife, Norma, a hot shot. Perhaps the knowledge that I had known and liked Norma, precluded Clark from admitting to me what he had done to her. Despite his not admitting to being involved in any foul play as far as Norma was concerned, I'm still crediting him with killing her.

The afternoon shadows were lengthening as we sat there drinking a high priced bottle of imported wine, both of us wearing expensive, well-tailored suits, our pockets full of $50 bills, but both of us morally bankrupt. While I was more interested in getting an after-dinner drink, Clark was just getting warmed up. I remember him leaning towards me as he started telling me about his next two victims. The next two killings he told me about are open to debate, as his version of events is contrary to what indemnified witnesses told Justice Stewart at the Royal Commission hearings into the Mr Asia syndicate. But I'll recount here what he said. He began by telling me that the previous year, 1977, was a very busy year for him as he had to kill four people. According to Clark, the first two were crewmen aboard the trawler *Konpira*, which had brought 400 kilos of smack down from Thailand in March for the syndicate. When he went on board to collect the smack, Clark said he was told two of the crew wanted more money for the trip. In an aggrieved voice as he was telling me, Clark said 'two of the cunts' came out on deck and started rambling on in broken English about wanting more money. After listening briefly to their complaints, Clark told me that he said to both men: 'I'll give you cunts more money all right.' I distinctly remember him laughing as he recounted how 'fucking shocked' everyone on board was when he pulled out his gun and shot both crewmen on the deck of the boat. He then told me they threw the two crewmen overboard.

The reason I am conflicted about Clark's version of events about what happened aboard the *Konpira* is the simple fact that a couple of Australian crewmen from that trip gave evidence at the Stewart Royal Commission and they never mentioned anything about Clark killing anyone. Or, for that matter, his even being aboard the *Konpira*. According to their testimony, he never even came on board. As they had indemnities from prosecution, it is logical to think that they would have mentioned something as significant as that. But then again, those two guys might have worried that their indemnities did not cover murder. All I can say about Clark is this: as he was recounting the killings, his eyes were shining. It was almost like he was reliving the whole experience again and enjoying that feeling. For what it's worth, if I had to choose between the *Konpira* crewmen's evidence and Clark's, I'd be inclined to believe Clark's version of events.

Dusk was falling as he started to tell me about killing Greg Ollard and Julie Theilman. He tried to justify the killing of his former Wi Tako prison associate and friend, Greg Ollard, by saying he had received information from the police that Ollard was ready to roll over and give him up. I doubt if that was true, but any excuse is better than none. Those two killings were still fresh in Clark's mind, as they had only happened six months previously, around the middle of September. His reason for killing Greg, he told me, was predicated by the fact that Greg had become a 'fucking liability.' Clark said he offered to buy Ollard out but 'the cunt refused my offer.' Because Ollard was using heavily and shooting his mouth off all over town, Clark thought he had become a loose cannon. Apparently Clark had received some information from the narcs – drug squad detectives – that Ollard was ready to roll. By Clark's warped reasoning, this meant he had no option: Ollard had to go. Being a cynic, I don't suppose all the money Ollard had coming to him from his share of the business with Clark had anything to do with his death. If you are a drug dealer, letting people run up huge debts with you can have fatal consequences. Rather than paying the debt, it is not unusual for a drug debtor to kill the person he owes money to. I sense that is what happened with Greg Ollard. Using the pretext of showing him where he had some heroin stashed, Clark lured Ollard to a location on a dirt road just off Cottage Point Road in the Ku-ring-gai National Park, on Sydney's northern beaches. To highlight how devious he was, Clark had not only buried a thermos flask full of heroin at the site, but had also dug a shallow grave nearby. He told me as Ollard bent down to pick up the thermos flask, he shot him in the back of the head. I remember him having a little chuckle as he recounted the fiasco that followed. Because he had forgotten how fat Ollard had become, Clark could not move him. He told me that after killing Ollard he had to find a phone box and call Wayne S to come over to help him clean up the mess. After meeting Wayne S at Church Point wharf the next morning, he said he took him out to where he had shot Ollard. Between the two of them Clark said, they managed to drag 'the fat fuck' over to the hole he had dug for him, covered him as best they could and left.

After telling me how he disposed of Greg Ollard, I recollect Clark sitting opposite me with a pensive look on his face. It was as if he was remembering something unpleasant. No doubt he was also wondering how I would react to him confessing to killing a woman. Back in the 1960s, women were sacrosanct, you did not involve them in crime and you certainly did not harm them. The guy was definitely an aberration there. No criminals I knew at that time, myself included, would ever have killed a woman, no matter how desperate the situation. After taking a few sips of his wine, Clark started to tell me in a cold, detached way, why he had killed Julie Theilman.

Obviously with the amount of time that has passed since that long lunch all those many years ago, my memory is not as accurate as it could be. Despite my scepticism at the time as to whether or not Clark was telling me the truth, however, his chilling confessions to me, particularly the brutal way he murdered Julie Theilman, have remained seared in my brain ever since. To the best of my ability, I am recounting what I remember of that conversation at Eliza's restaurant. I have been able to confirm much of what Clark told me from reading Justice Stewart's report. The guy who was with him when he shot Julie Theilman – Wayne S – gave a detailed account to Justice Stewart of what occurred on the day Clark murdered her, and it corresponds to what I remember Clark telling me. This witness, by the way, was given an indemnity from prosecution for his part in helping Clark murder

Julie Theilman. He also got an indemnity for selling large amounts of heroin every week for eighteen months. No wonder they lined up to get indemnities! I have often wondered what Julie Theilman's family felt about Clark's accomplice in her murder getting off scot-free. I'll wager they were not happy.

Shooting Julie Theilman, a woman, must have weighed on his conscience a little more than shooting his male victims, because once again he tried to justify to me what he had done. He began by telling me that he did not want to kill a woman, but she was a bad junkie and could have brought us all down by going to the police and telling them Greg was missing. Using his twisted logic, Clark opined that once he killed Greg, he knew that he could not leave his girlfriend, Julie Theilman, alive. It was his opinion that she would have become 'a fucking nightmare'. So the next morning after burying Greg Ollard, he said that he and Wayne went over to Greg's place at Avalon. According to Clark, they told Julie Theilman that Greg was waiting for her at Parramatta and wanted them to take her over there to meet him. Before they left, Clark said he gave her a couple of snorts of A-grade smack, after that she did not know what was happening. He said they then drove up to an area in the Blue Mountains where he used to plant smack; a very remote spot, situated well off the road. She was pretty wasted with the smack he gave her he told me, so 'I just pulled her out of the car, and shot her in the back of the head.' He could not hide his disdain as he told me how that 'weak cunt' Wayne whimpered and spewed everywhere after he shot Julie Theilman. As they were dragging her body into the bush, just behind a big tree, he told me that a shocked Wayne S said she was still alive, so he put two more bullets into her chest. After covering her with rocks, he said they left. He then told me a few days after he killed them, both he and Wayne went over to their house at Avalon, packed up all their belongings and put all their stuff into a storage spot he had in Artarmon. After he finished telling me about Julie Theilman, Clark just shook his head as he said to me: 'It's just fucking business Jim, just business.' Those cryptic words have stayed with me for all these years.

Before we left the restaurant we both had an Irish coffee. As we were drinking our coffee, Clark looked at me and casually said that about five months ago, he had returned to where Greg and Julie's bodies were and chopped off their heads. He said if their bodies are ever found it will be hard to identify them. He was chuckling as he told me how he went and buried their heads in another spot. It was the casual, jocular way he told me about chopping two people's heads off, even allowing for the fact that they were already dead, that really caught my attention. When he finished imparting this additional gruesome information to me, about what he had done to Greg Ollard and Julie Theilman, I recollect looking at Clark and thinking to myself once again, Is this guy for fucking real? I have to tell you, whether I thought his story was real or not, it put me off my Irish coffee and I left it unfinished. It was dark as we walked out of the restaurant into a warm March night, looking for all the world like two business-men who had just enjoyed a good meal at Eliza's, instead of two men who had spent most of the afternoon discussing multiple murders. As I stood on the street outside Eliza's waiting for a taxi, I clearly remember thinking to myself, I do not know if you were telling me the truth or not, but from this moment on I will never turn my back on you again.

For those readers who are wondering why I did not bolt out of the restaurant as fast as my legs would carry me after Clark started confessing all those murders to me, the answer is simply this. At that point in my life, I was completely desensitised to violence. Since I was sixteen I had been imprisoned in extremely violent prisons. The security block at Mt Eden Prison not only hardened me, it destroyed a lot of my humanity, and I left part of my soul inside that place. Unless it was my immediate family, what happened to others did not concern me in the slightest. So when Clark started to tell me about what he had done, he was talking to a man who was already morally and emotion-ally crippled. During my time in the NZ prison system I had been around numerous homicidal psychopaths: men who were multiple murderers, men who had killed police officers, men who had machine-gunned people to death, men who had killed their parents, men who had killed their wives, their children; men who had killed their victims with machine guns, shotguns, pistols, rifles, knives, machetes, axes; men who had strangled or drowned their victims, even one guy who had used a spade to kill his neighbour. So death and violence in its many guises was no stranger to me. I took the view with Clark, that many businessmen take: you do not have to like or love the person you are doing business with. Business is business. My business with Clark was earning me up to $100,000 a week. That type of money can make a man lose his morals very quickly. To my everlasting shame, that's what all that money did to me. My greed destroyed any last vestiges of decency or common sense that I had left.

The amount of time I have spent on Clark is a fair indication of how important he was to the Mr Asia syndicate. In fact, Clark *was* the Mr Asia syndicate. Without his drive and organisational ability, the Mr Asia syndicate would never have gotten off the ground. Although I have highlighted all his many defects and psychopathic tendencies, Clark did have a few redeeming features. For one, he loved his children, particularly his son Jarrod – whom he had with Maria Muhary. Like many psychopaths, Clark could be charming when he wanted to be. On the few occasions I went out and had dinner with him, he was always polite and well behaved; he was not a nasty drunk. From the first time I started working with him in mid-1977, until about July 1979, I found Clark to be very professional, particularly where drugs were concerned. What Clark did not know about hard drugs was not worth knowing. I found the guy to be surprisingly punctual in all his dealings with me. For a professional criminal, being punctual is a much desired and very necessary trait, especially when you are handling large amounts of illegal drugs. Clark was always on time, and always ready for business. Unlike my friend Skip Gardiner whom I spoke about in an earlier chapter, Clark did not have a charismatic personality. When the guy smiled there was no warmth in his smile or his eyes. I guess killing more than six people can do that to you. Clark always tried to dress well, but he was one of those men who could make a $1000 suit look second-hand. The three women he was involved with when I knew him – Maria Muhary, Allison Dine and Karen Soich – all loved the man, so he must have had some endearing qualities for them to have loved him like they did. It most certainly was not his good looks as Clark was not a handsome man. Maria, Allison and Karen were all attractive, intelligent women. Karen Soich was a solicitor when she met Clark, and Allison Dine a schoolteacher. That old saying 'love is blind' certainly fitted the bill with those two ladies.

Over the course of four years, between July 1975 and July 1979, it was compelling to watch Clark slowly disintegrate before my eyes. From the switched-on drug dealer I first met in 1975, to the incoherent cocaine addict he became in late 1979, was one hell of a journey for both of us. It was drugs that took him to the top, and it was drugs that destroyed him. I guess some people would call it poetic justice.

16

THE CONNECTIONS

The two most significant people besides Terry Clark and Martin Johnstone in the Mr Asia syndicate were, in order of importance, Chinese Jack Choo, a Singapore resident and Brian Alexander, a Sydney law clerk. The first supplied the top-grade heroin that was the group's signature, the second the police protection that enabled the syndicate to thrive. When you can supply top-grade heroin and get police protection at the same time, then you have the ingredients for making huge amounts of money in the drug trade. For two years, that is what transpired with the Mr Asia syndicate.

Chinese Jack was born in Singapore on 9 April 1939. His infant years were spent under the brutal Japanese occupation of Singapore, during the Second World War. Like me, Chinese Jack's upbringing after the war was tough. His parents struggled to put food on the table and at a very early age he had to go out and work. A limited education meant Chinese Jack had to learn what he could, where he could.

I do not know whether it is the result of being one of the earliest civilisations on earth, but I have always found Chinese people to have an innate intelligence and an instinctive feel for business. Despite his lack of schooling, Chinese Jack was a very shrewd man. Slim and of medium height, he was a heavy smoker, and always coughing. Although only a couple of years older than me, he walked like a man much older. His shoulders were always hunched and his eyes squinting behind his glasses. You would not want a buck for every time Chinese Jack smiled, because you would be struggling to pay for a bus ticket downtown. The guy was not a bundle of laughs. We spent a bit of time together at Parklea Prison and during my time there with him I found him to be a very bitter man.

As he only got twenty years, with a fourteen year non-parole period on the bottom when he was sentenced for his involvement in the Mr Asia syndicate – despite having more than double the amount of charges as me – Chinese Jack should have been doing an Irish jig every day to celebrate his good fortune. I guess the fact he fainted when Justice McInerney sentenced me to 25 years' hard labour helped him. Police officers had to hold him upright as he was sentenced. According to Justice McInerney's reasoning, Choo had shown contrition by pleading guilty to four separate conspiracies to import heroin and buddha sticks into Australia – as well as fainting with shock at my sentence – therefore he deserved a much lighter sentence than his co-accused, yours truly. I, on the other hand, had the audacity to plead not guilty on one charge of conspiracy to import heroin into Australia, therefore I deserved double the sentence. Chinese Jack ended up serving less than seven years; I served just under fifteen. Am I still bitter? Damn right I am! While he was doing time here in Australia, I made sure Chinese Jack was protected wherever he went, by friends of mine. When I saw he had an old black and white television set, I gave him a brand new remote colour television set I had sent in. My reward from this ingrate for not saying a word about him after my arrest in 1984 – despite inducements of a heavily reduced sentence if I did – as well as the protection I ensured he got while serving his sentence, plus the colour television set I gave him was not even one lousy Christmas card in eight years after he got out.

Now that I have got that little personal piece of bitterness out of the way I can continue with Chinese Jack's story. All the many trials, inquiries, media coverage, indemnified witness accounts, even Justice Stewart's Royal Commission into Drug Trafficking, have not understood or realised that Chinese Jack was Clark's equal partner. Because all the publicity about the Mr Asia syndicate has always focused on Terry Clark and his murderous deeds, no one has really looked at mild-mannered Chinese Jack. To all intents and purposes, he was just part of Clark's evil empire. That has always been the prevailing thought. Well I am here to say that was not the case. They were equal partners: Chinese Jack received half the profits of whatever Clark made. As he supplied all the heroin for the syndicate, he knew almost to the dollar how much money he had coming from his share of the profits.

I think the mistaken belief that because Chinese Jack had worked as a lowly ship's steward on Straat Line merchant ships, meant that law enforcement officials and many of Clark's own associates all viewed him as a subordinate and not someone capable of being Clark's equal. They were all wrong. To be able to supply the amounts of heroin he did – up to 600 kilos – as well as 400 kilos of buddha sticks, he had to be well connected. Having done a lot of business in Thailand in my early days in the drug business, I know first-hand how difficult acquiring large amounts of heroin can be. When I was in Parklea Prison with Chinese Jack, I asked him if there was any truth to the story that he was related by marriage to Khun Sa, the notorious opium war lord, whose troops at that time controlled most of the Golden Triangle, which lies between Thailand and Burma. From his base deep in the jungles of the Golden Triangle, Khun Sa has controlled the heroin trade for 40 years. I remember at the time he laughed off my question with the reply: 'Who told you that, Jim? I know who you are talking about, but that is not right.' Well I think it was right. I say that because Chinese Jack had access to unlimited amounts of heroin on credit. The bulk of heroin Clark received was on credit. I remember a meeting we had in

Fiji in March or April 1978 at the Regent Hotel in Nadi. Present were Terry Clark, Chinese Jack, Martin Johnstone and myself. When moves into the lucrative markets of the United States and United Kingdom were discussed, Chinese Jack was asked how much heroin he could supply for those markets if required. His reply was very succinct: 'A tonne if needed.' Now at that point in time there was only one person in the world capable of supplying that much heroin: Khun Sa. That is why I think Chinese Jack was related to him.

I do not know when Chinese Jack started working as a steward on one of the Royal Dutch Orient Line ships. These ships used to have a mixture of Dutch and foreign officers in command and were crewed by mainly Chinese seamen. Throughout Asia, all the Royal Dutch Orient Line ships were widely known as Straat Line ships. All these ships used to ply their trade throughout Asia, down the eastern seaboard of Australia and around the coast of New Zealand. The routes were perfect for any of the crew wanting to smuggle illegal contraband into Australia or New Zealand. For Chinese Jack, New Zealand was the promised land and buddha sticks would be the keys to his fortune. Between 1973 and 1975, Chinese Jack smuggled and sold hundreds of thousands of Thai buddha sticks in New Zealand. During those few years, I personally knew at least three guys who became millionaires through the sale of buddha sticks acquired from Chinese Jack. And that's when a million bucks really meant something.

In Thailand you buy buddha sticks for 10 cents each. To make for easier handling and hiding, the buddha sticks are pressed and compacted into blocks of a thousand. The first thing you had to do after buying the buddha sticks was use steam to make each stick expand. It was amazing to watch these buddha sticks go from being a flat piece of tobacco wrapped around a small bamboo stick, to a rounded, healthy-looking amount of marijuana after steaming. Once steamed, each buddha stick was worth up to $25 each. It used to work like this. Chinese Jack would sell the buddha sticks he had smuggled aboard whatever boat he was on at that time for $4 each, so buying directly from him, 1000 sticks would cost you $4000. He used to bring in 200,000 or 300,000 sticks each four-monthly trip. Not a bad return on his original 10 cents a stick investment. The NZ importers buying their sticks directly from Chinese Jack would in turn sell them for $9 each in lots of a thousand. The wholesalers then usually charged up to $13 per thousand. So by the time Chinese Jack's buddha sticks reached the consumer, they could cost up to $25 each. Capitalism working at its very best.

The methods Chinese Jack used to move the smuggled buddha sticks off the Straat ships were varied. In the beginning when they first started, Chinese Jack and other crew members would lower parcels of buddha sticks down the side of the ship by ropes while the ship was docked at either the Auckland or Wellington ports. Someone in a small dinghy or on a surfboard would retrieve the sticks and row or paddle quietly away. As it soon became obvious there was a huge market for buddha sticks in New Zealand, Chinese Jack, being a resourceful entrepreneur, dramatically increased the amount he smuggled in from Thailand. Thousands of buddha sticks became hundreds of thousands of buddha sticks. As a consequence of the larger amounts, the retrieval of the sticks became more sophisticated. Fast speedboats became the order of the day. When his ship was approaching, say, the port of Auckland, Chinese Jack would send a cable or make a ship to shore call to Martin Johnstone about the ship's estimated time of arrival at Auckland. This would enable Martin to be waiting in the shipping lane as Chinese Jack's ship came up the Auckland harbour channel heading for its anchorage. Whether it was daytime or night-time, Martin would pull up behind Chinese Jack's ship and wait for him to toss waterproofed packages of buddha sticks over the side. At night they used flotation devices with flashing lights attached to the large packages so they could be more easily retrieved. In Wellington, the same system worked, only the personnel were different. The Wellington crew in speedboats would follow Chinese Jack's ship as it steamed up the Cook Strait heading for Wellington harbour. The same procedures used for offloading the buddha sticks would then follow.

Business was so good in New Zealand that Chinese Jack had compatriots on other Straat Line ships off-loading large amounts of buddha sticks as well. Between 1973 till the end of 1976, New Zealand was awash in buddha sticks. It took the NZ government and the police a long time to realise what was happening. By the time they did, quite a few individuals had made fortunes from the sale of buddha sticks. In Auckland, Martin Johnstone and George the Greek were spending money like it was going out of style. In Wellington, Billy W was buying racehorses. Not bad on a seaman's wage. The Hare Krishna sect in Auckland suddenly found the money to build a new temple. The Hare Krishnas back in the early 1970s had quite a few members who were not averse to making money by selling buddha sticks. As Marianne Faithfull used to sing in one of her songs from that era, 'those were the days, my friends, those were the days we thought would never end.'

But end they did. To stop any buddha sticks from being off-loaded anywhere around the NZ coast, the government started using a Royal NZ Navy frigate to escort each Straat ship as soon as it arrived in New Zealand waters. The frigate would follow each ship as it sailed around the coastline discharging cargo at different ports and stay with the vessel until it left NZ waters. This tactic was very success-ful and helped dry up the sale of buddha sticks for a little while. One characteristic that many drug smugglers have, however, is that they are extremely resourceful. I am sure that any drug law enforcement officer will tell you the same thing. As soon as one door closes, drug smugglers will be looking for another avenue to bring in their illegal shipments. For Marty Johnstone and a team of investors, that new avenue would be a 36 foot yacht called *Brigadoon*.

Once again Chinese Jack would prove his worth. After meeting him in Singapore, Martin Johnstone arranged the purchase of 400 kilos of Thai buddha sticks. The purchase of those sticks in late 1975 would eventually lead to the establishment of the Mr Asia syndicate, as well as at least twelve people being murdered, includ-ing Martin himself. It is sobering to think how much damage those

400 kilos of buddha sticks caused. I guess you could also say that, without Chinese Jack Choo and Martin Johnstone, the whole Mr Asia scenario would not have happened. By supplying Martin Johnstone with buddha sticks while he worked on the Straat Line ships, Chinese Jack gave Martin the money he needed to progress as a successful drug dealer–importer. A year later, when Clark asked Chinese Jack to arrange the purchase of 400 kilos of heroin, he was able to accommodate him. So it is easy to understand where I am coming from when I say Chinese Jack Choo was an integral and vital part of the rise and fall of the Mr Asia syndicate.

To be able to operate all those many years in a country that executes drug dealers, Chinese Jack had to have protection at the highest level. You do not run around Singapore with the amounts of heroin that Chinese Jack used to have in his possession without police protection. I remember meeting Chinese Jack in Singapore around August 1978. He owned a crocodile farm back then and he took me out there during my visit. I remember commenting to Chinese Jack while he was showing me around his establishment: 'With so many hungry crocodiles, it would be a handy place to get rid of your enemies.' In one of the few times I ever saw him smile, Chinese Jack replied: 'I have thought of that.' I often wonder if he ever did use those crocodiles.

Considering the damage he caused, Chinese Jack Choo came out of the whole Mr Asia downfall in real good shape. Seven years' imprisonment for importing hundreds of thousands of buddha sticks into New Zealand when he was a seaman; plus organising the purchase of 400 kilos of buddha sticks for the *Brigadoon* importation into New Zealand; 100 kilos of heroin into the United Kingdom using couriers; and at least 400 kilos of heroin into Australia through the *Konpira* importation and the use of numerous couriers. Now that's what I call serious drug importation. All ancient history now, but I think I am correct in labelling Choo Cheng Kui as the one that got away!

17

THE *BRIGADOON*

The *Brigadoon* was the foundation stone on which the Mr Asia syndicate was founded. The money to purchase the *Brigadoon* and pay for 400 kilos of Thai buddha sticks was put up by a group of enthusiastic NZ investors who Martin Johnstone had brought together. Many of the investors were businessmen, others were his social and pot smoking friends. That old adage about using; 'other people's money,' was at play here, as Johnstone did not put up any of his own money for the enterprise. The interesting thing about this disparate group of investors was the fact that none of them were criminals. They were just a bunch of naive people, mistakenly thinking they were getting involved in an exciting and profitable drug smuggling caper. I am sure those misguided people who invested money in Martin Johnstone's *Brigadoon* importation back in 1975 would be horrified to know that, inadvertently, they were responsible for the Mr Asia syndicate as well as at least twelve murders.

For those people wondering why any sane business person could allow themselves to become involved in something so dangerous and illegal as drug importation, you have to first understand the prevailing drug culture in the early 1970s. There was no cocaine, ecstasy, ice or speed back then in either Australia or New Zealand. Heroin was available, but only in limited amounts. Marijuana, buddha sticks and hashish were the staple drugs. Rightly or wrongly, many people considered marijuana to be non-addictive, and anyone who sold grass was not regarded as a criminal but rather as a real handy person to know. There was not the wide media coverage back then about how destructive drugs can be, therefore the general public didn't have the aversion to drugs that is prevalent today. The police may say otherwise, but it was my experience through talking to many professional people back in the 1970s, that they regarded marijuana as a benign drug and definitely a drug that should be legalised. Many people took the view, wrongly, that marijuana was harmless. That's why Martin Johnstone was able to gather together a group of misguided investors to help fund his ambitious drug smuggling importation. They all viewed the smuggling of marijuana as a victimless crime, no more serious than drink driving.

To give some indication of how warped people can be, I remember dealing myself with a very successful Auckland businessman around 1975. This man had a thriving business with a large number of people in his employ. I will not go into what we were doing, but suffice to say, it was highly illegal and very profitable. One afternoon while we were sitting in his spacious office talking, I recollect saying to him: 'My friend, I know why I am involved in criminal activity, I am trying to get rich. But you, you're a successful self-made man, why are you doing this?' His heartfelt reply absolutely staggered me. 'I love taking on and beating the police. I get a real thrill out of it!' I shrugged my shoulders and thought to myself; You are definitely doing business with me for the wrong reasons. He was never caught and retired when I left New Zealand for good in 1977, and I'm fairly certain he never committed a crime again after that.

Before I continue with the *Brigadoon* importation, I would like to impart some knowledge about marijuana – grass, pot, weed, hash or whatever you like to call it – to any young people who are reading this book. This is knowledge acquired by me from being around marijuana since 1964 and analysing its effect on friends of mine who have been consistent pot smokers over that period of time. Marijuana is not harmless. I am here to say that it is both addictive and harmful. Because I have observed the effects of prolonged pot smoking among friends of mine – over a 40 year period of time – I can comment on the damage smoking pot can do. All my friends who smoked pot continuously are now seriously brain damaged. To a man, you cannot get a coherent sentence out of them. Whenever you ask any of them a question, all you get is a 'yeah man, yeah'. Sadly, their brain cells have been eroded, as well as their pockets, because not one of my long term pot-smoking friends has a dollar to his name. Some of these guys were successful businessmen when they started smoking pot, but now they are incapable of running a business even if they wanted to. It has been very sad to watch some of my friends slowly destroy their minds. I may not be the ideal person to lecture anybody about the dangers of smoking pot, especially when you consider my past, but unlike many of the so-called experts on drugs, I have been around drugs for 40 years and have seen up close and personal what smoking pot has done to my friends. So to any pot smokers who might be reading this book, please give my informed warning some thought.

But back to the *Brigadoon*. The skipper of the *Brigadoon* was a 30-year-old New Zealander named Peter Lawrence Miller. Although I never had anything to do with this importation, quite a few people who did gave evidence to the Stewart Royal Commission, and Miller was one of these people. In evidence he gave to police, Miller said he met Martin Johnstone and George Papaconstantinou, another New Zealander, in mid-1974. At first he thought Papaconstantinou was the mastermind of their drug organisation and not Johnstone. He met Terry Clark, but was led to believe he was only involved in a minor way. In early 1975, Miller formed a series of companies with

Martin Johnstone. They used one of these companies to purchase the *Brigadoon*, a 34 foot yacht for $50,000. The reason they chose the *Brigadoon* was the fact that Johnstone's father had helped design and build the yacht. It is obvious from the evidence presented to the Royal Commission that Miller was involved right up to his bootstraps in the *Brigadoon* importation. The fact that he purchased the yacht with Johnstone is clear evidence of this. So his lame excuse that he was only hired to sail the yacht up to Thailand does not stand up to close scrutiny.

After giving the *Brigadoon* a complete refit and overhaul in late August 1975, Miller set sail for Thailand. On board as crew were Michael Lampshire, a car sales manager, and his brother Kevin. Before this motley band had even sailed, NZ Customs and the police had notified all authorities in the Western Pacific and South East Asia that the *Brigadoon* was believed to be carrying drugs and requested that if sighted she be stopped and searched. Despite this early alert, the *Brigadoon* was able to sail around South East Asia and New Guinea untouched, carrying a full cargo of buddha sticks. It is a telling indictment about how little coordination there was between different countries back then, particularly when it came to passing on information about suspected drug smugglers. The *Brigadoon* and its illegal cargo should never have made it back to New Zealand.

The one vexing problem most criminals face is how to keep their criminal activity from being uncovered by law enforcement officers. When two people know something it is no longer a secret. That long established truism is especially relevant to criminals. If I had a buck for every criminal who has been brought undone by loose lips, I would not be a millionaire; I would be a billionaire. Even when you have a tightly run criminal organisation, it is still hard to stop information from leaking out. So it is easy to understand how information about the *Brigadoon* leaked out so quickly. With so many investors, particularly pot smoking investors, involved it is a wonder the *Brigadoon* ever set sail. Although I was not involved in the importation, I remember a fellow criminal telling me in late 1975 to stand by as there was a huge shipment of buddha sticks arriving by sea. Every drug dealer in New Zealand seemed to be aware of the *Brigadoon*'s imminent arrival. I guess the fact that the yacht arrived back in New Zealand four months behind schedule threw the police off track, because by the time it actually arrived, the police had abandoned all the coastal surveillance for it.

From the time the *Brigadoon* left New Zealand in late August 1975 until its arrival back in NZ waters some seven months later, on 21 March 1976, it is a fair comment to say that the yacht and its crew had more than their share of misadventures. On a stopover in Noumea, two of the crew were arrested for shoplifting. After paying a fine for the shoplifting offence, the two crewmen rejoined the *Brigadoon* and she set sail for Thailand. One of the crew, Kevin Lampshire, told the Royal Commission that after picking up 39 coal sacks of buddha sticks – weighing approx 400 kilos – in Bangkok in late October 1975, the *Brigadoon* set sail for New Zealand. Unfortunately for Kevin Lampshire and his brother Michael, they contracted malaria while travelling through the Indonesian islands. This resulted in both of them being hospitalised for three and a half months, as well as causing a long delay in the *Brigadoon*'s sailing schedule. While waiting for them to recover, the buddha sticks were off-loaded onto a uninhabited island and the *Brigadoon* put into Makassar, a port on the southern edge of Sulawesi in the Indonesian archipelago. All the crew had visa problems after arriving at Makassar and Martin Johnstone had to fly in personally to sort out their visa situation. A continuing engine problem on the *Brigadoon* meant the yacht was already two months behind schedule when they arrived at Makassar (now known as Ujung Pandang). However, Martin Johnstone and Peter Miller's luck changed when they met an Australian sea captain named John Chadderton in Makassar.

Born in Mornington, Victoria, on 10 June 1950, John Andrew Chadderton was the captain of the ex-Taiwanese fishing vessel *Konpira Maru* when Johnstone and Miller met him in Makassar. Although aged only 25, Chadderton owned the *Konpira Maru*, a vessel he had acquired through salvage in 1974 in Darwin. This vessel would play a pivotal role a year later, when Terry Clark organised his first major importation of heroin into Australia. Other expatriates living in Makassar had introduced the Australian skipper to Martin Johnstone. As Chadderton was looking for work at that time, he was only too happy to take on a 'no questions asked' job involving the towing of the *Brigadoon* back to NZ coastal waters. As John Chadderton did not want to wait any longer than necessary, the *Brigadoon* with the *Konpira Maru* escorting her, set off from Makassar in January 1976. The two sick Lampshire brothers were left behind, broke; they had to find their own way home to New Zealand. The abandonment of the Lampshire brothers was just another example of Martin Johnstone's poor organisational skills and lack of regard for the welfare of people working for him. After making one more stop at Gove, a small coastal mining town in northern Australia, where Martin Johnstone disembarked, the *Konpira Maru* and the *Brigadoon* slowly headed towards New Zealand.

When Martin Johnstone arrived back in New Zealand, the police monitored him very closely. All the publicity about him being the elusive 'Mr Asia' meant not only the police were watching his movements but also other criminals as well. It did not take long for word to leak out about the imminent arrival of the *Brigadoon* and its cargo of buddha sticks. The police and Customs issued alerts and conducted aerial searches of the northern coastline, but to no avail. The good fortune that had followed the *Brigadoon* since she left Thailand held. Because of constant engine trouble, the *Brigadoon*'s arrival back in New Zealand was delayed by a month. As a consequence of this lengthy delay, the police had discontinued their intense surveillance, which allowed the *Brigadoon* to limp, undetected, into Doubtless Bay, a secluded spot on the North Island.

The seven-month trip to Thailand had been arduous, dangerous and difficult, but with a huge amount of luck on her side, the *Brigadoon* had made it safely back to New Zealand with her cargo of buddha sticks. With close to a half million buddha sticks in her hold, everybody connected with the enterprise was about to make a whole lot of money. When he had paid off his investors, Martin Johnstone still cleared just over $1 million for himself, plus he retained possession of the *Brigadoon*. The coveted task of selling all the Buddha sticks was given to Terry Clark.

After his release from Wi Tako Prison in March 1974, Terry Clark had returned to a vastly changed landscape in Auckland. The old methods of safe-breaking and selling stolen goods were no longer a viable or profitable way of making money. Drugs were the main game and Clark started to learn the hard way about making money from dealing in cannabis and heroin. His first few forays into heroin dealing were a disaster, as he was sold some real rubbish. I guess the fact that his then wife, Norma Fleet, was a raging heroin addict, kept him involved for a short time in that commodity. But it didn't take him long to realise that the big money was being made in the sale of buddha sticks. Through a fortuitous meeting with Martin Johnstone, Clark was soon able to access large quantities of buddha sticks. As a consequence, his monetary situation not only improved dramatically but he also became a trusted business associate of Martin Johnstone. This burgeoning friendship was why Johnstone offered Clark the opportunity to sell all the buddha sticks from the *Brigadoon* importation.

Rather inconveniently for Clark however, while the *Brigadoon* had been away he had got himself involved in an ill-fated attempt to smuggle in a couple of pounds of heroin from Fiji, using a woman named Valerie Karau. I have always found it hard to understand why Clark risked a potential $1.5 million earn to try and import two pounds of heroin, worth about $150,000. Later, when we were working together, I didn't ask him why he got involved in that abortive heroin importation simply because no one likes to be reminded about their failures, and Clark certainly came into that category.

As a result of this abortive heroin smuggling attempt, Clark had been arrested and was on bail awaiting trial when the *Brigadoon* arrived in New Zealand. Rather than take a chance on being convicted, when his trial was due to commence in March 1976 Clark absconded while on bail and went into hiding. With so much money at stake from the sale of the buddha sticks aboard the *Brigadoon*, Clark was not about to let such a golden opportunity slip by. Using trusted associates like Douglas Wilson and Peter Fulcher, Clark was able to orchestrate the sale of all the buddha sticks off the *Brigadoon* despite being on the run. Although it took over six months to move all the shipment, the successful sale of at least 450,000 buddha sticks netted Clark just over $1.5 million. When you consider that in 1976 the average weekly wage was $100 and a house in New Zealand could be brought for $10,000, you get some idea about the sheer scale of money that was available to successful drug smugglers back then.

With a combined profit of over $2.5 million from the *Brigadoon* importation, both Terry Clark and Martin Johnstone were ready to go after bigger game. The fact that he was a wanted man just made the game more exciting for Clark. For Martin Johnstone, the belief that he and his friend Terry Clark were destined for great things meant he too was ready to roll the dice and outlay all their profits on a huge shipment of heroin into Australia. The Kiwi invasion of Australia was about to begin.

18

FAREWELL
NEW ZEALAND

The two of us, Terry Clark and myself, arrived in Australia because of slightly different circumstances. When Clark slipped out of New Zealand he was a wanted man, having absconded while awaiting trial on heroin charges. I, on the other hand, although not wanted by the police for any criminal offences, left my home country just one step ahead of the posse chasing me.

While the *Brigadoon* importation was under way I had been busy in Auckland and Wellington making money, illegally of course. To keep the police off my back, I had acquired a much-coveted seaman's ticket, which allowed me to ship out as a merchant seaman. Whenever any police officers or detectives queried me about employment, I would just say I was on the corner – a name given to the office where seaman go to pick up a ship – waiting for an available ship. A shame I never stayed there, as the seaman's union back in the 1970s was very strong and looked after their members real well. I shipped out a few times and really enjoyed it, but I was always thinking about how I could earn more money illegally.

In 1976, using some of the money I had invested with Robert, I became a silent partner with a lovely gentleman named Graham Smith, in an Auckland nightclub we named Pips International. We took the name from a famous Los Angeles backgammon nightclub called Pips. There was a club in Sydney called Pips at that time as well, evidently they had an agreement with the LA club to use the Pips name. As we were a long way from Los Angeles, we did not think permission to use the Pips name was necessary so did not ask. Although we had backgammon tables downstairs, we used to run the club primarily as a disco on Thursdays, Fridays and Saturdays. It was impossible to get a liquor licence back then, so my partner Graham Smith came up with an ingenious plan to get around the liquor laws. We would charge a $5 entry fee and give the alcohol away for free.

When he first suggested the idea to me, I thought he was stark staring mad. 'Are you crazy,' I said. 'The punters will drink us out of house and home!'

'Let's just give it a trial,' Graham calmly replied. So we did and the results were spectacular. As the owners of the premises we were leasing had a liquor licence, we could purchase, for example, a large bottle of whisky or rum for $4. Now there are not many people who can drink a large bottle of spirits. We found that most of the people who came to our club were already drunk when they arrived, and it averaged out that each person consumed only $1.20 worth of booze, which meant we made $3.80 on every punter who walked through our doors. We had two floors and the punters would be hanging from the rafters, it was that crowded. It was fucking hard to get a drink too.

On Wednesdays and Sundays when we were not open to the public, the disco floor became a mini casino for us. On those nights, we ran one of the biggest Manila card games in New Zealand. Manila is a lot like seven-card stud poker. A player is dealt two cards face down, which only he can see. Five cards are then placed face down in the middle of the table. As each card in the centre of the table is turned over, a round of betting ensues. By the time the fifth card is turned over there has usually been a lot of money bet, as you can have up to ten players at the table gambling. A card player can win, or lose, lots of money very quickly playing Manila. As we ran the game, we used to take $1 out of every $40 bet. I know it doesn't sound like much, but we would average $200 an hour.

The Wednesday night game used to run for 24 hours. On many a Thursday night, the card players would just be leaving as the first disco revellers were arriving. The Sunday night games sometimes went for two days. To protect the players and ourselves we had a reinforced front door to stop anyone bursting in. I also kept a steel-weighted baton and a sawn-off shotgun under the front desk in case of any unexpected trouble. As both Graham and I knew all the big punters in New Zealand, no undercover police or strangers could get past the front door. 'We are closed,' was our monotonous mantra.

For all our card players the food and drink was free. As an added attraction for them, we had gorgeous topless waitresses serving them any food or drink they ordered. The girls used to get around $500 a night in tips so there was no shortage of attractive women wanting to work our card game. The added bonus for us was the fact that Graham Smith was one of the best card players I have ever met. So besides our take from the card game we also made a lot from Graham's card playing ability. We pulled at least $10,000 a week, every week. That club was a veritable goldmine while it was open. Unfortunately it burnt down in late 1977. Some malicious people – that is, the police – suspected Graham and I of burning the joint down for the insurance money! The fact that by sheer coincidence I was dining at a restaurant called the Firehouse, on the night Pips burned down did not endear me to the police investigating the fire. But the truth of the matter was simply this: Graham and I were making too much money from our card games to want to burn the club down. No one was ever charged with burning down Pips, but my last ties to New Zealand went up with the flames that destroyed the club.

For me, New Zealand was getting too troublesome to live there comfortably. Because of all my criminal activity, the police, rightly, were determined to put me behind bars. Once the police get a 'hard on' for you they can make life very difficult, particularly in a small country like New Zealand. So for most of 1977 I had been making surreptitious trips to Sydney, to set myself up for a new life away from New Zealand. By the time the club burnt down, I was mainly domiciled in Sydney anyway, so the permanent transition went very smoothly. Over the years while I was in prison in New Zealand I had met a lot of willing Australian criminals, who for one reason or another had come unstuck in New Zealand and had served time there. Friendships forged in NZ prisons, meant that whenever I was in Australia, be it Sydney or Melbourne, there were always well-connected criminals I could look up. Quite often criminals on the run from Australia would come over to New Zealand and I would be asked to take care of them. I did this on many occasions and my help was much appreciated by my Australian friends. These connections were the main reason Clark wanted me to come over to Australia and work with him.

I first met Clark in 1975 at a private party in Auckland. Although I did not know him at that time, I was aware through the criminal grapevine that Clark was selling large quantities of buddha sticks. The lady with him when we first met, Maria Muhary, was an old friend of mine. In fact, I was quite surprised to see her with Clark, as back then Maria was an extremely attractive woman and he did not fit the mould of someone she would go out with. Even on his best day Clark was not an imposing figure, whereas Maria had the exotic dark looks of her Hungarian heritage. I used to take out a friend of Maria's and knew her very well. In a recent phone call with Duncan, my long departed friend Barry McFarlane's son, I reminded him that he used to go out with Maria before she hooked up with Terry Clark. His whimsical reply that he had even introduced them really brought home to me how interrelated all the events involving the Mr Asia syndicate were. Because it was Maria who suggested to Clark that he get me over from New Zealand, both for my expertise in moving money and my criminal connections. Despite my celebrated reputation with women, the fact that I had never slept with Maria also made it a lot easier for Clark to work with me.

The second time I met Clark was just before he left the country in early 1976. Once again it was a private function at a mutual friend's house. During the course of the evening, Clark pulled me aside and asked me about my Australian criminal connections. He was obviously already planning to disappear and Australia was firmly in his plans. The *Brigadoon* importation had not been successfully concluded at that time, but Clark was obviously thinking ahead, because he asked me if I was interested in working in Australia. When I asked him what he was intending to do over there, he just smiled and said: 'It will be hammer.' For someone yet to make his first million, that was a bold statement. I politely declined his offer. I was doing so well at that time that I had no intention of going anywhere. I did tell him that I had some great criminal connections in Sydney, however, and if he ever wanted to utilise them he only had to call me. My reason for offering Clark assistance, despite not knowing him that well, were twofold. First, he was involved with a woman I really liked; and second, the guy he had been charged with for the heroin importation, Ray B, was an old friend of mine from Invercargill Borstal. So as a mark of respect to them both, I made my offer of assistance to Clark. It was about eighteen months later, in July 1977, when Clark called me at my Auckland home. His request was simple: he needed police protection for himself and his new enterprise, could my Australian friends help? To my eternal regret I said yes, I'm sure they could. Arrangements were made for me to fly over and speak to a few people. One of those people was Robert Trimbole.

Invercargill Borstal. Where it all began for me. Do not let the pleasant-looking facade fool you. This was a brutal institution for young New Zealand criminals.

Mt Eden prison riot, 1965. If I live to be a hundred I'll never experience anything like the riot again. It certainly changed my life, and not for the better.

Before I became notorious criminal Diamond Jim Shepherd, I was, at the age of 32, just fun-loving Jim Shepherd.

Marty Johnstone in 1979. It was Marty's drug money that created the Mr Asia syndicate. It was his death that ended it.

Robert Trimbole. Despite all the allegations against him, he was a man I came to like and respect.

Meet Peter Heyfron. This picture was taken for one of Clark's numerous false passports.

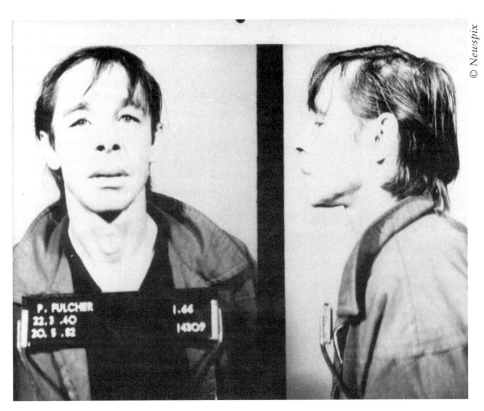

I first met Peter Fulcher in the late '50s in prison. A determined criminal; he ran the New Zealand operations.

Despite being found guilty of conspiring to kill Donald McKay and the murders of Doug and Isobel Wilson, James Bazley has always maintained his innocence.

The *Brigadoon*. The successful importation into New Zealand of 450,000 buddha sticks aboard this yacht gave Johnstone and Clark the money needed to set up the Mr Asia syndicate.

The *Konpira*. The size of the boat gives you some indication of how much heroin it could carry. I've always thought there was much more heroin aboard this vessel than was listed in the Royal Commission report.

Terry Clark's house in Opua. His dream was to retire here and live the life of an artist. He never made it.

Happier times for Terry Clark. This nondescript man does not look like someone who I believe killed at least twelve people.

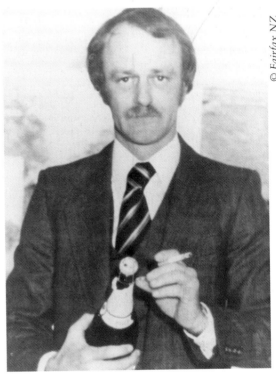

May 18, 1979. Police excavating the Wilsons' shallow grave in Rye on the Mornington Peninsula in Victoria. The beginning of the end for the Mr Asia syndicate.

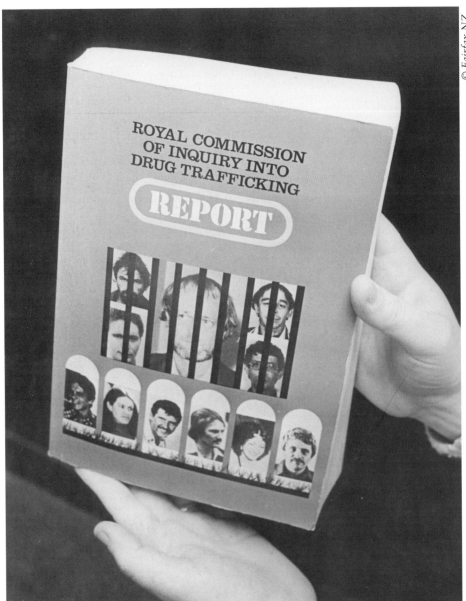

Justice DG Stewart's Royal Commission Report. Most of the people pictured on the cover were murdered. Although the R.C. Report was comprehensive, this book fills in many of the unknown details about the syndicate.

19

ROBERT 'AUSSIE BOB' TRIMBOLE

One of the greatest fallacies to come out of all the publicity and subsequent inquiries about the Mr Asia syndicate was the notion that Bob Trimbole was involved with Terry Clark in trafficking heroin. He was not. I am here to say, Bob Trimbole never got one gram of heroin off Terry Clark, ever. Bob Trimbole never paid Terry Clark one dollar for drugs during the whole time the Mr Asia syndicate was active. But do not take my word for those statements, just read the report of Justice Stewart's Royal Commission into Drug Trafficking. The report ran for 900 pages and over a two year period the Royal Commission interviewed hundreds of witnesses worldwide, including all those individuals who worked closely with Clark; yet not one indemnified witness gave any evidence that they supplied Bob Trimbole with even one gram of heroin. The only evidence presented to the

Royal Commission about Bob Trimbole being involved with the Mr Asia syndicate were the dubious statements made by Allison Dine and Maria Muhary. They both testified that Clark had told them that Bob Trimbole was taking over the Australian operations. The earliest mention of Bob Trimbole at the Stewart Royal Commission was by Allison Dine, who said she met him in April 1979 when he arranged to get her a false passport. And that is it! Yet had he lived and been arrested for his alleged involvement with the Mr Asia syndicate, there is no doubt he would have been convicted if had he been sent for trial. The sheer weight of all the negative press he received concerning his alleged illegal activities between 1977 and 1980 would have ensured a guilty verdict. Now I am not here to say Bob Trimbole was a Boy Scout, far from it. There has been a lot of evidence presented in different trials over the years that suggest Bob Trimbole was involved in the disappearance of Donald Mackay. But suggesting something and proving it are two different things.

I have trawled through my memory and I can only come up with four occasions that I am aware of when Terry Clark actually met Bob Trimbole. The first was around July 1977, when I introduced them; the second was at a dinner we had together in May 1978 at Tati's restaurant in Sydney; the third time was another dinner in April 1979 just before Clark left Australia; and the final time was in July 1979, when Bob Trimbole came over to London to see us. I accept that Bob Trimbole may have met Clark on other occasions, but I can only recount the meetings I am sure of. I will stress here, though, that I was the one who knew Bob Trimbole well, not Clark. That is why it was so amusing to watch the scenes on the *Underbelly* series where Clark and Trimbole were doing business together. In one scene the actor portraying Bob Trimbole tells the actor playing Clark: 'Don't cross me, Terry, or I will bury you.' Talk about creative television.

I first met Bob Trimbole in the beginning of 1977, at Randwick racecourse in Sydney. An old friend of mine from Auckland who had moved to Australia ten years previously and had business interests in Kings Cross introduced me to Bob as a long-time trusted friend from back home. In the criminal world, introductions like that carry a lot of weight because of the implied understanding that the person being introduced is a stand-up guy, someone you can do business with. Although I was still doing a lot of business in Auckland at that time, my nightclub being my main interest, I was increasingly spending more time in Sydney. Because there was no restriction on travel between New Zealand and Australia back then, one example being you did not need any identification, I was able to slip in and out of Australia at will.

A friend of mine from Wellington who owned a couple of slow racehorses in the mid-1970s was always bringing horses over to Melbourne or Sydney to try and beat the bookies, with no success. On more than one occasion after accompanying my friend on an unsuccessful punting trip to Melbourne or Sydney to back one of his horses, we would invariably fly home to New Zealand with empty pockets. But all those punting losses changed after I met Bob Trimbole.

Robert Trimbole was born in Australia on 19 March 1931 to Italian parents. When I first met him he was married and had four children. He had various business interests in Griffith and owned a supermarket in the Sydney suburb of Casula. Anyone who knew Bob Trimbole back in the 1970s, will tell you he was a likeable rogue. Although he was proud of his Italian heritage, he did not look like an Italian, or speak like one. He sounded very Australian; I guess that's why they called him 'Aussie Bob.' More times than not, he had a smile on his face whenever you met him. I know this may sound contradictory to what many people have read, seen, or heard about Bob Trimbole, but I always found Bob to be a real engaging man and good company. He was a character. Like me, Bob was not a tall man. Slightly balding, you would invariably see him wearing a short-brimmed hat and a three-quarter length coat. Although he had a paunch and was not a fitness freak, Bob had a lot of energy. The man was always on the go, always looking to make a buck, always on the lookout for a deal. A fearless gambler, his greatest pleasure in life – apart from his family – was winning money off bookmakers. At least twice a year Bob would fix a race and sting the bookies big time. I had the pleasure of sharing in a couple of his race stings.

I distinctly remember the first race winner Bob ever tipped me. I was at the Rosehill races in Sydney around March or April 1977, when I bumped into Bob again. He remembered me from our first meeting and after the usual pleasantries had been exchanged, he asked me what I was backing. I told him the horse I came over from New Zealand to back had already lost and cost me five grand. I said I still had five grand but I was going to use that money to have a good time and do some shopping.

'Racing is a hard game in Australia, Jim. We try to speed them up; the bookies try to slow them down. You have to get up very early to beat the bookies over here,' was Bob's jovial comment to me. 'I have a lot of respect for your Kiwi mate doing business up the Cross, so I'll give you a chance to get your money back,' was his next intriguing comment. Moving closer to me and speaking very quietly, he told me to 'back number five in race seven at Brisbane in two hours' time. If it won, I was to back number fifteen in the last race at Melbourne that day.' After checking I had the numbers right, Bob bade me a cheery goodbye and raced off into the crowd. Not wanting to risk all my money, I only put $3000 to win on number five in the seventh race at Brisbane, at odds of 5 to 1. When the designated race started, I was standing in the crowd watching the race on television.

'Where's number five?' I asked my slow horse owning friend from New Zealand who was with me.

'That's it ten lengths in front,' was his cheerful response. When the horse ended up winning by five lengths, Bob Trimbole's status grew tenfold in my eyes. Rather than risk all my winnings, I again put $3000 on number fifteen in the last race at Melbourne, at odds of 16 to 1. It ran nowhere, but I still ended up a big winner. After thanking Bob profusely for giving me a winning tip, I promised to look him up next time I was in Australia and buy him dinner. And that, as they say, was the start of my friendship with him. For a change, I flew home to Auckland with money in my pocket. I said to my friend on the trip home: 'If you cannot beat them, join them.' I rarely lost money on a racecourse in Australia after I met Bob Trimbole.

A few months after my second meeting with Bob Trimbole, I had to come over to Sydney again on some business. While there I had dinner with my Kings Cross friend, Phil L, and asked him about the tipster – Bob Trimbole – he had introduced me to. My friend was a very tough guy but I sensed he was reluctant to talk about Bob. It took some gentle persuasion and the usual fervent declaration from me that it would go no further, before my friend agreed to fill in a few details about Bob.

'There are a group of Italians operating out of Griffith. They are growing grass down there by the truckload and Bob is one of their top men. He handles most of the sales. They are all making fucking squillions, as they have got the law on side. These boys are not the Mafia, but they are the closest thing to the Mafia in this country. Although the crew down there are all nice guys, they will not hesitate to have you killed. So beware my friend, if you ever do business with them. If you ever need help with the law, Bob's your man. Now get me a fucking drink,' was his not so subtle way of saying, I've told you more than enough.

I have to be honest here and say that the last thing I thought Bob Trimbole would be was a major drug dealer. I had him pegged for a SP bookie, a professional gambler or a businessman with an interest in horses. So much for my ability to pick someone in the same line of work as me. The bit of information that really got my interest though, was Bob's ability to do business with the law. That was the connection Clark needed to operate in Sydney – access to corrupt police – and Bob Trimbole was able to facilitate that desire. It was just a short time after I was told this valuable information about Bob Trimbole's ability to do business with the law when Clark called me in New Zealand seeking help. If only I had said no. Now that would have saved me fifteen years of fucking misery, and would definitely have made a difference to how Aussie Bob's life evolved. And lest we forget, hapless law clerk Brian Alexander, the man who would become

Clark's conduit to corrupt police, the man Bob Trimbole arranged an introduction to. The same Brian Alexander who would be murdered in late 1981, simply because he knew too much about corrupt police. There is an old biblical saying, 'As you sow, so shall you reap.' I guess those prescient words in the Holy Bible could well encapsulate what happened to the four of us. One way or another, we all paid a heavy price for our sins. Three with their lives, me with 25 years' hard labour. I think it is fair comment to say that I am not looking forward to Judgement Day.

20

THE *KONPIRA*

In May 1976, Terry Clark was living with his second wife, Norma Fleet, in a flat at 104 Zilman Road, Hendra, which is near Brisbane. The *Brigadoon* had only arrived two months previously, but Doug Wilson and Peter Fulcher were handling sales of the buddha sticks efficiently and money was flowing in at a rapid rate. Despite being a wanted man, Clark told me that during that period he slipped into New Zealand on two occasions, heavily disguised, just to make sure the sale of the remaining buddha sticks was completed and all monies owed to him were paid. After splitting with Norma in July 1976, Clark made his liaison with Maria Muhary official and travelled with her to Penang in Malaysia, where they lived for five months.

Before the *Konpira* importation in March 1977, Terry Clark organised a couple of smaller drug runs himself during late 1976. Both he and his de facto wife at that time, Maria Muhary, made successful trips into Australia carrying heroin strapped to their bodies. It was the one and only time Clark ever put himself at risk by carrying heroin personally. He later told me the harrowing experience of having so much heroin strapped to his body while going through Customs made him think long and hard about more efficient ways of importing heroin into Australia. The *Konpira* importation was a direct outcome of Clark's personal experience smuggling heroin. He correctly ascertained that one large heroin importation by sea – something similar to the *Brigadoon* buddha importation in New Zealand – would be far more effective than making a hundred smaller drug runs using couriers.

According to evidence she gave to the Stewart Royal Commission, Maria Muhary stated that while living in Penang, she and Clark toured Malaysia and also visited Singapore and Thailand. It was more than likely on one of these trips to Singapore that Clark, Johnstone and Chinese Jack organised the *Konpira* importation of 400 kilos of white, number four heroin – widely regarded as the best heroin you can get – into Australia in March 1977.

Since 1975, Martin Johnstone had been setting himself up in Singapore. It was where he lived most of the time and where he controlled all his business interests. Although he had numerous companies in Singapore, it was his Cross & Mercer companies in Singapore, Hong Kong and Australia that he conducted most of his business through. After the successful *Brigadoon* importation into New Zealand, using some of the money made from that venture Johnstone and his then de facto wife Bronwyn Davies travelled around the world first class. In October 1976 they returned to Singapore and settled down in an apartment on Balmoral Point, an affluent area favoured by expatriates living there. For the next two years, Martin Johnstone lived out his boyhood dreams. He became known around Singapore as a high-flyer, a man of means, a man always ready to pick up the cheque, a generous host of parties where vintage champagne flowed and cocaine was freely available. The Marco Polo Hotel was where you would find him most days, particularly at The Club, a member's only enclave located in the hotel. Whenever Bronwyn was away, Martin had a steady stream of women to call on. Airline hostesses, nightclub singers, local beauties; if a woman was attractive, no one was barred. It was almost as if Martin knew what was awaiting him on 9 October 1979, because during those years he tried to sleep with as many women as he could.

Shortly after their return to Singapore in 1976, Martin Johnstone acquired a half share in John Chadderton's ex-Taiwanese fishing trawler, the *Konpira Maru*. He paid for his half share by paying for repairs to the boat in New Zealand and an additional cash settlement that was finalised in Singapore. Martin Johnstone and John Chadderton established a company with the grandiose name of Timor International Marine and Oceanographic Research Private Limited (Timor). This company never traded profitably and, by December 1980 had debts of $480,000. The only listed asset of the company was the *Konpira*.

A letter sent by Elaine Chadderton and dated 26 November 1976 was intercepted in Auckland a day later. In the letter, she confirmed they were staying with Martin Johnstone and Bronwyn Davies at 23e Balmoral Road while the *Konpira* was in dry dock in Singapore. From these dates we can conclude that preparations for the *Konpira* heroin importation were already well under way. They also firmly wash away any nonsense that John Chadderton was not heavily involved in that massive heroin importation. Just another one of the many indemnified witnesses who Justice Stewart let walk off into the sunset scot-free.

According to Terry Clark, who confided in me one afternoon while we were having a quiet drink in early 1978, the *Konpira* heroin importation was structured like this. In 1976, top quality number four – china white – heroin was available at $11,000 or $12,000 a kilo. But because of the large order they placed through Chinese Jack, they were able to get 400 kilos of heroin at $9000 per kilo, meaning they were up for $3.6 million, that being the total purchase price. It was agreed between the three of them that Johnstone would put up $500,000 plus supply the boat and crew to transport the heroin to Australia. His contribution, Clark told me, was $1 million in cash; in addition, he was to be responsible for all heroin sales in Australasia.

The remaining $2.1 million required to purchase the 400 kilos was carried by Chinese Jack and the organisation he purchased the heroin from. When you think about it, for that era, the size of the importation was staggering. According to Clark, it was agreed that all costs – that is, monies paid for heroin and so on – involved in setting up the importation would be taken from the profits first, then all subsequent money was to be shared equally between them. As Clark used to sell a ten-gram bag of heroin for $1000, each kilo of heroin weighing 1000 grams was worth $100,000 dollars to the syndicate. Therefore 400 kilos was worth $40 million to the three of them. After expenses, they stood to make $12 million each.

That was the game plan anyway, but like a lot of plans, they are only as good as the people implementing them. In an earlier chapter I described Terry Clark as a psychopathic killer; I should have also included in my description that he was extremely cunning and extremely greedy. Although he never told me, it is obvious to me now how Clark shafted Martin Johnstone and Chinese Jack over the *Konpira* heroin importation. By doing my figures I am able to come to this conclusion, because I am the only person alive who knows roughly how much heroin Clark sold between 1977 and 1979. At the end of this chapter, I'll explain how I believe Clark ripped off and robbed Martin Johnstone and Chinese Jack Choo.

To help facilitate the *Konpira* heroin importation, Martin Johnstone and his brother Stephen arranged for one of their companies, Cross & Mercer (Hong Kong), to deliver a load of pottery to the company's Australian base, Cross & Mercer (Australia). One of the crew on the *Konpira* told the Royal Commission that shortly before the vessel departed with its shipment of pottery, Martin Johnstone told John Chadderton that he would be carrying additional cargo to Australia. The crew member said that Johnstone supplied Chadderton with a specific latitude and longitude reference in the Gulf of Thailand – near the Thailand–Cambodian border – and also gave him half a torn dollar note. I'll quote from what the crew member told the Stewart Royal Commission:

That is the sort of thing you read in a second class novel, but there is where they get the ideas from, from things people have done. It is either what people read in novels or it is the other way around and when you look back at the history of the world people have been doing things like that for thousands of years. He said when we got this place another boat would come to meet us and they would have the other half of this note he gave Chadderton and if they were satisfied that was the other half of the note that they had, they would hand the stuff over.

After the *Konpira* sailed to the arranged rendezvous in the Gulf of Thailand, the crew member said they were met by a boat he described as a 45 foot cigarette hull, flat top type of boat with seven hp engines. The boat was crewed by Chinese seamen who loaded nineteen four-gallon kerosene cans onto the *Konpira*. They also gave Chadderton two M16 rifles and 1000 rounds of ammunition. At first the crew member thought they were carrying marijuana, but he soon realised because of the weight, that the additional cargo was heroin. It is absolutely amazing to me how many indemnified witnesses did not realise what was going on around them while they were involved with the Mr Asia syndicate!

To give the impression that the vessel was just going about its usual business of doing salvage and towing jobs in the South East Asian area, the *Konpira* headed to Kalaragung in Borneo, where it had a contract to tow two barges through the Philippines to a tug at Halmahera in the Maluku Islands. After completing the towing charter, the *Konpira* continued its southbound journey to Australia. Off Papua New Guinea, the *Konpira* developed engine trouble and John Chadderton had to make an unexpected stop for engine repairs. Fortunately for all on board the *Konpira*, Chadderton anticipated that the vessel might be searched in Papua New Guinea, so he astutely off-loaded the nineteen kerosene drums onto a nearby deserted island before they pulled into Wewak. Because of Chadderton's foresight, disaster was averted: a thorough search of the vessel by PNG Customs officers found nothing. After repairs were completed, Chadderton retrieved the cans off the island and the *Konpira* continued its journey down the east coast of Australia.

Soon after the *Konpira* entered Australian waters, Chadderton became aware that the vessel was under aerial surveillance. Under the codename 'Operation Tuna', the Australian Federal Police were watching the *Konpira* using RAAF Orion aircraft as it sailed slowly down the Australian coast. This Australian police surveillance was a complete rerun of the NZ debacle that allowed the *Brigadoon* to bumble ashore. It is amazing that informants exposed both importations at an early stage, yet both were successfully concluded. That would not happen today: the police, particularly the federal police, are now extremely competent and skilled when it comes to handling importations like what occurred with the *Konpira* in March 1977. Nowadays you would not see those Orions tracking you, because all the Federal Police need to do is utilise overhead satellite surveillance. The advent of overhead satellite surveillance has made movement by sea a very dicey proposition for any would-be drug smugglers. The days of the *Konpira* importation are long gone.

Because of the aerial surveillance, Chadderton knew the *Konpira* could not stop. To do so could have led to the likelihood of police and Customs officers boarding the *Konpira* to search the vessel. The plan he had devised with Johnstone before he left Singapore called for Chadderton, when he reached a prearranged point off South Solitary Island, about 15 kilometres northeast of Coffs Harbour, to send Johnstone a telegram. The telegram was to let Johnstone know they had arrived, and the message was to read along the lines: 'We had water in the fuel and were moving slowly and we were changing the injectors.' As per his usual modus operandi, however, Johnstone was not where he was supposed to be and according to a crew member on the *Konpira*: 'It was panic stations all round.' From this point on there are many conflicting stories about what happened to the 400 kilos of heroin carried aboard the *Konpira*. However, I will attempt to separate the wheat from the chaff in regard to what happened when the *Konpira* reached Australia; or, in plain English, fact from fiction.

When the *Konpira* arrived in Australian waters around 20 March 1977, Terry Clark was back in Australia and living with Maria Muhary at 32 Toorak Road, Hamilton, a Brisbane suburb. In anticipation of the *Konpira*'s expected arrival, Clark enlisted his old Wi Tako Prison mate, Greg Ollard, to rent a flat near Coffs Harbour. Records show a Phillip Scott and Lois Haslett booked Flat 1 at 129 Main Street, Wooli, for six weeks in February 1977. These two individuals were Greg Ollard and Julie Theilman. Within seven months of signing that lease, Terry Clark would murder them both. Why he murdered them emphasises what a truly despicable and nasty person he was. Everyone has assumed that Clark killed Ollard because as he told others: 'Greg had talked to the police, and could not be trusted.' His puerile excuse for killing Julie Theilman was that she was a junkie, and with Greg missing she could not be trusted to remain silent. At least four indemnified witnesses told the Stewart Royal Commission that Clark used those excuses to justify killing both Ollard and Theilman. He even laid that excuse on me when he recounted killing them over lunch at Eliza's restaurant in March 1978. I am now firmly of the belief, however, that Clark was tidying up loose ends when he murdered them. They were killed so they could not reveal Clark's duplicity in ripping off Johnstone and Chinese Jack.

It had always puzzled me when reading the Royal Commission transcripts that quite a few of Greg Ollard's associates said they were under the impression that he was Terry Clark's partner when he disappeared. Up until the time of his disappearance in September 1977, Greg Ollard himself told many of his associates that he and Clark were partners. I clearly remember Clark telling me at Eliza's, the day we had lunch: 'I offered to buy him out but the cunt refused my offer.' Other witnesses who gave evidence at the Royal Commission also said Clark told them that he offered to buy Greg out but he refused. The big question for me has always been this: Why would Clark – as even his own statements to me attested – have had as a partner a sorry-arsed, slovenly, fat, loud-mouthed drug addict who never put any money into the *Konpira* importation? The only logical and feasible explanation that could have brought this unlikely partnership about is what I suspect occurred after the *Konpira* reached Australia.

According to two crewmen on the *Konpira* who both gave evidence to the Royal Commission, when they reached the arranged rendezvous point off Coffs Harbour, Martin Johnstone was nowhere to be seen, heard, or found. They both maintained that because of the aerial surveillance and Martin Johnstone not contacting them, the nineteen kerosene drums were tied together by John Chadderton, attached to scrap steel and thrown overboard. It was their belief that the drums would have broken open in the heavy seas and as a consequence, the heroin would have been lost. If you believe that, you may as well start looking for little pink pigs to come flying past your window. I'll tell you this for free. If John Chadderton had jettisoned 400 kilos of number four heroin over the side of the *Konpira*, just weighted down with scrap metal as the two crew members attested, Terry Clark would have made it his mission in life to kill him, that is for sure and certain. I would have done the same. The mere fact that he did not do so indicates to me that Clark retrieved all the heroin. The only person who ever said the heroin was lost overboard was Clark! The two crewmen in their sworn testimony just assumed the heroin would be lost, because of the way it was dumped overboard. And we should not forget Clark telling me during that long lunch at Eliza's restaurant in March 1978 about going aboard the *Konpira*.

This operation was meticulously planned over four months in Singapore, and marker buoys with radio transmitters attached to them were always part of the plan. Martin Johnstone may have lost his nerve at the last minute, but not Clark. Locals from around Wooli told Royal Commission investigators that they recalled Terry Clark and Ian Henry going out in a Bertram speedboat every day, despite heavy weather. When federal police raided Clark's Brisbane address at 54 Highview Terrace, St Lucia, on 20 May 1977, two months after the *Konpira* arrived in Australian waters, they found two marker buoys fitted with radio transmitters marked *Konpira*. Two cartons containing walkie-talkies were also found on the premises. In his report, Justice Stewart said the marker buoys could be accounted for. What did he think, Clark was going to take those marker buoys and radio transmitters out to the *Konpira* after it arrived in Australia? Now that does not compute or make sense. Why would you have equipment needed for an importation in your house, instead of aboard the *Konpira*? No, no, no. You do not travel the distance the *Konpira* did, carrying the huge amount of heroin it had aboard, and not have marker buoys and radio transmitters available. The marker buoys found by federal police officers at Clark's Brisbane address clearly indicate that there were marker buoys aboard the *Konpira*.

Indemnified witnesses told the Royal Commission, that Terry Clark, Ian Henry and Greg Ollard went out to retrieve the nineteen kerosene drums of heroin in a Bertram speedboat. Justice Stewart was of the belief that the heroin was probably lost after being thrown overboard. Despite being on opposite sides of the fence, I have a lot of respect for Justice Stewart; he is that most dangerous of all law enforcement officials, an honest man. But on this point, he got it wrong. What Justice Stewart and the police investigators failed to pick up on was, why would a man who had just made $1.5 million take on as a partner a loud-mouthed, drug addict with no assets?

Quite a few indemnified witnesses gave evidence that they heard from Clark and others that 100 kilos had been retrieved from the heroin thrown overboard. Before he was murdered, Doug Wilson told Brisbane police that Clark retrieved 200 kilos of heroin from a sea importation. It is my firm belief that Clark got all those nineteen drums of heroin safely ashore, then put out the story that most of it had been lost in the sea. Many of the confirmed reports about how much heroin was saved from the *Konpira* seem to be around the 100 kilos range. Here is what I suspect transpired, and the heroin sales figures I am aware of support this theory.

After landing the 400 kilos of heroin, Clark put out the story that most of the load was lost bringing it ashore. If, as quite a few indemnified witnesses have claimed, 100 kilos was recovered, that would have netted Clark, Johnstone and Chinese Jack, $10 million. After taking off $4 million for expenses, they would have cleared around $2 million each. If what I believe is correct, that would have left Clark with 300 kilos for himself. Both Henry and Ollard would have been promised half the 300 kilos, leaving Clark with a minimum $15 million profit from selling his half of the heroin rip-off. Now the only people who would have been aware of this scenario would have been Clark's best friend Ian Henry, Greg Ollard, and his girlfriend Julie Theilman who accompanied him up to Wooli. I do not think it is any coincidence that it is only after the *Konpira* importation in March 1977 that Greg Ollard started referring to himself as Clark's partner.

To add weight to this proposition, I have only to revisit the amounts of heroin that I know was sold during 1977, 1978 and 1979. One indemnified witness – Wayne S – gave evidence at one inquiry that, between 1977 and 1978, he sold one kilo of heroin a week for eighteen months. That equates to 75 kilos with that one person. Another indemnified witness – Steve M – told the Royal Commission that he bought up to $300,000 of heroin off me every week for a year. That equates to at least 100 kilos. During 1978 alone, I am aware of another 100 kilos that was sold. Then you have the people Clark was dealing with personally, like his man in Brisbane, and two others in Adelaide and Perth. Now without even adding on the amounts Clark sent across to New Zealand, I can come up with 250 kilos sold quite easily. By comparison, when you add up all the heroin that the indemnified couriers brought into the country in suitcases, you would be lucky to total 70 kilos. The large discrepancy can only be accounted for in one way: Clark successfully brought ashore those 400 kilos of heroin.

All these observations throw a different light on the Ollard and Theilman murders. They both knew Clark had ripped off Johnstone and Chinese Jack. The fact that they were both hopeless addicts would have worried Clark. It was not the police he was worried they might tip off with loose talk, it was Chinese Jack, who would not have let Clark get away with such a blatant rip-off. Therefore by killing both of them, he not only disposed of a definite threat to himself but also got to keep Ollard's share of the *Konpira* rip-off. As I have mentioned earlier, the drug world, particularly those involved in the heroin trade, is abundantly populated with treacherous people. Such rip-offs as the one I believe Terry Clark perpetuated are not a rare occurrence. Honour is nonexistent amongst the denizens of this heroin netherworld.

It's all ancient history now. No one was ever charged with this, the largest heroin importation ever into Australia at that time. The *Konpira*, after off-loading its illicit cargo of heroin near Coffs Harbour slowly proceeded to Sydney, where the vessel was thoroughly searched. But to no avail. The horse – excuse the pun, as horse is another name given to heroin – had well and truly bolted by then. The *Konpira* sailed to Eden on the NSW south coast, where she undertook repairs, before sailing off back east.

After becoming indemnified Crown witnesses, John Chadderton and his crew gave their disjointed and self-serving evidence to the Stewart Royal Commission, then walked off into the sunset, unscathed, unapologetic and definitely unpunished. Who says crime does not pay?

21

BRIAN ALEXANDER

For any large criminal organisation to flourish it is very important that they have access to the best legal advice, the best financial advice and, if at all possible, access to corrupt police officers. For a criminal group these are the basic resources needed to succeed against the honest forces of law and order. For the Mr Asia syndicate, Brian William Alexander, a law clerk employed by the Sydney law firm of John Lawrence Aston, was the man able to supply unlimited access to corrupt state and federal police officers. Between July 1977 and July 1979, not one senior member nor even a low level member of the Mr Asia syndicate served more than a day behind bars in the state of New South Wales. That startling statistic can be put down to one man: Brian Alexander.

Brian Alexander was born in Sydney on 5 April 1939. When he was ten years old his parents separated and he was sent to live with his paternal aunt. He spent his adolescence years in Sydney's eastern suburbs, where he was educated at St Anne's Marist Brothers Catholic School at Bondi. His school years were not very distinguished, as he was not a diligent student. In fact, he did not pass his leaving exams. After leaving school, Alexander obtained work in a clerical capacity, at a Sydney law firm. He married at an early age but the marriage did not last long and there were no children. A few years after obtaining a divorce, Alexander remarried and had two children with his second wife. The couple were divorced just before his disappearance in December 1981.

During his tenure at the law firm, Alexander met and became a protege of Philip N Roach, a well-known Sydney solicitor in the 1960s. Most of Philip Roach's extensive clientele were either engaged in prostitution or minor criminal matters. Most of his practice was conducted at Sydney's Central Court of Petty Sessions and other inner-city lower courts. For any aspiring lawyer, low-level criminal cases are a great training ground for a successful career in law. Alexander failed to complete the exams that would have qualified him as a fully fledged solicitor, however. Despite failing at his legal exams, because of his work with Philip Roach, Brian Alexander became well known to a large number of Sydney criminals, both inside and outside prison. The same applied to police officers. Constant appearances around Sydney courtrooms representing clients over many years meant Alexander got to know a huge number of police officers. It has been my experience after 50 years of watching countless lawyers interact with their police counterparts in court, that quite a few of these court-room protagonists are very cordial to each other outside court. In fact, I know many good lawyers who are friends with police officers outside working hours.

As drug-related crime increased in the 1970s, Brian Alexander became more professionally associated with criminals involved in illicit drugs. While representing clients on drug-related matters, it was only natural that Alexander would meet numerous police officers engaged in drug law enforcement. These officers included members of the state drug squad, members of the then Federal Narcotics Bureau and Customs officers. When you are constantly meeting law enforcement officers on a daily basis it's not too hard to work out whom you can do business with and, just as importantly, whom you cannot do business with. Over the twenty years he worked with Phillip Roach representing countless criminals in courts all over Sydney, the mind boggles at the legions of corrupt and honest police officers Brian Alexander would have met. Between 1970 and 1985, if you were a criminal with money in New South Wales there was usually a corrupt police officer willing to work something out regardless of what your crime was.

When I first started doing business in Australia in the mid-1970s, my former Aussie cell mates who I did time with in NZ prisons, explained to me how it worked over here. If for some reason I was arrested while committing a crime in Sydney, the first thing I should do on being arrested was ask the arresting officer 'if we could do some business.' If I got a clip around the ears from an honest cop, I was to just keep asking that same question until I got a sympathetic police officer – a polite way of saying a corrupt cop – who would agree to see what he could do. I know it is hard to believe in this day and age, but that is exactly how the system used to work back then. Terry Clark once drunkenly boasted to a group of friends: 'The New South Wales police force; the best police money can buy.' As I stated earlier, the fact that not one of us involved in the Mr Asia syndicate ever spent a day behind bars in New South Wales between July 1977 and July 1979 says it all.

In 1975 Brian Alexander transferred his employment from Philip Roach to the legal practice of John Lawrence Aston, an urbane solicitor, with plush offices located at 54 Park Street, in the Sydney CBD. I am fairly certain that at that time 54 Park Street was owned by the late Kerry Packer. I'm sure Mr Packer would have had no knowledge of the criminal activity that was going on at the offices of John Lawrence Aston & Associates. The move to John Aston's firm was definitely a step up the legal ladder for Alexander, who became his managing clerk. Before Alexander started working for

John Aston, most of Aston's law practice involved commercial law and corporate crime. With the advent of Brian Alexander joining his practice, however, there was an influx of drug-related cases and an even greater influx of petty criminals wanting to be represented by the firm. Criminals are very adept at finding legal people who can make their problems go away. Once word gets out among the criminal fraternity that such and such a lawyer can either get you off or, at the very least, get you a good deal then invariably, that lawyer will have clients queued up around the block. That is what it was like with Brian Alexander. If you were a well-known criminal in the 1970s and needed to make your legal problems go away, then Brian Alexander was your man. If he could not fix your legal problems, then it was simply a case of making sure you had a toothbrush in your suitcase as you headed off to prison.

When Terry Clark rang me in New Zealand around July 1977 and asked for my help to arrange a few introductions to some of my criminal associates in New South Wales, I flew over to Sydney to meet him. I think he was living at McCarrs Creek, near Church Point, at that time. We met at the Crest Hotel in Kings Cross and Clark carefully outlined his plans to me. There was an abundant supply of top quality heroin available at a generous price if I was interested. The markets in Sydney, Melbourne, Brisbane, Adelaide and Perth would have to be established, but he was confident that could be done very quickly. If I was not interested in the supply side, then he also needed someone trustworthy, with the expertise to move large amounts of money overseas. When he told me that I would get five per cent of all monies I transferred overseas, I readily agreed to the money transfer offer. To give some idea how inflation hits not only normal folks, any criminal wanting to move money out of the country today – if he can even find someone – has to pay the intermediary 20 per cent of his ill-begotten money to be able to do so.

After we shook hands on the money transfer agreement, Clark asked me: 'Can any of your Aussie mates get me some police protection?' I remember shaking my head and vehemently saying to Clark: 'What do you want to deal with those arseholes for? You cannot trust them.'

Clark just smiled at my reply and said: 'It's just business, Jim. That's how they operate over here. It's just like taking out insurance on your house, a prudent necessity.' With the benefit of now knowing that in the 1960s, Clark worked as a police informant in New Zealand, I have no doubt that the irony of having police officers working for him would have also been a motivating factor in his desire to hook up with corrupt police. Despite my reservations, even all these years later, I can still recall myself instantly thinking about Bob Trimbole. The information my friend Phil L from Kings Cross had told me was still fresh in my memory. 'If you ever need help with the law, Bob's your man.' Before we parted company, I told Clark I would talk to some people and get back to him in a few days. It was agreed between us that I could go as high as $20,000 in getting a successful introduction.

That night I had dinner with Phil L and sounded him out about approaching Bob Trimbole with the view to obtaining his assistance in acquiring police protection. If a meeting could be arranged fairly quickly and a recommendation made, there was $5000 fee immediately payable to my friend. That payment for just organising a meeting saw my friend reaching for the phone before I had finished the sentence. Within ten minutes of me offering him the money, he had contacted Bob Trimbole by phone and a meeting was hastily arranged for 4pm the next day at my friend's Kings Cross office. 'Easiest five grand I ever made in my life,' my friend chuckled as he put down the phone. That $5000 phone call was to cost Brian Alexander his life four years later and earn me a 25 year stint as Her Majesty's guest at Long Bay Prison in Sydney.

The following afternoon at 4pm sharp, I met Bob Trimbole at my friend's Kings Cross office. When he walked in, Bob was wearing what I would come to recognise as his daily uniform, a three-quarter length fawn raincoat and a short-brimmed hat. After the usual pleasantries were exchanged, Phil L once again reiterated to Bob that I was a man he had known for many years and someone he trusted implicitly. There were matters I wished to talk to Bob about which did not concern Phil L, so he left the room. Although I was a little nervous, I stated my case calmly: 'I have some friends over here in New South Wales. They have been operating here for a little while but would like to get some police protection. Personally, I am against it, as it goes against my principles but my friend is not of the same mind, and he would like to get some protection if he could. I know your time is valuable, so if you or anyone you know could make my friend's request happen there is a $10,000 introduction fee.'

During my short speech, Bob just sat there staring at me impassively. I now realise that, at that time, $10,000 to Bob Trimbole was not even a losing bet. He had met with me simply out of courtesy to my friend Phil L. The first question he asked me was very brief: 'What is the product?' When I replied that it was heroin, he shook his head vigorously from side to side and said: 'That could be a problem, mate. We have a very clear understanding with the pollies and police in this state. Grass is okay, so is illegal gambling, SP bookmaking, even prostitution, but hard drugs like heroin are a definite no-no. They will not wear hard drugs. All the people I know stay well away from the hard stuff.' If only I had listened to his warning.

Despite his assessment about the problems associated with dealing in hard drugs, I pressed on: 'Bob, if there is anyone willing to work around this aversion to dealing in hard drugs, there could be a lot of money available to the right people.'

After looking at me for a few seconds, Bob stood up, shook my hand and said in a matter-of-fact manner: 'I may know someone who can help. He's a bad drunk and a hopeless gambler, but he is well connected and has no scruples. I cannot promise anything, but I will make a few calls. If I have any luck, I'll let your buddy know and we will meet back here tomorrow at the same time.' The meeting was over in less than ten minutes. As I got to know Bob Trimbole better, I came to realise that was his normal behaviour. No hanging about for chitchat after your meeting was over; Bob was the original 'gone in 60 seconds man.'

Around noon the next day I called my friend Phil L and he had some positive news for me. Mid-morning he had received a call from Bob asking that he contact me and organise a meeting for 4pm at his office. I was to bring my friend with me. After assuring Phil L that I would be there at 4pm sharp, I called Terry Clark and arranged to meet him at the Crest Hotel in Kings Cross at 3.30pm. 'Bring fifteen thousand dollars,' were my closing words. At precisely 3.30 pm, Clark and I were shaking hands. I gave him a brief run down on Bob Trimbole and how the pollies were dead set against hard drugs. Clark just shrugged his shoulders and said: 'What's new?' Before we headed over to my friend's office, Clark handed me an envelope containing $15,000. The money was in $50 bills.

We were both sitting in Phil L's office when Bob Trimbole walked in just after 4pm. This meeting was the only time Terry Clark met Bob Trimbole in 1977. After the introductions had been made, my friend excused himself and left the three of us in his office. As I remember, it was quite amusing as the three of us sat there warily eyeing each other off. It was Bob who began proceedings by telling Clark and I that he had spoken to someone about getting some protection. If the money was right, then he was assured it could be arranged. 'Some of those people would sell their mothers,' he lamented. 'Mate, that is great news, thank you,' was Clark's happy response. 'How do we go about organising this?' was his immediate query. At that time none of us could have ever imagined the disaster awaiting the three of us when Bob replied: 'His name is Brian Alexander, he is in his office waiting for a call from me. Shall I give him a call?' When Clark replied in the affirmative, Bob asked him: 'What name would you like to use?' It only took Clark a few seconds to come up with the name 'Robert James.' Moments later 'Robert James' was arranging to meet Brian Alexander at his office the next day.

After thanking Bob profusely, Clark asked him if he was interested in doing some business? 'Thanks, but no thanks. I already have more on my plate than I can handle,' was Bob's terse reply. Obviously, with the passage of time it is difficult to remember exactly what we all said.

But I am certain that what I am repeating here is reasonably accurate. Our meeting ended with us all shaking hands. It would be at least ten months before the three of us met again for dinner at Tati's restaurant in Sydney.

I stayed back after Clark left my friend's office as I wanted to pay both him and Bob for helping out. My friend gratefully accepted the $5000 I had promised him for his assistance, but Bob respectfully declined the $10,000 with this comment: 'It's not about money, Jim, it's about respect. Your friend Phil has been able to do me a few favours in the past, I was just returning the favour.' That is the kind of man Bob Trimbole was. In all the years I've been in Australia, I have never heard of anyone being ripped off by him. The forces of law and order may have loathed him, but I both respected and liked Robert Trimbole. For anyone wondering, no, I didn't give the $10,000 Bob declined back to Terry Clark. Clark was not that good a friend of mine and I figured my time was pretty valuable too.

Before I left Sydney to fly back to New Zealand, I met once more with Terry Clark at the Crest Hotel. Over a drink he told me about his first meeting with Brian Alexander at his office in Park Street. 'Very nice offices, Jim,' he began. 'The guy certainly knows what he's about. I told him I'm prepared to pay $10,000 a month, but I expect fucking first class service for that much cash.' Then in an aggrieved tone, Clark told me that Alexander had said: 'It will cost a lot extra if any of your crew are arrested, old son. That is how it works here.' Despite the thought of paying extra, Clark was pretty happy with how the meeting went. For a drug dealer, the comforting thought that you are a protected species gives you a false sense of invincibility. For drug dealers like Clark, paying for police protection was just a necessary business expense. When you are making up to $1 million a week, even paying police $10,000 a week, plus extras, is nothing. By the time he left Australia, that is roughly how much Clark was handing over to Brian Alexander every week. For the two years that the Mr Asia syndicate was heavily active in Australia, however, it was money well spent.

What did you get for your money? For starters, Clark was given a daily bulletin on police activity, particularly any activity involving the drug squad. There was an understanding that any members of the syndicate would have a 24-hour head start if they were wanted on a serious crime. If any of the syndicate's names were mentioned in dispatches, then Clark was informed immediately by Alexander. The police never dealt with any of us personally; they were too smart for that. All information was channelled through Brian Alexander. None of us ever met – thankfully – any of his contacts. If we had, we would more than likely be resting on the ocean floor with the unfortunate Brian Alexander. How much of the money Clark paid him actually ended up in police wallets I do not know. Being a profligate gambler, Alexander more than likely kept most of that money for himself. However much he paid them, at the end of the day no amount of money could have saved him, because he knew too much.

I have often been asked about what sort of a person Brian Alexander was. Over a two year period I would have met him a dozen times. Most of my meetings with the guy were just to pay him money, usually late at night, and usually in a deserted back street. Not once did I meet the man for a social drink, or have dinner with him. It was strictly business with Brian Alexander and me, nothing else. I personally never trusted the man. Like quite a few lawyers I have met who deal on a regular basis with tough, hardened criminals, Brian Alexander thought he was of a similar ilk. Without ever having killed, shot, stabbed, beaten or robbed anyone, let alone committed a serious crime, there are people like Brian Alexander, who actually think they are tough guys. That's a very serious mistake. While he was a likeable enough person, Brian Alexander always struck me as being hyper tense. Whether it was a combination of his heavy drinking, his gambling addiction or the subversive double life he was leading, the guy always appeared to me to be on the verge of a nervous breakdown. There is no way this man would have stood up to a serious police interrogation, or for that matter, cross-examination at the Stewart Royal

Commission. Obviously there were others who thought like me, because Brian Alexander disappeared on 21 December 1981.

There was an excellent drama series called *Blue Murder*, written by Ian David, that was shown on Australian television some years ago. The series' two main protagonists were notorious Australian gangland figure Arthur 'Neddy' Smith and disgraced ex-police detective Roger Rogerson. For a television series it was fairly accurate. I can say that with some certainty, as I knew the actual history of the events being depicted. In one of the concluding episodes, they had Brian Alexander tied to a chair on the deck of Neddy Smith's cabin cruiser, surrounded by drunken police and pleading for his life. His pleas fall on deaf ears and a drunken Neddy Smith pushes Brian Alexander over the side of the boat. Neddy Smith's cell was directly opposite mine in Long Bay and despite his progressive Parkinson's disease he was always hobbling over to my cell, as I was one of the few old-school criminals he knew still in the prison system. I remember asking Neddy Smith about Brian Alexander one day and how his murder was depicted on the *Blue Murder* television series. His reply was very enlightening: 'The first thing that show got wrong was him being murdered on my boat. The police confiscated my boat three weeks before Alexander disappeared. I did not know the man that well and had no cause to kill him. The boat was right, the only difference being, Alexander was taken out to his death on a police boat. He was due to give evidence to the Stewart Royal Commission, and the word was out that he was ready to start signing people up, so he had to go.' Although Neddy Smith may have known the names of the police officers who murdered Brian Alexander, he never told me.

There was a lot of speculation when Alexander disappeared that members of the Mr Asia syndicate had murdered him. My answer to anyone who thought like that is simply this: What could Brian Alexander have done to harm us? The answer is nothing. We did not know who he dealt with, and furthermore, we did not want to know. We had far more serious crimes like murder, drug importation and drug supply to worry about. Bribing unknown police officers was the least of our problems. The police officers who gave Brian Alexander a copy of the tapes that Doug and Isabel Wilson unknowingly made at the Brisbane Police Station on 12 June 1978, which Alexander then sold to Terry Clark; well for my money, you need look no further to find out who murdered him.

On page 874 of the Stewart Royal Commission Report there is the heading 'APPENDIX C The Whereabouts of Brian William Alexander':

> Brian William Alexander is potentially one of the most important witnesses to the Commission's present terms of reference. He is currently not able to be located and has not been sighted since 22 December 1981.

The above reason is why Brian Alexander was murdered. Come Judgement Day, I expect to have quite a few police officers lined up alongside me answering for crimes that they have committed. One of those crimes will be the murder of Brian William Alexander.

22

THE MR ASIA SYNDICATE BEGINS

Despite his trepidation at carrying drugs himself, one thing his earlier 1976 drug runs did achieve was to give Clark his first tentative foothold in the burgeoning Australian heroin market. At the beginning of 1977 Clark had a developing market in Brisbane that he handled personally. Through his old Wi Tako Prison mate Greg Ollard, he was able to tap into the rapidly expanding Sydney drug market. The six kilos he successfully smuggled into Australia became 600 ten-gram bags worth $1100 per bag: after expenses, a clear profit of around $600,000. As he later expounded to me in private one evening: 'My first lots of heroin, the buyers nearly ripped my arms off wanting to get more of my product, simply because I never cut it. The speed with which I was able to move that uncut heroin showed me that was the way to go.'

To give him his due, in all the time I dealt with the man, Clark always insisted very forcefully that I sell all the heroin I handled for him uncut. The man took a perverse pride out of the fact that his heroin was uncut. He even had a red dragon stamp made, and inside every ten-gram bag of heroin, before he heat-sealed it, he would put a stamped red dragon card. That stamped red dragon card was Clark's certification that this bag of heroin was both uncut and top quality. Over the years I was in the NSW prison system, I met quite a few old drug dealers from the seventies and, to a man, they all said there has never been any heroin available since as strong as the stamped, red dragon product Clark sold.

Besides the high quality of the heroin he was selling, Clark offered something that was equally as important to drug dealers: a consistent and unlimited supply of heroin for those buying drugs off him. If you are a drug dealer, a regular supply line of top grade heroin is a licence to print money. To be able to access heroin from Clark whenever they needed it was an unheard of occurrence in the 1970s. That factor alone would have been enough to corner the market for you, and that is certainly what happened with Clark.

The best analogy to use when describing Clark's deliberate decision to sell his heroin uncut, is what is now happening with big department stores worldwide. Big department stores sales are being seriously affected by discount stores selling the same designer labels as them for much cheaper prices than what they charge. If you are a savvy buyer and want to buy a designer label suit – lets say a Pierre Cardin – that is selling at Myer department store in downtown Sydney for $1000, why would you pay that when for $600 you can get the same suit from a discount store in the suburbs? With savings like that, only a fool would buy his suit from Myer. Unlike other major drug traffickers of that era, Clark sold his heroin at discount prices and that is why he was able to corner the market. Many of our dealers, believe it or not, made more money than us. Nevertheless, Clark regarded selling his heroin uncut as good business practice.

Although many people – particularly the police – would disagree with me, selling drugs is a business. Just as big import-export companies do, importers buy their drugs, be it heroin, cocaine, ecstasy, or ice, from suppliers overseas, as cheaply as they can. They then import those drugs into a targeted country, where they sell their highly marked up product to a designated distributor. Sound familiar? The distributor then sells that product to wholesalers with his – drug dealers at this level are usually men – percentage added on. The wholesalers then repackage the product and sell to retailers – mid-level dealers. They in turn use salespeople – street dealers – to get that product out to the market place – the public. Obviously by the time some of these products like heroin or cocaine hit the streets, with all the additives they have been cut with, those drugs can be extremely hazardous to your health. Nevertheless, that is how it works.

For those people not aware of what happens after a major drug dealer purchases heroin from an importer, this is an example of what wholesaler occurs. Say the purchaser buys, for argument's sake, one kilo of uncut heroin for $120,000. The quality is so good that he can cut that heroin one and a half times using Glaxo baby food or some other white-coloured substitute like crushed codeine tablets. Now the buyer has two and a half kilos, which he then re-bags into 250 ten-gram bags. Those bags are then wholesaled to other dealers for $1000 a bag, giving the wholesaler a return of $250,000 on his original investment of $120,000. Obviously the heroin being purchased is far from the best quality, so it's easy to understand why Clark's wholesalers were extremely happy to buy his uncut heroin. The profit margins on uncut heroin are huge. You do not have to be a maths genius to work out how much money you will make if you are a drug dealer able to buy one kilo of uncut heroin every week for a year. But that is exactly what the people who dealt with Clark were able to do. There were at least two dealers who moved a minimum of one kilo a week, every week, all year round. None of them were ever arrested; and I'm willing to bet that they never paid any taxes on their ill-gotten gains either.

After the heroin from the *Konpira* was landed, Clark went into overdrive. Despite not having any police protection for the first seven months of 1977, Clark moved about Australia freely as he set up potential markets. With his best friend, Ian Henry, looking after Brisbane for him, Clark moved down to Sydney. The close shave he had when federal police officers searched his house at 54 Highview Terrace in Brisbane on 20 May 1977 made the move south to Sydney both prudent and necessary. Being the largest city in Australia meant that Sydney was where the real big money was. He and Maria stayed with Greg Ollard for a few days before renting a property at McCarrs Creek, near Church Point. By the time Clark and Maria Muhary moved to 76 Grosvenor Road in Wahroonga, around September 1977, she was heavily pregnant with their son Jarrod. Her pregnancy, however, was not about to stop or slow Clark down.

Whenever you try to open up new drug territories anywhere, be it in Auckland, Melbourne, Sydney, London, or even Timbuktu, there are always serious problems that have to be overcome. Other drug dealers do not take kindly to anyone trying to take business off them. It then becomes a case of the strongest survives. People buying drugs from Clark would usually point out their opposition dealers to him and request assistance. That assistance usually came in the form of heads having to be busted, arms and legs broken or the occasional person being shot before the opposition was either driven off or wiped out. On a couple of occasions when I was in Sydney in 1977, both myself and a few tough criminal friends of mine accompanied Clark while he battered, threatened or cajoled aspiring young drug dealers into taking their business elsewhere. Baseball bats, iron bars, a .357 Magnum handgun and a sawn-off shotgun were all the persuasion we needed. Dealing in heroin is a particularly nasty business, populated by particularly nasty people, and if you are not strong enough to hold onto your territory or markets, you will be overrun by other tougher, stronger and more dangerous criminals. Think of the laws of the jungle, where only the fittest survive: that is what it is like to be a major drug dealer.

To help move his product, Clark brought Peter Fulcher and Patrick Norton-Bennett over from New Zealand to help set up his Sydney markets. In the early days, Clark tried to have only New Zealanders working with him because he did not trust Australians. Why, I do not know, but he had a fixation about Aussies. He was always mumbling: 'The bastards cannot be trusted.' Perhaps in another life, or maybe before he left New Zealand, an Aussie must have robbed him, because he certainly maintained that attitude for as long as I knew him. As some of my best friends back then were Aussies – even more so today – I did not support his irrational dislike of Australians. When I started out in Australia however, I must admit that all the people working with me were New Zealanders.

In mid-1977 I had already made a few trips to Singapore to set up false bank accounts for myself, so when Clark asked me to move some of his money around in July 1977, I was in a position to be able to start that money transfer process fairly quickly. The first lot of money I moved was not large, just $50,000 to get the ball rolling so to speak. I went around a few banks in Sydney and had no difficulty transferring the cash. Remember back then, banks were not required by law to report any large money transfers going overseas. Through my friendly bank manager in Singapore, I arranged to have the money transferred on arrival to one of Clark's designated bank accounts in Hong Kong. Over the next two years, that initial small money transfer would balloon into millions. We had money going out with couriers; we had money going out through banks, like Nugan Hand; we bought shares and gold overseas; we sent suitcases full of $50 bills out of the country by ship and air; we even did direct swaps with wealthy Chinese entrepreneurs. All this entailed me giving a Chinese businessman here in Sydney, say, $1 million in cash, and him having the equivalent amount paid into a Singapore or Hong Kong bank account. It's very, very difficult to do any of this nowadays, as the police have become adept at following the money trail. I guess that's why people are always talking about the good old days!

It must have been about November 1977 that I rented a third-floor, two-bedroom apartment in Oxford Street. After having extra heavy locks installed on the apartment's front door, I used that secret little hideaway for my money and drugs stash. When I got into business with Clark full time towards the end of 1977, it was not unusual for me to have one room in the apartment full of garbage bins containing bundles of $50 bills, and the other room full of garbage bins containing ten-gram bags of heroin. Coming from an impoverished childhood where my family didn't have much money, I never thought I would see the day when I got sick of counting money. But believe it or not, that's what happened to me during those halcyon days in 1977, 1978 and 1979.

Because law enforcement officers, be they federal, state or the Australian Crime Commission, have become so proficient at following the money trails of criminals, it has become a huge problem for modern-day crooks to conceal the large amounts of cash in their possession. In recent years in Australia, I have read about criminals being arrested with up to $10 million in their homes. I guess with so many people struggling to pay their bills today that is a dilemma some people would like to have. For a criminal, however, having nowhere to park your ill-gotten money can become a serious problem. What often happens with criminals in the drug trade is that not many of them are prepared for the sudden upsurge of money that can start flowing their way. If you are a drug dealer with a regular supply of top-quality heroin or cocaine, within six short months you will have more money than you know what to do with. That is why nowadays you see so many criminals getting caught with huge amounts of cash. They have not given any thought to what they will do after they have made large amounts of cash from their illegal activities.

By contrast, for me back in the 1970s it was simply a case of remembering what my old friend Skip Gardiner had taught me in Paremoremo Prison. The fiscal advice he gave me back then proved to be invaluable when I started moving money for Clark. After setting up numerous bank accounts in Singapore and Hong Kong, as well as putting in place company structures to receive that money, I went a step further. Although it cost me close to $40,000, I had a lawyer fly over to the Netherlands and the Netherlands Antilles – a tax haven in the Caribbean – to set up tax structures for me so that I could move money freely around the world. I also used this company to send money back into Australia to help fund a land development project I was involved in on Bribie Island in Queensland. It became obvious to me at an early stage that the massive amounts of money we were accumulating could become a problem. Hence the numerous overseas bank accounts, the tax havens, the safe houses and even a bank vault.

Besides the apartment in Oxford Street that I used as my personal money safety deposit, I also rented a bank vault from Westpac – or the Bank of New South Wales as they were then – in George Street. During the course of my trial in April 1986, evidence about the bank vault was presented. Although it was not funny at the time, I can certainly laugh about it now. A representative from Westpac gave evidence about the vault I had leased from the bank. When the Crown prosecutor asked the gentleman about the bank vault, he began by saying: 'Mr Shepherd rented a safety deposit box from your bank, is that correct?' 'Yes sir,' was the reply. 'How big was his safety deposit box? Was it a normal size safety deposit box or slightly larger?' the prosecutor asked. 'It was larger, sir,' the bank official replied with a smirk on his face.

'Bigger, how do you mean bigger?' the prosecutor queried. 'Could you tell the jury please?'

The bank official stood up in the witness box and spread his arms wide to denote five feet wide, and then raised his arms above his head to denote seven feet high. Then, with a dramatic flourish to the jury, he declared: 'Mr Shepherd did not have a safety deposit box, he had a large vault.'

Those twelve jurors' heads instantly swivelled as one and stared at me in disbelief. You could almost see their brains working. A fucking vault, how much money did this guy have? Like I say, I can laugh about it now, but that was a damning piece of evidence against me, that vault. At the recess, after the bank official had made his dramatic disclosure about the vault, my barrister asked me: 'What the fuck were you doing with a bank vault, Jim?'

With tongue firmly planted in cheek, I told him: 'I figured that by the time I filled it up, it would be time to retire.' The real truth of the matter was a little more mundane; it was just another safe place for me to stash large amounts of money before transferring it overseas.

Justice Stewart's Royal Commission did an excellent job, the most comprehensive investigation into the Mr Asia syndicate by any judicial inquiry. Yet even he could not find out where all the cash went, because none of his indemnified witnesses knew the full story. Some of them handled small amounts of money, but they were just pawns, not important pieces on Clark's chessboard; particularly where his money was concerned. When he was murdered in 1983 in Parkhurst Prison on the Isle of Wight, the shadowy people looking after Terry Clark's financial affairs in Singapore, Hong Kong and Switzerland would have rubbed their hands together in glee and stamped his files 'Deceased estate, no living relatives.'

23

THE ORGANISATION, FIJI AND ME

Although Terry Clark confessed to killing Greg Ollard and Julie Theilman to me in March 1978, when I was doing business with him in September 1977 – around the time he actually killed them – he never said a word to me about it. In fact if I remember correctly, during that period of time Clark actually seemed to be in good humour most of the time. I guess the comfort of knowing that two witnesses to his *Konpira* treachery were dead and buried, as well as the additional money he stood to make from Ollard's share of the spoils, kept him in a good humour for months. I have racked my brains over the years and I cannot recall ever meeting Greg Ollard or his lady, Julie Theilman. As they were both heavy drug users, they would not have come into my social or business orbit. Back in those days I did not even smoke grass; my personal choice of self-destruction was alcohol, copious amounts of it.

Despite knowing all the facts as well as I do, I am still amazed that Clark managed to keep the murders of Greg Ollard and Julie Theilman away from me at that time. Had I known them, then their disappearance would have set alarm bells ringing with me. The chilling fact that Clark was able to do business with me unaffected by what he had done, demonstrates very clearly in my opinion, what a callous, cold-blooded individual he was. Do not get me wrong, I am no pacifist. If someone hurt me or anyone I love or care about, I will not go to the police for justice. I have no qualms about dealing with people who have hurt anyone I love. They get no mercy from me. But I have never been an advocate, not even in my wildest years, of killing for no reason.

Loyalty was not one of Terry Clark's strong points, however, as evidenced by his killing his old prison mate Greg Ollard as well as orchestrating the murders of his two supposed best friends, Marty Johnstone and Doug Wilson. Throughout his brief, murderous career, Clark made a habit of taking over drug markets set up by erstwhile friends of his. After murdering Greg Ollard, he assumed control of all Ollard's dealers. It was Martin Johnstone who opened up the London drug markets through his connections there. By eliminating Johnstone – if fate had not intervened – Clark would have had control of the London markets. As for the thriving Sydney and Melbourne markets, I'll talk more about them a little later. What I am trying to illustrate here was the cold-blooded treachery Clark used against all his so-called friends once they had established lucrative drug markets. Nobody was immune to his ruthless tactics, not even me. In September 1977, however, all that nastiness was still two years in the future. In between times there was a lot of drugs to sell, a lot of money to be made, a lot of champagne to be drunk, a lot of bets to wager, a lot of women to sleep with, as well as five murders to come.

By late 1977 it was obvious to Clark that the two men he had brought over to work for him in Sydney, Peter Fulcher and Patrick Norton-Bennett, were not doing well. Despite their best efforts, they could not crack the Sydney markets. If you do not know people, the Sydney illegal drug markets can be both difficult and dangerous. After four or five months of desultory results, they both pulled the pin and returned to New Zealand. From that point on, Peter Fulcher assumed control of all the NZ markets, distributing heroin purchased from Clark or me in Australia. After buying heroin here in Sydney, it was his job to personally get that heroin back to New Zealand. Patrick Norton-Bennett was convicted on a charge of murder after his return to New Zealand. Some of Clark's nastiness must have rubbed off on him while he was here in Australia.

Because heroin sales with Fulcher and Norton-Bennett had been slow, Clark approached me again in late 1977 about using my Australian contacts to move some product for him. He explained to me that despite their best efforts, both men were not coming up to expectations. At that point in time I could have saved myself a lot of grief and heartache by just saying no, but to my eternal regret I did not. The lure of unlimited credit, a constant supply of top quality heroin, the millions that could be made, proved too irresistible for me to refuse. I told my conscience to 'shut the fuck up,' and accepted Clark's offer. To get the ball rolling while I went back to New Zealand to tidy up my affairs, I left a trusted friend of mine with 50 ten-gram bags of heroin that I had acquired from Clark. I told my friend I did not care what he did with the uncut heroin, but I wanted $1300 per bag. As I was paying Clark $1000 for each bag, it equated to a profit of $15,000 for me.

For anyone wondering about me leaving a friend with $65,000 worth of heroin while I went back to New Zealand for two weeks, I should explain how credit works in the drug trade, particularly at the top. It is not unusual for major drug importers to give their main distributors large amounts of drugs on credit. Once again, just like a normal business does. When you buy merchandise from a company, say, watches from a jewellery store, you normally get a monthly account from the company you purchased those watches from requesting payment for the merchandise. Major drug importers follow those same principles. It is not unusual for a major drug importer to give his main distributor up to a million dollars in credit. As soon as the product has been sold and the distributor paid, a new line of credit is given. Unlike the real business world, however, non-payment for any illegal drugs acquired this way can often prove fatal. In the drug world, drug dealers who owe large sums of money do not have to worry about getting taken to bankruptcy court by their creditor. They just end up in a shallow grave, debt paid in full.

When I returned to Sydney in early November, I was pleasantly surprised to find my friend waiting for me with $65,000 and a request for more of the same product. Despite my friend having the money available for me on my return, Clark was not convinced that giving credit was the way to go. It was his belief that giving credit was a sure-fire recipe for disaster. He surmised – correctly – that once you gave someone credit, you were very much reliant on that person's dependability and trustworthiness. There were three ways you could lose money by giving credit Clark opined; one, the dealer could be arrested, thus your drugs were lost to the police; two, the dealer could be ripped off by other criminals, once again leading to the loss of your drugs; or three, the person you had advanced credit to could do a runner on you. Because of these concerns, Clark came up with a very innovative way to get around the 'giving credit problem'.

At a meeting between us in Sydney around that November, Clark and I came up with eight potential drug dealers we could use in Sydney. It was Clark's plan that we advance each of those dealers, 10 ten-gram bags of heroin. For one month we would carry them, and each dealer was told that they could come back as often as they liked to both pay us and replenish supplies. After one month of credit, however, all of them would have to pay up front for any heroin they wanted to purchase from us. It was Clark's belief that after one month of selling the uncut heroin he was offering them, they would have more than enough money to pay for future purchases. Within a week, many of the dealers were back to pay their bills and get more supplies. Within the month, at least four of them were ordering twenty bags at a time. We were also able to assess which of the dealers we wanted to continue working with. Three of the dealers had barely managed to sell fifteen bags over the month, so we assigned them to the other more productive dealers. We decided that the minimum order had to be ten bags, cash up front.

The process worked like this. First, the dealers we decided to work with were told we would only be open for business on Mondays, Wednesdays and Fridays. Orders and cash would be taken between 2pm and 4pm on those days. Taking orders that early gave us a chance to count their money and make sure it was all there before deliveries were made. If one of the dealers were even one dollar short with his cash, we would deduct one ten-gram bag for that mistake. We only accepted twenty and 50 dollar bills. These were the old paper notes in use before plastic notes were introduced in 1988–92. Anything smaller and we deducted one ten-gram bag for not following our guidelines on money. If their money was not bundled up right, with all the heads of the different denominations of $50 and $20 bills pointing in the one direction, then we deducted one ten-gram bag. Our dealers soon learnt our rules. Because our product was so good and they were making so much money through us, had we asked them to iron the banknotes before paying us they would have gladly done so.

Our delivery system was also very innovative as well. Say one of our dealers ordered twenty bags off us. After checking that his money, in this case $26,000, was all there the order would be passed on to my delivery man. That night between 9pm and 11pm, the purchaser had to be near his phone. After calling him, my delivery man would instruct the purchaser to go to such and such street, and outside a designated house address he would find his order in the gutter or sometimes in the letterbox there. The delivery man would wait until the purchaser had picked up his order before going on to his next stop. The buyers never saw him and he never had any physical contact with them. To help evade detection from honest cops, he never used the same street twice, or the same suburb. As I was the only person who knew who my delivery man was – I never told Clark who he was – the system worked very well. In all the years we were operating, I only ever lost 10 ten-gram bags. When you consider the millions of dollars' worth of heroin that was sold in three years, a $13,000 loss was more than acceptable.

The guy I used to take orders and pick up cash was a little more vulnerable than my delivery man, as he had to have direct contact with the drug dealers who purchased heroin off us. On the designated days, anyone who wanted to purchase would call my man between 2pm and 4pm and place their order. He would then go out and meet them and collect their purchase money. After returning with the buyer's orders and cash, we would both sit down and check each buyer's money to make sure it was accurate. When I first started counting out the large sums of money involved, I got a real thrill at seeing all those bundles of cash. When it got to the stage that I was counting out hundreds of thousands of dollars every other night, however, it became a tedious chore.

What really amazed me about the Sydney heroin scene was how quickly it exploded. By early 1978, Clark was moving 400 ten-gram bags of heroin a week. His business was booming, money was rolling in by the bucket load from all over Australia. Because of the upsurge in business, Clark increased the minimum buy to 20 ten-gram bags. Between January and June 1978, both Clark and I were constantly on the go. If we were not bagging and weighing heroin, we were counting money that was being transferred overseas.

When I first came on board with Clark, he used to get Steve Muhary – Maria's brother and his delivery man – to drop off garbage bags full of already bagged and weighed ten-gram plastic bags of heroin to me. For deliveries of up to 500 bags, Clark always used Maria's brother. As business started to take off in early 1978 and more product was required, however, Clark would personally deliver to me garbage bags full of solid blocks of heroin. No doubt this heroin was from the *Konpira* importation. I now realise why Clark used to impress upon me the need for only him and I to know about the large amounts of heroin he was delivering to me. It is also obvious to me now why more money used to go to his bank accounts, than to Chinese Jack's or Martin Johnstone's bank accounts. As I was taking my cut out before Clark actually received any moneys from me, I did not give a flying fuck what he did with the money I paid him.

Breaking down and bagging those blocks of heroin was a laborious, time-consuming and unhealthy job. The blocks were so hard and solid we had to use hammers to break them into small pieces. Once that was done we would put the small pieces into blenders and mash the heroin into powder. Those blenders used to take one hell of a beating. On an average day we would go through six to ten blenders, because the blocked heroin was so hard. While we were doing this, myself and the two men I usually had helping me would be wearing surgical masks to keep out the overpowering heroin fumes. We would get half stoned from the fumes. Unlike Clark who paid his workers a pittance, I looked after my team real well. To compensate my two workers, before weighing and bagging, say, 20 kilos of heroin, I would take half a pound of Glaxo baby food and spread it evenly over the crushed heroin. That allowed me to give both my workers eleven bags of heroin each which, when sold, equated to just under $15,000 per man for their day's labour. I figured as the dealers were making small fortunes off Clark, they would not mind me amply rewarding my employees for the stressful work they were undertaking. As for Clark and his crusade to supply uncut heroin to his dealers, I simply took the view that what he did not know, would not hurt him.

It was not all work, though. In March 1978, Terry Clark, Maria Muhary, their baby son Jarrod, Maria's sister Angelique and myself all travelled to Fiji together. In March 1978, prior to Colonel Rambuka's military takeover, Fiji was a sun-drenched, fun-filled place; a lovely country to visit. Ostensibly, the trip was to look at some land on an outer Fijian island called Taveuni. The land being offered for sale was the last freehold land in Fiji, so Clark and I between us ended up purchasing 36 acres, plus six apartments being built on a land project there. One of the benefits of purchasing the land on Taveuni was the fact that for each acre of land purchased, you were given a free plane ticket to Fiji as well as accommodation. For Clark and I that equated to 36 free trips to Fiji. A favourite ploy of mine back then was to offer some attractive lady I had just met an all-expenses paid trip with me to Fiji for a romantic weekend. The lady and I would then fly into Fiji from Sydney on a Friday and fly back on Monday. It was exhausting, but I managed to use up all those tickets.

For Clark, however, the Fiji trip was more about an opportunity to meet up with Chinese Jack Choo and Martin Johnstone, at a location well away from the inquisitive eyes of honest Australian or New Zealand police. Well that was the plan anyway. But who should be staying at the Regent hotel in Nadi when we checked in? The New Zealand Police rugby team, who were touring Fiji at that time. That was a rude shock. I do not think Clark even unpacked his bags, he just moved himself and his family to the Hyatt hotel, further up the coast from Nadi.

It was at the Hyatt, dining under the palm trees with a full moon overhead and Fijian native dancers performing that the plans were laid for expansion into the UK and the US drug markets. Over bottles of expensive imported French wine, we discussed the best ways to go about achieving these aims. Although the Australian markets were still being established and only a year had passed since the *Konpira* importation in March 1977, here were Clark, Johnstone, Choo and myself discussing future ventures in other countries. If we were a legitimate business entity, I guess our discussions would have come under the banner 'forward planning'. It was Clark's estimation – correct as it turned out – that by March 1979, because of our superior product, we would have total control of the Australian markets. When that happened, it would be time for further expansion.

It was also at this meeting that Chinese Jack showed Clark a sketch of the new suitcases he had been working on. Up until then, the preferred option for smugglers was a false-bottomed suitcase. Chinese Jack's model was like a magician's illusion, however. The bottom of the suitcase was normal, but the heroin was secreted in the back wall of the suitcase. Looking at that suitcase, everything about it appeared normal. To get at the fibreglass-encased heroin you had to literally destroy the suitcase. Chinese Jack told us that he would have his modified suitcases rolling off the assembly line within two months. These clever suitcases, he surmised, would be ideal for use into the United Kingdom and the United States.

During our discussions it was agreed between the four of us that I would continue to control the Australian markets, Chinese Jack would stay in control of purchases and shipments of heroin in Singapore, Martin Johnstone would spearhead the push into the UK drug markets, and Clark would try and develop the US markets. While we were in Fiji, Clark met an American musician, a guy called Alvin – for the life of me I cannot recall his last name – and foolishly as it turned out, thought this unknown musician could be his ticket into the lucrative US markets. It must have been the cocaine Clark snorted with Alvin that gave him this grandiose idea. My attitude back then was that you did not do business with anyone you did not know. When I raised this point with Clark, his flippant reply was: 'You have to speculate to accumulate, Jim.' For me, Alvin the musician was the first crack to appear in Clark's persona.

When we got back to Australia, Clark acquired another false passport and jetted off to San Francisco to meet with Alvin and see what could be done. I believe he took a sample of heroin over with him to show Alvin's supposed contacts just what he had. In San Francisco in those days there was a legal drug-testing facility where drug users could send their drugs to have them tested free of charge. No joke. Evidently, Clark sent a sample of heroin off to this service to show Alvin how good his dope was. The testing program gave a rave review to Clark's heroin sample. Despite this, no business was concluded, simply because Alvin was just what he purported to be, a failed musician. Although they did not do any business together in San Francisco, Alvin was instrumental in planting the seeds of Clark's downfall by fuelling his liking and subsequent addiction to cocaine. If you suffer from delusions of grandeur like Clark did in those days, then cocaine can amplify your feelings tenfold. There was talk of shipments of heroin into the United States, possible shipments of drugs through Alaska; none of which eventuated. His failed US trip did not dim Clark's enthusiasm to find an American connection, however, and he vowed to try again.

Having lived in the United States for six years after leaving Australia in 1979, I now realise how unrealistic and fanciful Clark's plans were back then. Anyone trying to sell heroin in the States without the mob's permission better have a fully paid up life insurance policy, because those boys do not mess around with unconnected people trying to muscle in on their markets. They will make you disappear and take your dope before you have even unpacked your bags. I met a few mob guys while I was living in the States and they certainly impressed me. Ruthless with a capital R, we would have stood absolutely no chance against those guys. It took me three years just to establish myself over there, so I know how impossible it would have been for Clark to set himself up as a drug distributor in the States. But then again, that's another story; this book is about the Mr Asia syndicate.

24

1978: WHAT A YEAR

For those of us involved in the Mr Asia syndicate, 1978 had everything. From the start of the year to its end, the business really boomed. I'll start this chapter with a light-hearted, humorous anecdote about the power of cash. After my brief vacation in Fiji with Terry Clark and his family, on the flight back to Sydney I was flipping through *Time* magazine and an advertisement for Patek-Philippe watches caught my eye. When I observed that there was a jewellery shop in George Street, Sydney, that sold these watches, I decided to pay that shop a visit. After entering the shop and inquiring about them, I was shown a tray of exquisite and extremely expensive Patek-Philippe watches. One gold watch on the tray really caught my eye and after trying it on, I said to the shop assistant: 'I really like this watch, how much is it worth?' The shop assistant in a decidedly condescending manner said to me: 'That watch is valued at ten thousand dollars, sir, but I am afraid an order has already been placed for that particular watch.' When I immediately said to him: 'I have cash,' there was a marked change in his attitude towards me.

Without the slightest trace of embarrassment, he straightened up, looked me in the eye and said: 'In that case, sir, the cash buyer must always come first.' The funny part was, I did not have $10,000 on me, but I told the shop assistant I'd be back in ten minutes and I sprinted down to a bank where I had a safety deposit box at that time and pulled out $10,000, then raced back to the jewellery store and paid for my first gold Patek-Philippe watch. As I did not own a car back then, I used to consider that watch as a car on my wrist. I really loved that watch and was extremely upset when it was stolen from me in London the following year.

Another humorous incident in 1978 is also worth retelling here as it illustrates not only how well I was going back then, but also how well my crew were doing. During the years 1977, 1978 and 1979, because I liked expensive, imported clothes, I was regarded as a valued client by the managers and owners of a few exclusive menswear shops in Double Bay. Consequently, when any new lines of men's clothing were brought in from overseas, they would call me to come down and have a look at what they had just imported. On this particular day, I received a call about some stylish new jackets that had just arrived. When I turned up at this particular shop I was shown a beautiful, soft, fawn-coloured doe-skin jacket. I have to say it was a lovely jacket. The shopowner told me that because I was a valued client, for $600 the jacket was mine. I immediately snapped it up. Before I left the shop, the owner told me there was only one other jacket like mine in Australia. That evening while having dinner at Tati's restaurant and proudly wearing my new, exclusive, fawn-coloured, doe-skin jacket, who should walk in with his girlfriend for dinner but one of my crew. Let's call him John. You guessed it; he was wearing the only other fawn-coloured, doe-skin jacket in Australia. We had a good laugh about it over dinner. As he was with his girlfriend, I did not pull rank; I just took my jacket off and put it over the back of my chair. I do remember thinking to myself at the time though, I'm definitely paying my crew too much money!

By contrast to those two humorous anecdotes, the attempt on my life in late April 1978 was deadly serious and nearly succeeded. Because of all the money I was making at the start of that year, I had become careless and was extremely fortunate to survive the bullets fired at me. It would have just been four weeks or so since Terry Clark made his horrific murder confessions to me at Eliza's restaurant in March when I nearly became a statistic myself. Many successful criminals have a bad habit of becoming complacent after years of profitable criminal activity and I certainly fell into that category. I thought I was bulletproof, invincible and above the law. It took three bullets to bring me back to earth with a thud.

At the time the attempt was made on my life, I was living in Waratah Street in Elizabeth Bay, an affluent inner-city suburb close to the water. I was leasing a lavish, two-bedroom apartment off a couple of gay guys who had gone to Europe for a year. These guys were ahead of their time: there were remote control switches beside the huge bed that activated everything. For instance, I could open the window curtains from the bed, as well as the leopard skin curtains running around the bed. The place was comfortable enough but a little gaudy for my still formal NZ sensibilities. The interior design would not have been out of place in a brothel, with all the leopard skin rugs and thick black shagpile carpet. Still, at that time of my life, I thought I was doing just fine in my ornate bachelor pad.

Whenever I went out drinking with my buddies, I would invariably catch a cab home and get the driver to drop me off at Roslyn Gardens, a street just above where I lived. I would then make my way down Waratah Street to my address. It was around 3am after a heavy Saturday night out drinking with friends that the attack took place. My favourite weapon at that time was a small, six-shot .25 automatic pistol that I owned. It came with a shoulder holster and fitted unobtrusively under my armpit. When I put a coat or jacket on, you could not see that I was carrying a weapon. This evening was no different;

I had the gun in a holster, under my coat. The only problem with my security precautions was the fact that I was blind drunk. And that is what saved me.

To this day I do not know how the gunman knew where I lived, as my address was known to only a few people at that time. That aside, I guess it is fair comment to say you would not have had to be an Aboriginal tracker to follow me back to my Waratah Street address, particularly after I had been out drinking. The truth is, I got sloppy. No doubt some of the people I had helped Clark rough up, or other opposition drug dealers had observed my drunken behaviour and decided I was ripe to be taken. They were certainly right there; the only mistake they made was in contracting an inexperienced gunman to kill me.

At the front of the apartment complex I lived in there were a couple of large bushes and the gunman had positioned himself behind one of them to await my return home. That early Sunday morning as I stumbled down Waratah Street to my apartment block, my only thoughts were of the comfortable bed that awaited me. I had just crossed the street and, in my drunken haze, did not even see the gunman as he stepped out from behind the bushes and positioned himself to shoot me. An instant before he fired I tripped on the gutter and fell face forward. They say you never hear the sound of the bullet that hits you, only the sound of the ones that miss. Well that was certainly the situation with me. The sound of the gunshot so close to my head was both loud and disorientating. As I hit the pavement another two shots boomed out close to me. My immediate reaction was 'What the fuck's going on?' Despite being very drunk and disorientated, my survival instincts kicked in. I rolled to the left and reached for my gun. Well that is what I tried to do, but in my drunken state I could not quickly pull my small gun out of its holster. Fortunately for me the gunman was not a professional, otherwise I would not be relating this incident today. If the gunman had been a professional, he would have simply walked over to where I was ineffectively trying to pull my gun out, calmly put a bullet in my head and then another behind my ear just to make certain. After firing three shots at me, however, the gunman bolted up Waratah Street towards Roslyn Gardens and disappeared. After regaining my feet I managed to loose one shot off at him but it just ricocheted harmlessly off the pavement. All these years later, I still thank my lucky stars that being drunk caused me to trip on the gutter just as the gunman fired.

If you want a sure-fire recipe to sober up, have someone shoot three bullets at you from close range, that will do the trick every time. Visibly shaken, I made my way into my apartment. The amazing thing about the whole incident was the fact that despite four shots being fired in a deathly quiet street, not one person stuck their head out of a window to say: 'What's going on down there?' I guess if I had been left lying on the street in a pool of blood, then the police and media would have got involved. Yet the very incident that could have ended my misbegotten life in April 1978, went unreported.

As soon as I got into my apartment I replaced my small .25 automatic with a more lethal .357 Magnum handgun I also had at that time. After barricading the front door to my apartment, I managed to get in a few hours of fitful sleep. By 9am that Sunday morning I had Bobby Dunlop, an Australian ex-professional boxing champion who held titles in the middleweight, light heavyweight and heavyweight ranks, standing in my lounge room. A big, powerful man, Bob was always superbly fit. A vicious street fighter, Bob was afraid of no one. I had met Bob in Auckland in the early 1970s when he was living over there. Along with Bob and I, was Cec McQuillan, another former Australian lightweight boxing champion, who was a tremendous puncher for his size, and another fighting machine who I knew back then, a super tough Maori named Terry Brown, who made a formidable fighting unit. Between us, we busted a lot of heads in pubs and clubs around Auckland during 1972–74. My three friends were the kind of guys who would never leave your side when you were outnumbered. Fortunately for me, Bob was back in Sydney and answered my early morning call to arms immediately. Although he was never involved in any drug dealing or criminal activity with me, Bob was always prepared to help a friend in need.

To give you some idea of what a loyal friend Bobby Dunlop was, I will digress here briefly and recount what happened in Auckland during a violent incident in 1972 which nearly got both of us killed. At the time Bob was going out with a Samoan lady and had been invited to her uncle's home one Saturday night for a birthday celebration. Against my better judgement, I decided to accept Bob's invitation to accompany him to the birthday party. Having grown up with many Pacific Islanders in my youth, I was well aware of their low tolerance of alcohol. Even guys I had known since my childhood, I found difficult to handle once they'd had a few drinks. So going to a party where everyone was a Pacific Islander was, I thought, a recipe for trouble; and so it proved. We had only been at the party for an hour when a burly Islander approached me and accused me of chatting up his girlfriend. Now you can accuse me of many things but chatting up an Islander lady in a room full of drunken Islander men is not one of them. Crazy, I am not! This guy would not be mollified by my protestations of harbouring no lustful intentions towards his beloved, however. While the guy had been raving on in front of me, I had been sitting on a sofa in the main lounge room of the house. When the guy walked away from me I thought the worst was over but I was sadly mistaken. About five minutes later he came back into the room through another entrance, walked up to where I was sitting and king-hit me from behind. Although his punch sent me sprawling into the middle of the lounge room, I was more surprised than hurt. After quickly regaining my feet, I was able to avoid his next drunken attack and quickly put paid to him with a left–right combination of punches. The next thing I knew, I was being attacked by every Islander male in the room. Without any thought for his own welfare or safety, Bobby Dunlop came to my assistance. I was told by a witness later that we managed to drop six of our attackers before we were overwhelmed. They punched us, kicked us, hit us with chairs, bottles and anything else handy. Someone produced a carving knife and stabbed Bob in the head. I was semiconscious on the floor at the time, my jaw fractured. Our lives were saved by Bob's

Islander girlfriend and a few of her cousins who placed themselves over our semiconscious and badly injured bodies and managed to form a shield around us as we were carried out to a car and taken to Auckland Public Hospital. A doctor at the hospital said Bob was extremely lucky to have survived his stab wound, as a fraction further to the left and he would have been dead. About ten days after our beating I saw Bob and suggested we back up and get some revenge by blowing the house up. His philosophical reply to my suggestion really surprised me: 'Jim, over the years we have handed out plenty, it was our turn to get some. Let's leave it at that.' Such was my respect for Bobby Dunlop that I agreed, albeit reluctantly, to his philosophical acceptance of the beating we suffered. Consequently, I too did not seek revenge for one of the worst beatings ever inflicted on me.

That was certainly not the case, however, after the botched attempt on my life. I badly wanted the person who had attempted to kill me. Around 10am a concerned Terry Clark, along with my personal driver Phil, arrived at my apartment for a hastily convened war council. After recounting the episode to Clark and my friends, it was decided that Clark and I would put out a large reward among our dealers for any information about the gunman. It was agreed that we would offer a reward of $20,000 for any positive information on the gunman. Although the lease on my apartment was paid up for six months, it was also decided that to continue living at that address would be both foolish and unwise. So for the next month I lived in hotels and motels, constantly moving and constantly armed, and always with two friends not far from my side. From that early Sunday morning on, as long as I was in Australia, I slept with a gun beside my bed.

We never found out who the gunman was. Although I was really angry at the time and would have shot him in a heartbeat if I had been able to identify him, I was nevertheless also a realist and understood that being shot at by other criminals was just one of many dangers associated with being a successful drug dealer. It's not a nice way to live. You have your moments – like spending or gambling large amounts of cash, buying nice cars and jewellery, eating at the best restaurants, drinking fine wines and bedding attractive women but at the end of the day, is the loss of your liberty for fifteen years, or having people constantly trying to rip you off or kill you, worth the price? Take it from someone who has been there and done that, the answer is a resounding no!

With the benefit of hindsight I can be philosophical about how I should have lived my life but back in early 1978, I was too busy counting my illicit drug money to worry about future consequences. Many criminals, and I was certainly one, lead excessive lives: they drink too much, spend too much, gamble too much, chase too many women, all with no thought as to where it will end. It is almost as if we know that prison or death is just one mistake away and we better live life to the hilt before either one of those disasters catches up with us. Like a shooting star, some criminals have their moment in the night sky, but invariably their light fades away, or is extinguished.

During 1978, Tati's restaurant in Oxford Street became my home away from home. The food was sensational and the owner of the restaurant, Robert Fionna, became a close personal friend. If you wanted to catch me on a Thursday, Friday or Saturday, you only had to call Tati's after 10pm to find me. In Justice Stewart's report, among my assets he listed a half share in Tati's restaurant. That is half correct. What transpired back then was simply this. My friend Robert Fionna needed to borrow a large sum of money around August 1978 to help facilitate a real estate deal he was involved in, so he asked me if I could loan him $60,000. As a surety for the loan he put up a half share in the restaurant. Nothing was ever put in writing, but because I liked the man so much, I had no hesitation in loaning him the money. A rather expensive way to get free meals I know, yet I would do the same thing today if Robert Fionna asked me and I had the money. The guy was without peer as a restaurant owner and friend.

It must have been around May – a few weeks before Clark murdered Harry Lewis – that we both had dinner with Bob Trimbole at Tati's. The dinner was our way of saying thank you to Bob for all the help he had given us, especially for the introduction to Brian Alexander. While we were eating, Bob told us about his plans to open up an illegal casino in Sydney. I guess with all the money he had lost in illegal casinos over the years, he figured he may as well own one. Then, surprisingly, Bob told us he was experiencing financial problems. Evidently the heat he was getting at that time from both federal and state police over Donald Mackay's disappearance was making it nigh on impossible for him to access or make any money whatsoever. For the moment he had to sit tight and just wait for the situation to cool down. Without hesitation we both offered Bob a bridging loan until he could get his business interests going again. Bob gratefully accepted our offer and we ended up loaning him $100,000, which we gave him in two lots of $50,000. The money was repaid within two months and as a token of his gratitude, Bob let me in on his next two racecourse stings.

I will not mention the fixed races we were involved in or which racetracks they happened at. Neither will I mention the names of the horses, or the trainers and jockeys who participated in Bob's elaborate stings. All these events took place over 30 years ago and I am not here to trash other people's reputations. I think most fair-minded racing people would agree with me when I state that the racing industry in the 1970s was rife with corruption and fixed races. And before any indignant racing officials come pounding on my door, when required, I have a very poor memory.

Today, horse racing is so well policed it is next to impossible to fix a race. You could not do today what Bob Trimbole used to do back then. And even back then fixing a race wasn't easy, so you could not do it too often. The process worked like this. First you had to have a horse capable of winning a race. Next a trainer willing to give a horse something to speed that horse up. Then you had to have a top jockey with a win at all costs attitude riding your horse. No use having a horse filled with juice if your jockey could not get it past the post first. Then you had to select a suitable race, preferably a race with only eight or ten runners. Once the race had been selected, you had to pay at least four jockeys in that race to help your horse win. Those jockeys would usually be paid $1500 up front and the same again after the horse won. In the designated race, Bob usually had the two jockeys riding the favoured horses on side. The other two jockeys he paid rode interference and blocked any other runner from winning. Once all this was done, you would have to have commission betters ready on and off the racecourse to bet at least $200,000 on your horse. All the bets had to be coordinated so that all the commission agents put their wagers on at exactly the same time. Before making a single buck, you were up for a quarter of a million dollars. A huge amount of money back then, and today for that matter, so it's easy to understand why I say that fixing a race was not only difficult but also very expensive.

I remember one horse that Bob had set for a race that year – must have been around August or September because Clark was still in prison – that nearly gave me heart failure. Both Bob and I had put a small fortune on this horse and were at the racetrack to watch it win. During the race everything went to plan, our horse was full of juice and flying at least five lengths in front of the other horses as they entered the final straight. I was rubbing my hands together with glee and doing a little jig down by the winning post as the horses thundered towards me. Then about 200 metres from the winning post our horse started to slow down. Whoever administered the 'go fast' juice that day, hadn't given the horse enough. Fortunately for us, the jockey riding the favourite, which was rapidly overtaking our horse, was part of the sting. First the jockey dropped his whip, and then he pulled the left rein of his horse, causing the favourite to end up racing alongside the outside rail. These evasive tactics allowed our horse to flop in and win by a head. We celebrated long and loud at Tati's that evening. There is nothing better in life than getting a book-maker's money!

25

ONE MURDER, TWO ARRESTS

Harry Lewis was born in Wymondham, England, on 12 July 1942. Not much is known of his early life, except he got married in England in 1965, had a son in 1968, and immigrated to New Zealand with his wife, Janet, in 1974. I first met Harry Lewis at the Foundry, an Auckland nightclub, in 1975 or 1976, when he was supposedly working as an advertising consultant with Martin Johnstone's alleged drug-dealing friend, George Papaconstantinou, at his *City Girl* magazine. Although George the Greek was never convicted on any major drug trafficking charges, the criminal dossiers on him that have been compiled over the years by various law enforcement agencies would be substantial.

Harry was a good dancer and I can still see him and his girlfriend, a Maori girl named Lois Haslett, prancing around the dance floor together. I also remember Harry as being a natty dresser, always wearing brightly coloured shirts, tight pants and flash, stylish shoes.

For me, Harry was the quintessential English wide boy. By that I mean, someone who was a bit of a rogue, always looking to make a dodgy buck and prepared to bend the rules to get that dodgy buck. Having said that, I did not mind Harry as he was a gregarious, outgoing man, always good company to have a drink with. I guess my liking for him was the reason why Terry Clark never told me about killing him. Another significant trait Harry Lewis had was his ability to keep his mouth shut. I am embarrassed to say that, while Harry Lewis was working with Terry Clark in 1977 and 1978, I was unaware of this fact. The man never even hinted as much to me, although he must have known I was working with Clark from 1977 on. While we were drinking together in early 1978, he must have been saying to himself: 'If only you knew, Jim.' It's a shame he did not tell me, as he might still be alive today, because I would have certainly told him to watch his back at all times when he was with Clark.

From documents I have read, it would appear that Harry Lewis had been organising and handling couriers for Clark and Chinese Jack on the Bangkok–Singapore run in 1977–78. He was also carrying money out of the country for Clark before I came on the scene. On 8 May 1978, however, Harry Lewis's world slowly started to implode. A female courier he was using named Vivian Sharp was searched at Kingsford-Smith Airport in Sydney and found to have 35 kilos of cannabis in her luggage. It did not take the authorities long to find out that her boyfriend, Frederick Broadhurst, and the man who had employed her, a certain Harry Lewis who was using the false name Stanley John Weinert, would both be arriving in Sydney on 13 May. Being the helpful, save yourself type she was, Miss Sharp also informed the authorities that the men would most certainly be carrying drugs. Unwittingly, by handing Harry Lewis over to the authorities, Vivian Sharp helped sign his death certificate.

After being stopped and searched by Customs officers at Kingsford-Smith Airport on 13 May, Frederick Broadhurst was found to have 40 kilos of cannabis in his luggage. As Clark had long since moved away from cannabis – particularly the small amounts found in Vivian Sharp's and Frederick Broadhurst's luggage – I can only assume Pommy Harry was trying to become a fledgling drug entrepreneur himself. Definitely a bad career move. A body search of Harry Lewis uncovered ten grams of cannabis in his underpants. Although a nice guy, Harry was not super intelligent. What happened during his interrogation after being arrested at the airport is very contentious. Before he was released on bail on 19 May, however, Clark was of the opinion that Harry Lewis had spoken to the authorities about him. On 19 May, the Federal Narcotics Bureau opened a file on Terry Clark. As Harry Lewis was arrested on 13 May, it can reasonably be assumed that he was the reason for that file being opened. It is also beyond doubt that any information about a file being opened on him could only have come from one source: Brian Alexander. Whoever told Clark that they thought Harry Lewis had talked most assuredly hastened his death, because within four days of being bailed out, he was murdered. I believe it was Wayne Shrimpton who Clark got to bail Harry Lewis out. To further highlight how ruthless he was, Clark put up the $5000 bail money just so he could get Harry Lewis out to kill him. With friends like that, who needs enemies?

After he bailed Lewis out, Wayne Shrimpton drove him to the Travelodge hotel in Rushcutters Bay, where they met up with Terry Clark. According to testimony Shrimpton later gave to the Stewart Royal Commission, a fierce argument ensued about whether or not Lewis should leave Australia. Clark wanted him to go, Lewis wanted to stay. Unfortunately for Harry Lewis, after a few days of consideration, he decided to go along with Clark's suggestion that he travel north with him to Brisbane and get on a ship leaving the country from there. The trip north was postponed for a day, however, so that Clark could take advantage of Wayne Shrimpton's departure overseas to buy gemstones and spend a drunken, lust-filled night with Allison Dine in a luxury suite at the Hilton hotel in Sydney. In later testimony, Allison Dine was to relate that when Harry Lewis came around to the hotel room the morning after he seemed very pensive. As he had less than 24 hours to live, Harry Lewis had good cause to be pensive. I guess some subliminal instinct was warning him that his life was in peril.

One of Harry Lewis's bail conditions was that he report twice a day to the Narcotics Bureau at Customs House in Circular Quay. His last reported check-in time and date was 7.20pm on 21 May. It is believed he headed north with Clark the following day, in a new purple Jaguar that Clark had just purchased for $29,000. Despite being a new car, somewhere along the mid-north coast they hit a bump in the road and damaged the exhaust pipe. After pulling into a garage and getting the exhaust pipe repaired, Clark later told Allison Dine, they decided to head back to Sydney. There are conflicting stories as to what happened after they left that garage. In the sanitised version he told Allison Dine, Clark claimed he acted in self-defence after Harry Lewis tried to kill him. As only Clark knew the real story as to how he murdered Harry Lewis, and later gave a few different versions of what happened, we can only hypothesise as to what actually occurred. For what it's worth, this is what I was told transpired.

After leaving the garage and heading back towards Sydney, the two of them got into an argument over money. Evidently Harry Lewis wanted more money to go away with. To bolster his argument and show Clark he was not a man to mess with, Lewis grabbed a spare gun Clark had in the glovebox of his car and threatened him with it. To placate Lewis, Clark said more money would be forthcoming. As Clark later told friends: 'He visibly relaxed after I told him he would get more money to leave the country with.' A short time later he told the same friends: 'I stopped the car on the pretext of engine trouble. With my spare gun tucked in his pants, Lewis got out of the car and walked around to my side of the car. Using the pretext of getting a spanner from under the seat, I reached down and pulled out a .357 Magnum handgun I had hidden there. With his back towards me, I simply walked up to the mongrel and shot him in the head. For good measure I put another two bullets into him, then dragged his body over to a nearby ditch and left him there.'

Although he would never admit it, I believe Clark panicked, because he drove off without properly concealing Harry Lewis's body. It was not until he had travelled 100 kilometres down the highway that he had second thoughts about leaving Harry's body so exposed and close to a busy road. According to Allison Dine when giving evidence to the Stewart Royal Commission, Clark told her he drove back to where he shot Harry Lewis, put his body in the boot of his car and then drove off to find a more secluded area to dump his remains. At a spot not far from Port Macquarie on New South Wales's north coast, he drove up an unsealed road for a distance, then carried Harry Lewis's body about half a mile into the bush, where he dumped it. After chopping off Lewis's hands and smashing in his face to help make identification difficult, Clark headed back to Sydney and his lover Allison Dine. As the body was found on 15 March 1979 and quickly identified as missing drug suspect Harry Lewis – aka Stanley John Weinert – it would appear that Clark's gruesome handiwork was to no avail.

On the way back to Sydney, Clark stopped and made a call to Allison Dine that, in my opinion, epitomised how callous, cold-blooded and unaffected Clark was by killing people. I know this call happened because at my trial in April 1986, my barrister asked Allison Dine these questions.

'Miss Dine, after killing Harry Lewis in late May 1978, Terry Clark made a phone call to you, is that correct?'

'Yes it is,' she replied.

'And what did he ask you to do, when he called?' my barrister then asked.

In a very sheepish voice, Allison Dine replied: 'He said he was on his way back to Sydney and he asked me to cook a roast pork dinner with all the trimmings.'

'And did you?' my barrister inquired.

I can still see the embarrassment on Allison Dine's face, her head bowed low, as she replied: 'Yes.'

During further cross-examination, my barrister was able to further elicit from Allison Dine that, over dinner, Clark confessed to her that he had just killed Harry Lewis in self-defence and had dumped his body in the bush. She also admitted to washing Clark's bloodstained clothes in her washing machine. I think it is fair comment to say that, on the night she cooked Clark a roast pork dinner with all the trimmings, washed his bloodstained clothes and listened as he related to her how he had murdered Harry Lewis, any last vestige of her assertions that she was just a prim, proper and naive kindergarten teacher from Rotorua disappeared. I have often wondered over the years if, during their roast pork dinner, Clark ever told Dine where he disposed of Harry Lewis's severed hands.

The most chilling aspect for me about the murder of Harry Lewis was the fact that barely two weeks after he killed him, Clark invited me to accompany him on a drive to Brisbane to see our mutual friend Ian Henry. I had actually known Ian Henry much longer than Clark, as he and another brother of his went to the same primary school as me in Auckland. A few years younger than me, Ian was in the same class as my younger brother, Brian. Had I known that Clark and I would be travelling to Brisbane in the same car that he had recently used when disposing of Harry Lewis, no doubt I would have thought twice before accepting his invitation. For me, the trip was a chance to catch up with an old friend from my primary school days. For Clark, the Brisbane trip was, I now believe, far more deliberate and complicated. He made that fateful trip for a reason, and that reason I believe was a salvaged fishing vessel called *Anoa*.

As we were driving up the coast, we unknowingly drove into a huge police, army and navy surveillance operation that was awaiting the arrival of a fishing vessel carrying a massive cargo of buddha sticks, destined for Australia. The name of the fishing vessel the authorities were waiting for was the *Anoa*. Now this is why I believe Clark was up to no good. Before being renamed the *Anoa*, this ex-Korean fishing boat was called the *Choryo Maru* No 5. The boat was salvaged from Wellington harbour in New Zealand, where it had run aground. The man who salvaged the boat was John Chadderton. Records show that John Chadderton sold the salvaged *Choryo Maru* No 5 to a gentleman named Graham Lyall Cann, who then renamed it the *Anoa*. To demonstrate how interwoven all these events were, as a young boy in Auckland, I played junior rugby league with Graham Cann. Another guy who played in the same team was a chappie named Ray Brunnel, who would later be charged – and acquitted – with Clark on heroin charges in New Zealand. Because of the Chadderton–Cann–Brunnel connection to Clark, I am now convinced that he was very much aware of the *Anoa* drug importation. It is too much of a coincidence that the very weekend we travelled to Brisbane on a supposed trip to visit a friend, the *Anoa* sailed down the coast of Queensland with a huge shipment of buddha sticks on board. Obviously Clark never trusted me enough to tell me what he was up to but I am of the firm belief that some of the *Anoa's* drug shipment belonged to him. I also believe the reason he asked Doug and Isabel Wilson to come up to Brisbane that weekend was so that they could drive his share of the drug shipment back down to Sydney. It is the only scenario that makes sense, because there was no other reason for the Wilsons to be in Brisbane on that crucial weekend.

On the drive up to Brisbane, Clark and I were blissfully unaware of the massive security surveillance operation going on concerning the *Anoa*. I was, however, very much aware of Clark's penchant for killing. His unsolicited accounts to me while having lunch at Eliza's restaurant in March, of having murdered numerous people, had me keeping a wary eye on him at all times. Also tucked into the back of my pants, under my shirt, was my trusty little .25 automatic. It was never needed, but provided a comforting sense of security for me.

What happened when Clark and I arrived in Brisbane was this. In what he thought was an innocent joke, Ian Henry had booked Clark into the Gazebo hotel as Joh Bjelke-Petersen, MP. The staff did not think it was a joke and notified police that there was a possible trick-ster staying at the hotel. On the Thursday evening – 8 June – that we arrived, Terry Clark, Ian Henry and a few other friends of his plus myself gathered for an all-male drinking session in the lounge bar of the Gazebo hotel. Around 1am, after many beers had been drunk and many drunken stories had been told, we all called it a night. Being an early riser, I was dressed in a tracksuit and out jogging by 8am the next morning. On returning to the hotel 30 minutes later, I noticed a large contingent of men, who looked suspiciously like police officers in the foyer. I cannot remember what floor we were on but Clark and I had adjacent rooms. On reaching our floor I went immediately to Clark's room and knocked on his door. When he answered the door, I voiced my concerns to him. 'Look mate, either I'm paranoid or there's a police convention going on at this hotel because the lobby is full of armed police.' Before I had finished the sentence, Clark raced over to his bedside table, grabbed his briefcase, which contained $10,000 in cash as well as a .357 Magnum handgun and raced out the door. As he bolted towards the elevator he called back to me: 'I'll be at Ian's.'

What happened next was told to me by Clark that night in the cells at the Brisbane watch-house. As Clark, briefcase in hand, was waiting for an elevator, the door of one of the elevators opened and out poured a large contingent of burly, overweight and heavily armed Brisbane police officers. None of them noticed Clark with his brief-case standing quietly beside the elevator doors as they thundered en masse down the hallway to our two hotel rooms. Clark calmly walked into the elevator they had vacated, travelled down to the first floor and exited the Gazebo hotel via a window. He made it safely to Ian Henry's Brisbane workshop, but then made the error of sending one of Henry's workers back for his Jaguar. The police simply followed the car back to the workshop, where they later took into custody Clark, Ian Henry, Kevin Gower and Stephen Johnstone – Martin Johnstone's brother. Before he was arrested that day, Clark, unaware that I had been taken into custody, went out for a short trip on Ian Henry's Bertram boat – sound familiar? – with all the above mentioned. So while the Queensland police were using me as their personal punching bag, Clark and company were drinking beer and practising firing his .357 Magnum handgun at seagulls. To save the others, after being arrested, Clark admitted to owning the gun. If my memory serves me correctly, I believe Clark, Henry and I were the only ones arrested and charged with any offences that day.

While the police were searching Clark's hotel room, the phone rang and one of the officers answered the call. The phone call was from Doug Wilson wanting to know what Clark's plans were for the day. The enterprising officer asked a severely drug-dependent, drug-addled Doug Wilson where he was staying. As he and his wife Isabel had just recently completed a drug rehabilitation program in a private Sydney hospital, Doug's befuddled brain was still not functioning properly. Without hesitation he told the officer the name of the motel he was staying at, thus enabling the police to go around and take him and his wife in for questioning. None of us knew it then, but that questioning of the Wilsons was the beginning of the end for the Mr Asia syndicate.

If there was one glaring weakness in Clark's organisational skills, it was his dependence on women – that is, Maria Muhary, Allison Dine and Kay Reynolds – and weak, drug-dependent individuals like Greg Ollard, Wayne Shrimpton and Doug Wilson. It came as no surprise to me, therefore, that of the many people he had working for him, only one person – Errol Hincksman – never became an indemnified witness against Clark. No doubt Clark was able to easily control and terrify his compliant workers, but unlike the battle-hardened criminals who I used to work with me, Clark's soft and weak-willed crew melted like butter even before the blowtorch was applied. I actually told Clark in early 1978 not to send Doug Wilson around to collect any money off me as I did not want to have any business dealings with a junkie. To his credit, Clark respected my request and used to send Steven Muhary over to see me instead of Doug Wilson. It is almost with perverse pride that I can state that no one associated with me in New South Wales in 1977, 1978 and 1979 ever went to prison. What was the cost to me, however, of that perverse pride? Twenty-five years of hard labour with a specified non-parole period. Maybe I should have taken that indemnified offer and walked away footloose and fancy free like so many others. But I just could not bring myself to do it.

At 8.30am on 9 June 1978 at the Gazebo hotel, however, thoughts of weak-willed employees were the furthermost thing on my mind. As Clark had already decamped, my hotel room was the next logical stop for the police. As they were pounding heavily on my door and asking me to open up, I thanked my lucky stars that I had hidden my .25 automatic in the hotel's car park. On entering my hotel room, the farcical excuse the police used for questioning me was that they had been informed that the management were concerned that I might not be able to pay my hotel bill. On being told this, I immediately walked over to my bedside table, opened a drawer and showed them the $4500 I had lying there. I gave them a false name and told them that I was just in Brisbane for the races, but I could tell from their belligerent attitude that nothing I said was going to make any difference. By hook or by crook, I was heading to the police station. So I then did what any self-respecting crook does and told them to go fuck their mothers. My rude, insulting comment about their mothers was instantly followed by a resounding blow to my head that knocked me sideways. It was the first of many blows that rained down on me that day.

To put into perspective the punishment meted out to Terry Clark and me that Friday in the Brisbane watch-house, the 1970s in Queensland were the glory days of Joh Bjelke-Petersen, the premier of that state. Thirty years ago Queensland was a police state, corruption was rife and heaven help anyone who took on the police there, because they were a law unto themselves. The belief that they might have two international drug dealers in their custody spurred those officers on as they redoubled their efforts to batter information out of Clark and I.

Fortunately for me, at that time of my life I was 37 years old and superbly fit. With my hands handcuffed behind my back, I could only grimace and absorb all the punches being directed at my rock hard stomach. Between each blow was the question: 'You're here for the boat, aren't you?' As I honestly did not know anything about the *Anoa*, I was able to truthfully say: 'I don't know what you are talking about. I'm here for the fucking races.' My continued denials seemed only to infuriate them more, because one of them went off and got an aluminium bucket, which he placed over my head. One of the officers then proceeded to hit the bucket with a baton at regular intervals. Each bang was accompanied by the question: 'You're here for the boat, aren't you?' Because I did not know anything about the boat, my eardrums took one hell of a pounding that day. The pain was excruciating every time that baton slammed into the bucket. Between workouts I would be taken back to the cells so that I could reconsider my position. Excuse the pun, but I was on a hiding to nothing, as I really did not know anything about the *Anoa* importation.

After Clark was arrested that afternoon, at least I had company as those overweight, unfit officers tried to elicit information from me. While they were tickling me up in one room, Clark was getting the welcome to Queensland treatment in another room. He was to tell me later that at one stage two huge police officers picked him up by his feet and proceeded to dunk him head first into a bucket of water. 'Welcome to Queensland, boys.' Every time one of them made that comment they all laughed. Despite their best efforts, Clark and I managed to withstand all the punishment meted out to us. The same, however, could not be said of Doug and Isabel Wilson.

Many people have asked me over the years why I thought the Wilsons spoke to the Queensland police as freely as they did on June 12, 1978 at the Brisbane watch-house, without the police having any evidence against them or even a valid reason to hold them. Well I believe the real reason they spoke to the Queensland police about Clark and others involved in the Mr Asia syndicate was this: fear, pure primal fear. At one stage during my fistic interrogation, with my hands handcuffed behind a chair and a big, burly copper punching me in the stomach, I distinctly remember looking up and seeing the terrified faces of Doug and Isabel Wilson being forced to watch as the police battered Clark and myself. Both their fear-stricken sets of eyes were like saucepans as the police held their faces against a glass panel for a good ten minutes, just to let them know what treatment awaited uncooperative people. It was real strange at the time, looking at both of them and seeing the fear in their eyes despite the fact that my hands were handcuffed behind a chair and I was being beaten. I tried to reassure them by smiling and nodding at them. Unfortunately, fear had paralysed them and I had an uneasy feeling as they were led away that it would not take much to break either of them. Two days later while being interviewed by Queensland detectives, my worst fears were realised, as Doug Wilson, without a hand being laid on him, not only confessed to all his crimes but also gave the detectives a detailed account of the murders committed by Terry Clark as well as information about Clark's drug dealing activities in Australia. His account of huge drug importations by sea; multiple murders; and the millions being made by Clark, myself and others selling heroin must have seemed highly fanciful to the detectives who interviewed him, but as they say, sometimes truth is stranger than fiction.

It is all ancient history now, but what those Queensland detectives did to the Wilsons that weekend was very wrong and ultimately led to them being murdered nine months later. To begin with, they had no valid, legal reason to hold the Wilsons. On the Friday that Clark and I were arrested, the police illegally confiscated the Wilsons' money and possessions, thus forcing them to return to the Brisbane watch-house on Monday 12 June to retrieve their belongings. Then, despite the Wilsons saying they were not prepared to make a written statement because they were fearful for their lives, the Queensland detectives interviewing them contemptuously dismissed their pleas and surreptitiously taped their conversations. They did this by illegally hiding a tape recorder behind a curtain as they interviewed both Doug and Isabel Wilson. After pouring their hearts out to the detectives questioning them, both the Wilsons were solemnly assured by their interrogators: 'No one outside this room will ever know what you have just told us.' Tragically for the Wilsons, Clark did find out. For 30 pieces of silver, their fates were sealed.

It did not take the Queensland police long to uncover our real names. The funny thing was, as soon as they did, they stopped pounding on us. No doubt a call to their NSW counterparts would have confirmed that not only were we suspected drug dealers, but also *rich* suspected drug dealers. When Clark and I were later put in a cell together that Saturday evening, we laughed as we compared war stories about our less than friendly interrogations. In a resigned voice, Clark told me he had offered the senior police officer interrogating him $100,000 to let him go, but to no avail. Unfortunately it was too late; Clark was told that the NZ police had already been notified of his arrest and were sending a man over forthwith to arrange his extradition. However, Clark was told that if we both signed over all our money to them – about $14,000 – I would be charged in the morning with having goods in custody, fined a minimal amount and then be allowed to leave the state. And that is exactly what happened. The following morning I was charged, convicted and fined the princely sum of $45. As I walked unshaven and bleary-eyed out of court, one of the police officers who had been tap-dancing on my stomach the day before walked up to me and said: 'Don't ever come back to Queensland, because next time you may not leave.' I could tell by the cold, deliberate way that he spoke to me that he was deadly serious. So I said: 'Thanks for the warning,' and immediately caught a taxi to the airport. For Clark it would be another week in the Brisbane cells before he was extradited to New Zealand to face his old heroin charges.

During the Friday night after we were arrested, Clark and I were placed in a cell together. At my trial, two Queensland detectives gave evidence that on 9 June 1978 they were on undercover duty in a cell with Clark and I and heard me make incriminating statements while whispering to him. Both my barrister and I maintained that those two detectives were lying about being in a cell with Clark and me on that night. One salient point people have to realise is that, as the Wilsons did not make their startling allegations about the Mr Asia syndicate until three days later, on Monday 12 June, there was absolutely no reason for the Queensland police to have two undercover officers in a cell with Clark and I. Once again it's all academic, but I'm still pissed all these years later that those two detectives were allowed to get away with getting me convicted. Why am I still upset? Because the two detectives gave sworn evidence at my trial that, on the morning of 10 June 1978, after being taken from the cells, they both went straight to an office in the police station and typed out a five page statement of conversations that they claimed to have overheard between Clark and me during the night. Although they said they were on opposite sides of the cell, by a miracle, they both heard the exact same conversations. This, despite the fact they had no microphones or took no notes during the night. When questioned by my barrister, neither detective when asked could even remember the last question put to them by my barrister. It beggars belief to think that both men could remember the same, identical five pages of transcript without taking any notes. And to add insult to injury, the most galling fact about their sworn testimony was the statement they tendered to the court as being an accurate account of what they heard in the cells on the night of 9 June 1978. The only problem was, this statement was dated 23 April 1983! The two detectives said they had lost the original statement dated 10 June 1978. If that was the case, how did they make the April 1983 statement? I have always maintained that if those two Queensland detectives had produced a statement in court dated 10 June 1978, it would have proved beyond doubt that they were indeed in that cell with Clark and me; and I was guilty of making those incriminating comments. The mere fact that they did not produce a statement dated 10 June 1978 reinforces, in my opinion, my assertion that they lied. They would not get away with what they did to me today. Now that judges are more aware of police fabricating evidence, they would not allow statements into evidence made five years later. In his summing up at my trial, Justice McInerney told the jury: 'If you believe the two Queensland detectives, then you can find Shepherd guilty, because their evidence can be used to link him to the conspiracy to import heroin into Australia. The indemnified witnesses cannot corroborate one another, but you can use the two Queensland detectives' evidence to corroborate what they have said. If you believe the two respected Queensland detectives, you can find him guilty.' After deliberating for two days, that is what the jury did.

One of the jurors later told a lawyer in a discussion they had about my case that the reason they convicted me was the judge's comments that if they believed the Queensland detectives, they should find me guilty. Interestingly, the juror said the jury did not believe Allison Dine or any of the other indemnified witnesses who gave evidence against me. In the late 1980s the Fitzgerald Inquiry into corruption in the Queensland police force found that corruption was endemic in that state. One of the serving officers named as being heavily involved in corruption in the 1970s by the Fitzgerald Inquiry was a certain Detective Sergeant Peter Le Gros. I wonder what my jury would have made of the fact that one of those respected police officers who gave evidence against me, Detective Peter Le Gros – as Justice McInerney so astutely described him – was, four years after my trial, convicted of corruption during the 1970s and sentenced to six years' imprisonment. Unfortunately for me, as my lawyers were preparing an appeal on the grounds that Le Gros was corrupt when he gave evidence against me, he had his conviction overturned on an absurd technicality and the Crown did not proceed with the corruption charges against him. I may be cynical and obviously biased, but if the federal or state government of the day had a choice between keeping me in prison or a corrupt Peter Le Gros, who would they choose? Me, of course.

Before I left Clark on 10 June 1978, he asked me to make sure I kept the business going. He was confident that despite being in prison, he would be able to ensure that I had a plentiful supply of product. After finalising details about where he wanted his money to go, I wished him good luck as I left the cell for my court appearance and freedom. I guess I could have saved my family and loved ones a lot of grief by retiring right then, but the lure of easy money kept me going relentlessly towards a cold and lonely Goulburn Prison cell.

26

BUSINESS AS USUAL

On my way to the airport I made two stops. One at the Gazebo hotel to retrieve my trusty .25 automatic, the second at a Brisbane hotel where I borrowed $200 from a publican who was a friend of Ian Henry so that I could pay for my airline ticket back to Sydney. When I arrived at Sydney airport late on Saturday afternoon, I figured there would either be a police welcome party for me, or at the very least, police following me. I was right on the last count. Fortunately for me, the Queensland undercover detective who had followed me on the same flight from Brisbane, did not get much cooperation from the NSW drug squad, because they were all involved in the *Anoa* drug surveillance operation. From information gleamed from different police reports I have read over the years, it seems the Queensland detective was allocated only one drug squad detective to help him track me in Sydney. Evidently they both followed me to a building in Randwick, where they watched me go inside. Unfortunately for them, the building I entered had a rear exit. I simply walked out the back way, down another street, hailed a passing taxi and was gone. From one of the reports I read, it was two days before the police tracking me realised I was not coming out of the building they had so patiently been sitting in front of.

Unlike the *Brigadoon* and *Konpira* drug importations, which were successfully concluded – all the crew aboard the *Anoa*, including my old friend Graham Cann who was the captain, were arrested a few days after our own Brisbane arrest, further down the coast in New South Wales. The *Anoa* drug importation had been masterminded by a former rogue police officer, a charismatic criminal named Murray Riley. Although I have never met Murray Riley, his criminal deeds are legendary in the Australian underworld. For someone who was an ex-cop, he made one hell of a crook. I believe he won a bronze medal rowing in the double sculls at the Melbourne Olympics in 1956. His rowing partner was none other than the NSW police commissioner Merv Wood, widely reputed to have been one of the most corrupt police commissioners in that state's history. Graham Cann ended up getting ten years as a guest of Her Majesty, as did Murray Riley and other members of the crew. One of those crew members, whose name was John 'Jack' Lawrence, would become a good friend of mine in later years. Unfortunately, Jack Lawrence, along with Bruce 'Snapper' Cornwall, was arrested and convicted in 2000 over a 120 kilo cocaine conspiracy and is currently working his way through a fourteen year prison sentence. A shame really, as Jack is one of those men becoming increasingly hard to find in the criminal underworld: a real stand-up guy.

After my brutal weekend in Brisbane, I decided to treat myself. I went out and leased a luxury apartment in the exclusive suburb of Point Piper, bought some new furniture and a fantastic sound system, fully stocked my bar with beer, spirits and imported champagne, and then went out looking for women to help me forget the nasty, deadly business I was involved in. At the time I had a half share in a bookmaking business, so I used to pass myself off as a bookmaker, racehorse owner and successful punter. Whenever I went out, I was always very well dressed, always had a pocket full of money and, as I was a sociable person and presentable, I used to have a fair amount of success with the ladies. Shortly after I moved into my new apartment in Point Piper there was a very humorous incident that is well worth retelling here. As I recall it was a Friday evening and I had taken an attractive young woman named Karen out to dinner at Tati's. After a delightful meal and a lovely bottle of wine, I invited Karen back to my place for a glass of champagne. In the taxi on the way back from Darlinghurst, we started to get amorous in the back seat. On sliding my hand under Karen's dress, I discovered to my surprised delight that she was not wearing any panties. It may not be a big issue these days, but back in the 1970s, a woman not wearing any panties was a rarity. As soon as we got in the old style elevator at my apartment block, I could not restrain myself any longer. Within moments I had Karen's dress up around her waist, my pants down around my ankles and her astride me, with her legs wrapped around my waist. When the elevator stopped at my floor, I managed to open the door, shuffle into the corridor with her still wrapped around my waist and my pants around my ankles, close the elevator door and continue our sexual encounter along the corridor to my apartment. No mean physical feat, because Karen was not only taller than I was but very well endowed. Just as I reached my door and was struggling to put my key in the lock, the next door neighbour, an elderly gentleman named Mr Smythe, opened his door to see what all the moaning and groaning was about out in the corridor. Well you can imagine dear old Mr Smythe's shock when he saw us going at it in the corridor of this exclusive apartment complex. All I could manage before I got the door open was an embarrassed: 'Good evening, Mr Smythe.' The poor guy was so shocked he just stood there with his mouth agape. No doubt thinking, there goes the fucking neighbourhood!

Because I had a huge stash of heroin at my Oxford Street hideaway, I was well placed to keep all our dealers happy for a few months. By the time my supplies started to run low in August, Allison Dine, who had become Terry Clark's surrogate in Australia while he was in prison, had couriers she had personally selected bringing in suitcases packed with concealed heroin.

Up until Clark went to prison, I had not had much to do with Allison Dine. I had met her a few times with Clark as he was sleeping with her at that time. Born in Rotorua on 20 April 1954, Allison Dine was an attractive, wide-eyed and naive kindergarten teacher when she first came to Australia with Wayne Shrimpton in late December 1976. Being around a drug user and drug dealer like her boyfriend Wayne Shrimpton, however, meant she soon lost any innocence she may have once had. According to his own testimony to the commission, Shrimpton sold a lot of heroin for Terry Clark in 1977, so Allison would have been very aware how he earned his money. No doubt she also saw very early on who had the most money and the most influence. For someone who liked to play on her reputation as a naive kindergarten teacher, it did not take Allison Dine long to change horses and jump into bed with her boyfriend's supposed friend. As Clark was no Brad Pitt in the looks department, it must have been his large penis and equally large bankroll that induced her to fall so passionately in love with him. Because Maria Muhary was a good friend of mine, I kept my distance from Allison Dine. I was respectful to her because she was Clark's lover, but I was never her friend.

However, Clark's arrest on 9 June 1978 forced me into closer contact with her. After visiting Clark in Mt Eden Prison in Auckland, Allison Dine arranged a meeting with me. During her visit, she had managed to smuggle out a letter from Clark that was addressed to me. The letter detailed what Clark wanted Allison Dine, Steve Muhary, Chinese Jack and myself to do while he was inside. Allison Dine was to recruit couriers to bring in heroin in the suitcases that Chinese Jack had specially prepared, from Singapore to Sydney. On arrival in Sydney, Steve Muhary was to collect the suitcases from the couriers, dismantle them and deliver the concealed heroin to me. My job was to weigh and bag the heroin as usual, then sell it. All money received was to be sent out of the country through the usual channels.

And that is what we did for the six months Clark was on remand in Mt Eden Prison.

Unlike Clark, it had always been a policy of mine not to work with women, so I was very uncomfortable about working with Allison Dine. To get around this I used Steve Muhary as a buffer while Clark was in prison. Having said that, I have to admit that she did a good job in recruiting couriers for the Singapore–Sydney run while Clark was in prison. If I remember correctly, on one run Dine had four couriers in Singapore at the same time, waiting to travel back to Sydney.

The system used to work like this. On arrival in Singapore, the courier would check into a prearranged hotel. Chinese Jack liked the couriers to stay for a minimum of three or four days so as not to alert any observant Customs officers in Sydney as to how brief their trip had been. The swap over of suitcases was very simple. On the day they were checking out, Chinese Jack would come to the courier's hotel room with either Allison Dine or her friend Kay Reynolds to oversee everything. After giving the courier or Dine the money to pay the hotel bill, Chinese Jack would go downstairs separately and wait for them outside the hotel in his car. On leaving the hotel with Kay, Allison or the courier, Chinese Jack would keep their suitcases in the car and drop them off at a nearby shopping centre. When he returned in a few hours' time, the courier would find their clothes packed into new tartan suitcases. Chinese Jack would then take them to another hotel, where they could check in and wait for their flight back to Australia. Before heading out to the airport the couriers would be shown how to casually pack their clothes, usually with their lingerie on top, in the tartan suitcases. As another ploy, Chinese Jack liked to break an ornament to place on top of the courier's packed clothes. It was his belief that Customs officials, on seeing the broken ornament, would more than likely treat that person in a sympathetic manner while searching their luggage. For any couriers who might be suffering from nerves, Allison Dine would give them sedatives to calm them. On the flights to Sydney, Dine used to oversee the couriers travelling in economy class from her seat in the first class cabin. No slumming with the workers for this kindergarten teacher. I guess I could go so far as to say that she took to crime like a duck to water. Within a short period of time, thanks to Dine, it was business as usual. Once again our dealers had to dig new holes to bury their illicit drug money and, once again, I got sick of counting money.

As well as all the heroin that Allison Dine was supplying through couriers, Steve Muhary was also delivering to my apartment black garbage bags full of sealed ten-gram bags of heroin that he had been digging up from some of Clark's many hiding places in the bush. Clark had a penchant for burying large stashes of heroin in the bush. I remember one evening early in 1979, Clark and I were travelling by car to see a mutual friend who lived on the north shore. Because I did not know the north shore area too well, I was completely at a loss as to where we were when Clark stopped the car near bushland in Ku-ring-gai Chase National Park. He pointed to a heavy area of bushland beside the road and said to me: 'I have 100 kilos of smack buried in there.' Why he told me, or why he took me there, I do not have a clue. All I know is that if my life depended on it, I could not find that location again.

Despite the venomous snake that was the Mr Asia syndicate having its poisonous head temporarily chopped off with Clark's arrest, the body of the snake was still able to function. For me and all the dealers who purchased heroin from the syndicate, it was business as usual. If anything, the business grew while Clark was away. Because of our ability to supply product to our dealers on request, their orders became larger and more frequent. An old sea-going friend of mine from New Zealand, Darryl Sorby, who was living in Melbourne, became an active drug dealer in Victoria. Before you could say 'pass the salt', he was buying a minimum of 50 bags every week. Within six months, thanks to his thriving drug business in Melbourne, Darryl was able to purchase a luxurious house in Toorak. That wasn't one of Darryl's smarter moves, because at that time he had no visible means of support. The beautiful, large home in an exclusive part of Melbourne did not go down too well with the jury at his trial for conspiracy to supply drugs in 1984. He was a very entrepreneurial man though, Darryl. I remember him paying an American theme park designer from Dallas $30,000 to come over to Queensland in the early eighties to do a feasibility study for a water theme park near Brisbane. Whenever I see people on television cavorting at the extremely successful Wet'n'Wild on the Gold Coast, I often think of Darryl and his early vision. He was certainly ahead of his time there. He also bought up large tracts of land on Bribie Island in Queensland for property development, before the island became the fashionable destination for holiday homes and the resort area it is today. Darryl did not get away with any of his ill-gotten gains however. After being convicted at his trial, Darryl was sentenced to thirteen years' imprisonment and all his assets were confiscated by the government. The Victorian police also ensured his time in prison was extremely difficult by labelling him a potential escape risk, thus giving prison authorities a mandate to keep Darryl confined in Pentridge prison's notorious punishment block – H Division – for the first four years of his sentence.

While myself, my crew, and all those dealers doing business with us were living the high life, Clark was restlessly pacing up and down a prison yard in Auckland's (rebuilt since the 1965 riot), Mt Eden Prison. It was there he would meet the woman whom he would spend his last months of freedom with, Karen Soich. At that time, Soich was an ambitious young associate solicitor working for New Zealand's top criminal lawyer, Peter Williams. During the years I was on the wrong side of the law, Karen Soich was certainly not the first female lawyer or intelligent woman I have met who has had her life ruined by falling in love with a career criminal. I guess some women are just attracted to dangerous men, men willing to flout the law and live outside normal society rules.

As I have not spoken to Karen Soich since 1979, I am unsure what she now thinks about the brief fifteen months she was romantically involved with Clark. During the few times I saw them together, she seemed totally smitten. As Soich came from a wealthy family, had a privileged childhood and had enjoyed a good education, it is hard for me to fathom how she fell for a degenerate like Clark. My earlier assessment that 'love is blind' when discussing Maria Muhary's, Allison Dine's and Karen Soich's love for Terry Clark certainly pertained more to Soich than the other two women. Of all the people associated with Clark and the Mr Asia syndicate in the 1970s, Karen Soich has fared the best in later years. After returning home to New Zealand in 1981, she married a successful businessman and with her husband became involved in the entertainment industry. A company she formed with her husband produced the highly successful and critically acclaimed NZ film *Once were Warriors*. A film, by the way, I personally enjoyed watching. A few years ago she was reinstated to the NZ bar and allowed to practise law again. I believe she is now highly respected as a lawyer specialising in the NZ entertainment industry. I recently spoke to a very old and close friend of mine in New Zealand, who has fallen on hard times. Many years ago he had a personal relationship with Soich and they have remained friends ever since. On hearing my friend was not travelling too well, she recently surprised him by turning up at his apartment with some home-cooked food, $1000 and a big hug. That was a very kind gesture. If I have ever said anything unkind about you in the past Karen, I apologise.

Over the years, the lawyer that Karen Soich worked for in 1978, Peter Williams, QC, has come in for unwarranted criticism because he got Terry Clark acquitted of the heroin charges he was facing in October 1978. At the time the Mr Asia syndicate was active Peter Williams was, in my estimation, the best criminal lawyer in Australasia bar none. I believe at one stage Peter Williams – he was not a Queen's Counsel then – had ten murder acquittals in a row. I do not know of another lawyer in the world who can match that achievement. If you are the CEO of a large corporation and need legal advice about company law, you will invariably go to a top corporate lawyer for that advice. Criminals are no different. Those criminals who can afford the money to retain them invariably seek out the best criminal lawyers to defend them in any legal matters they are facing. Wherever I have been in the world, whether it be Auckland, Sydney, London, San Francisco or Los Angeles, I have always had a top lawyer on a retainer, just in case of unexpected trouble. Although I have known Peter Williams since the 1960s when he was an aspiring young lawyer making a name for himself in Auckland, I have never been out with him socially and I would certainly not class myself as a personal friend of his. But if back in the seventies or eighties I had to have a lawyer defend me on a murder charge where I was facing the death penalty, Peter Aldridge Williams, QC, is who I would have wanted defending me. That is why Clark got him for his heroin trial in October 1978: Peter Williams was the best criminal lawyer in New Zealand at that time, nothing more, nothing less. He was paid well for getting Clark acquitted of his heroin charge, but that is par for the course as far as top criminals and their high-powered lawyers are concerned. When you pay top dollar, you expect nothing less than a successful outcome to your legal problems.

Despite having quite a strong circumstantial case against Clark, through judicious questioning during the trial Peter Williams was able to exploit weaknesses in the Crown's case and, to the surprise of many, win an unexpected acquittal for him. Following his acquittal in the Wellington Supreme Court in early November 1978 there was a huge celebration that night at an inner-city hotel. Many bottles of Dom Perignon champagne were consumed as Clark celebrated his acquittal. A few days later, Clark bought a white Jaguar and made a showy return to his old alma mater – Wi Tako Prison – to visit a friend doing time there. The new car would have been Clark's not so subtle way of saying to his former jailers: 'Look at me now!' That acquittal also meant that within a year, Doug and Isabel Wilson as well as Martin Johnstone would be dead; and I would be starting a new life in the United States.

27

1979: THE END APPROACHES

In December 1978, when Clark was still in Wellington, he decided to show in a bold move that his five months in prison had not slowed him down or caused him to lose his nerve. He did this by getting Allison Dine and her ex-boyfriend's sister, Wendy Shrimpton, to carry over from Sydney on Christmas Day two tartan suitcases that Wendy had just days previously successfully brought in from Singapore. As an incentive to do the extra trip to New Zealand, they were both paid an additional bonus of $5000. On arrival in Wellington late on Christmas evening, Allison Dine watched as Wendy Shrimpton went through Customs without any problems. Unusually for Clark, he took an active interest in this importation and was waiting in the car park at Wellington International Airport for Allison Dine to emerge from the arrivals exit. After picking up Dine in his car, they followed a taxi carrying Wendy Shrimpton and Maria Muhary's young sister Angelique, who had met her at the airport, to the White Heron hotel in the city. Once Wendy Shrimpton had checked in, Clark arrived a short time later with Dine to retrieve and break open the two tartan suitcases. After smashing the suitcases to get at the concealed heroin, Clark left the hotel with over a million dollars' worth of heroin in his possession. A man later identified in the Royal Commission reports as Dennis Williams then came around to the hotel to take away the smashed suitcases and help clean up the mess. As Williams left the hotel he only just avoided police officers arriving to search Wendy Shrimpton's hotel room.

By working backwards, Wellington drug squad officers were able to ascertain where Wendy Shrimpton had stayed. A thorough search of her White Heron hotel room by drug squad detectives revealed traces of heroin in the carpet. The presence of residual heroin was a significant indicator to the police and Customs officers that a large drug transaction had more than likely just gone down in that hotel room. It was simply by sheer good luck that Terry Clark, Allison Dine and Wendy Shrimpton were not caught red-handed with that large amount of drugs at the White Heron hotel.

After checking out early the next morning, Wendy Shrimpton and Allison Dine travelled out to the airport to catch a domestic flight to Auckland. Unbeknown to them, however, NZ Customs and police had received prior information about their heroin smuggling operation. As a consequence they were both detained and searched at the domestic terminal while awaiting a flight to Auckland. Both Allison Dine and Wendy Shrimpton were found to have entered New Zealand using false names and were charged with that crime. A search of Wendy Shrimpton uncovered some marijuana she was carrying for her personal use and she was also charged with drug possession. At later court appearances they were both fined small amounts for their misdemeanours and allowed to walk away untroubled from the Wellington importation, because the authorities didn't have enough evidence to hold either of them. After her court appearance, Allison Dine slipped back into Australia early in January 1979. She was not through with the Mr Asia syndicate just yet. Her friend Wendy Shrimpton, however, had decided after the close shave in Wellington that life on the wild side was not for her and she disappeared into the Auckland suburbs for a life of marriage and domesticity. The next time I would see her would be in the witness box at my trial in April 1986.

Clark told me later that he hid the heroin he retrieved from the suitcases in a schoolyard located directly behind the White Heron. After police involved in searching Dine and Shrimpton's hotel room left, Clark calmly went back to retrieve the heroin he had stashed in the schoolyard the night before. Rather fortuitously, he had just missed being arrested by the police earlier that morning. Instead of heeding the warning signs, Clark interpreted his narrow escape as a sign from the gods that luck was on his side. His luck held that Christmas, but it would not last to the next.

A very interesting footnote to all of this is the fact that the very lady who wrote the introduction to this book, Glenda Hughes, was one of the police officers who arrested Allison Dine and Wendy Shrimpton on 26 December 1978. As I said earlier, it has never ceased to amaze me how different events concerning members of the Mr Asia syndicate have become interrelated over the years. I remember that time particularly well because 1978 was the last Christmas I ever spent with my mother and family in Auckland. Sadly, I have not been back to the land of my birth since then.

Both Allison Dine and Wendy Shrimpton gave evidence against me at my heroin importation trial in 1986. When Allison Dine gave her version of a large – four couriers – 23 December 1978 importation into Sydney from Singapore, I was upset, but I accepted she was just trying to save herself. The remarkable thing to me about her evidence though, was the fact that she actually believed her version of events. I have a theory about a lot of those indemnified witnesses who gave evidence in many court cases, judicial inquiries, Royal Commissions and trials like mine, and it is this. After being schooled by the police on how to give credible evidence – what to say and how to say it – and then repeating their version of events like a mantra through all the judicial processes I have just mentioned, many of these indemnified witnesses not only knew their prepared stories off by heart, but had brainwashed themselves into believing that what they were saying was 'The truth, the whole truth and nothing but the truth.' When I read the comment in the papers: 'they are rewriting history,' I often think of all those indemnified witnesses who gave evidence against me.

When Wendy Shrimpton got in the witness box to give evidence against me, it was very distressing. Around August or September 1978 I had a brief relationship with her. Due to my reluctance to sustain a meaningful relationship at that time, we remained friends but drifted apart. When she broached the possibility with me of doing a drug run with Allison later in the year, I strongly voiced my opposition to such a course of action. I advised her not to do it. I even told her I would be extremely upset if anything happened to her, as I was still very fond of her. To help pay her rent and bills I would get Wendy to pick up money for me, nothing dangerous or major. For doing next to nothing, I used to give her $300 a week. Unfortunately, Allison Dine was a better salesperson than I was, and got Wendy to do the December run from Singapore with three other couriers. 'Do not tell Jim what you are doing,' Dine told Wendy Shrimpton before she jetted off to Singapore. To her credit, Wendy Shrimpton repeated that statement at my trial. It did not help alleviate the disappointment I felt though, at seeing her standing in the witness box giving evidence against me. That image still hurts. I felt the same way as I watched my friend Maria Muhary in the witness box, helping to put another nail in my coffin. Freedom will beat friendship every time when the alternative is a cold and lonely prison cell.

Before returning to Sydney on 3 January 1979, I flew down to Wellington to meet with Terry Clark. At a meeting held at a mutual friend's house, we discussed his imminent return to Australia and the possibilities of us increasing our market share in Adelaide and Perth. It was agreed that I should return to Sydney as soon as possible and get business underway again. And that is exactly what I did. With fresh supplies of heroin from the December importation available, my crew quickly got back to work. Within two weeks, it was as if we had never stopped for a Christmas break.

My apartment in Oxford Street was soon awash with money. At least once a fortnight I had to send money overseas through different banks. Even Brian Alexander was getting in on the act. He was getting 2.5 per cent to move large amounts of money for us, to specified bank accounts nominated by us in Hong Kong. The guy had great contacts in the banking sector. Surprisingly, we never lost a cent using him to move money for us, which, considering his drinking and gambling habits, was amazing. For the first three months of 1979 it seemed like the party would never end. Business was booming, money was rolling in, women were plentiful, even the horses were winning. Little did I realise in March 1979 that the sun was already starting to set on the Mr Asia syndicate. The illegally taped record of interview that Doug Wilson gave to Queensland detectives on 12 June 1978 in the Brisbane watch-house was about to have disastrous consequences for all of us involved with Clark.

On returning to Australia in mid-February 1979, Clark was given a copy of the illegal tape recording that Queensland police surreptitiously made of Doug Wilson's admissions by Brian Alexander. I know, because Clark told me that Alexander had given him a copy of the tape. Over the years the figure that has most often been bandied about concerning how much Clark paid for the Wilsons' tape has been $200,000. A few people have given evidence to different judicial inquiries, that Clark told them he paid $200,000 for the tape. That is a fallacy. In late February, Clark asked me for $100,000 and that is the only large amount of cash he got off me during that period. Remember, I handled all the money the syndicate made, so I would have been aware of it if Clark had requested that amount of money. If he told others he paid $200,000 for the Wilsons' tape, he was big-noting. As the $100,000 was the only large sum of money he requested off me at that time, I can only assume that is what he used the $100,000 for, to pay Alexander for the Wilsons' tape.

After hearing the tape Clark was extremely upset and angry. Despite the fact that Doug Wilson was a junkie with a raging heroin habit, Clark really liked him. Because Doug Wilson had a university background and could discuss art him as well as other intellectual topics, Clark enjoyed his company. I believe Clark thought they were on the same intellectual level. As Clark considered himself a talented artist – his dream was to retire and live as an artist – it would have really hurt his ego to hear Doug Wilson on that tape denigrate his ability as an artist. There is nothing a pseudo-intellectual artist like Clark would have hated more than hearing someone say he was not smart and had no artistic ability. I know it would have pissed me off. I believe Clark confronted Doug Wilson a couple of times about the rumours he was hearing concerning him making admissions to the Queensland police. According to what Clark told me, a clearly agitated Doug Wilson denied the allegations both times.

Despite Doug Wilson informing NSW drug squad detectives in March that Clark was back in Australia, they discounted his information. They incorrectly told Doug Wilson that NZ police had Clark under surveillance over there. A fatal oversight for the Wilsons, because Clark was already in Sydney and paying Wayne Shrimpton $200 a day to keep a watch on their apartment at Rose Bay. Because he was now well known to the federal police, Clark had to keep a low profile while he was in Australia. He spent a lot of time moving between Adelaide and Sydney, always staying in hotels or motels. I can say from personal experience that it is not a great way to live, and definitely not the way to run a drug empire.

Clark came over to my new apartment in Sutherland Crescent, Darling Point, in early March 1979, to discuss what he had heard on the tape. The apartment I was leasing at that time had a spacious outdoor terrace overlooking the water, and we sat out there having a quiet beer while we discussed the ramifications of what Doug Wilson had said. I was shocked when Clark told me that Doug Wilson had kept a record in a diary of all the dates as well as the amounts of money he had collected from me. The police now had that information. As we were confident that the police protection we had would keep us safe in New South Wales, we were concerned but not fearful about what Doug Wilson had said. As I expected, Clark wanted Doug Wilson dead, and the sooner the better.

My motives for not wanting to kill Doug Wilson were both monetary and personal. I argued that as our business was thriving, the sudden disappearance of two people could put the spotlight on us. I made a point of mentioning how much damage Donald Mackay's disappearance had caused to the Italian boys in Griffith. I also knew that at that time there were already three bodies – Greg Ollard, Julie Theilman and Harry Lewis – lying around the countryside; another two bodies, if found, would almost certainly destroy us. I told Clark that the police currently protecting us would find it very difficult to continue doing so if the Wilsons turned up dead. We had too much money at stake to take such a risk, I argued. That was my monetary argument against killing Doug Wilson; my personal reasons were a little different.

Although he was a hopeless junkie and had made a statement against me, I remembered Doug Wilson as he had been when I first met him in the laundry at Mt Eden Prison in 1971, a drug-free, quiet, intelligent man who was always willing to discuss any worldly topic with me. To my way of thinking, Doug Wilson was a gentle, non-violent man. All my life I have fought against men who were bigger or stronger than me. One of my few redeeming qualities is the fact that over a lengthy criminal career, I have never preyed on nor stood over other criminals weaker than myself. I guess that predilection was always the chink in the armour I built around myself back then: my reluctance to attack or kill those weaker than myself. That is how I saw Doug Wilson, as someone weaker than myself. To me, Doug Wilson was a weak, ineffectual junkie who should never have been allowed to work with us in the first place. I blame Clark for that. When Clark asked me what I would do with him, I suggested giving Doug enough cash so that he and his wife could travel overseas to Britain or Europe. He could either do that, or give them enough money to relocate to Victoria or Tasmania and live quietly there. I firmly stressed to Clark that to my way of thinking, letting them quietly disappear somewhere else was the smart option. I can still see him now, a cigarette in one hand and a cold glass of beer in the other, looking out towards the water, deep in thought. After a few minutes of contemplation he turned to me and said: 'I'll think about it.'

Obviously my forceful arguments on Doug Wilson's behalf did not resonate with Clark's thoughts. He had no doubt already made up his mind at that stage to kill Doug Wilson. For him, Doug Wilson's betrayal was personal and he wanted him dead. Looking back on it now, I realise nothing I said at that stage would have saved Doug or his wife. Clark was one of those individuals who, once they make up their mind to do something, do not deviate from that course of action. His decision to order the murders of Doug and Isabel Wilson in April 1979 would eventually bring us all down.

28

FAREWELL AUSTRALIA: HELLO LONDON

Before he left Australia in late April 1979, Clark, Bob Trimbole and myself had dinner at Tati's. It was during this dinner that Clark told us he was moving to the United Kingdom. He told us that he felt he had run his race in Australia, that it was becoming too difficult for him to move around undetected and it was time to move on to bigger, greener pastures. It was his belief that London was a huge untapped market. He figured that what he had done here could be multiplied many times over in London. It was agreed between Clark and myself that I would continue handling the Australian and New Zealand end of the market while he was in London. Little did we know then that within two months of that dinner, I would be hiding out in London with Clark. We also discussed with Bob Trimbole the possibility of getting involved with him in an illegal casino in Sydney. We all agreed that an illegal casino – providing an accommodation could be worked out with George Freeman and company – was a sure-fire money earner. For anyone not familiar with the name George Freeman, in the 1960s and 1970s he, Stan Smith and another associate named Lenny McPherson controlled all the illegal casinos, slot machines and bookmaking in Sydney. During those years, no illegal casinos were allowed to operate in Sydney without their permission. It was decided after a lengthy discussion that Bob would do more groundwork on the casino project – that is, discussions with senior police and Freeman's crew to get permission for such an enterprise – then get back to us. That dinner should have been a warning sign to me, but I guess all that good food and fine wine had dulled my senses. The fact that Clark was discussing our business in front of Bob Trimbole should have alerted me to the developing friendship between them. Not for the first time, I got sloppy.

It was less than a month after Clark left for London that the Mr Asia syndicate officially began to fall apart. Like rotten fruit that has been hanging on the tree for too long, we started dropping to the ground, one by one. On 13 May one of Allison Dine's couriers, a lady named Joyce Allez, was arrested coming into Sydney airport carrying two tartan suitcases with four kilos of heroin concealed inside them. Joyce Allez was not arrested through a tip-off or information received, she was apprehended simply through an alert Customs official. When she presented her luggage for inspection, instead of lying her suitcase on its back so the Customs official could open it for inspection, she stood her suitcase upright. When her suitcase fell over because of the imbalance of the heroin packed in the sides, the Customs official picked it up, only to see it topple over again. This aroused his suspicions and a subsequent forensic examination of her suitcase revealed the concealed heroin.

After the heroin was discovered, she was taken to a police station and formally charged with importing heroin. The same afternoon as Joyce Allez was arrested, a clearly distraught Allison Dine rang me to both alert me as to what had happened and ask for my help. Within an hour of her ringing me, I had Brian Alexander down at police headquarters trying to calm down an obviously distressed and fearful Allez. Acting on our behalf, Alexander was instructed to tell Allez that all her legal fees would be paid, as would be the money she was owed for the trip, $10,000. I do not know if she ever received the money that I handed over to Alexander for her. Knowing how shifty he was, there is a big chance she never got a cent for her failed effort. Even if she did get her fee, $10,000 is not much when you consider that, after pleading guilty, she had to serve a minimum of five years in prison. Two thousand dollars for each year in prison. She would have earned more money a year in unemployment payments and benefits from Centrelink. It's a pity a lot of would-be criminals do not think about those figures before they go out and commit an armed robbery worth a few thousand bucks, whereby if they are caught, a guaranteed five or six years in prison awaits them.

It did not take the police long to zero in on Dine and her good friend Kay Reynolds. Before they knew it, federal police officers were raiding their apartment and questioning them over the Allez arrest. After questioning at Central Police Station by drug squad detectives, they were both released without any charges being laid. During this difficult and stressful time, Dine was constantly on the phone to me asking for my help. As Clark had already left the country and could not be contacted, it fell on me to try and settle the situation down. To assist in this, I enlisted the help of Bob Trimbole to keep Dine and Reynolds moving from hotel to hotel. I also asked Bob to arrange for Dine to get a new passport, which he did. Despite our encouragement and support, however, the constant police pressure proved too much for Dine and she had a nervous breakdown. Even for someone like me who is used to full-on police searches and covert police surveillance, coping with the pressure of an all-out investigation into your everyday activities and movements can be very disconcerting and daunting. For someone like Allison Dine who was not a hardened criminal like me, having the federal police hounding her everywhere would have been frightening. I think it would have been about this point in time that Dine would have started to realise that being involved in a massive drug ring with a psychopath like Clark and villains like me was not a good career move for a kindergarten teacher from Rotorua. Equally as frightening for her would have been the discovery of Doug and Isabel Wilson's bodies on 18 May in Victoria. That would have really terrified her.

On Friday 18 May, a meat inspector named Dennis Brown was out walking his part-cattle dog through vacant scrubland not far from his holiday home on the outskirts of Rye, a small holiday town situated on the Mornington Peninsula, about 80 kilometres from Melbourne, when he noticed something unusual. About a year earlier, while out walking his dog through the same area, the scrub-covered vacant lot 59 on Danny Street not far from where he had his holiday home, he had spotted about 20 metres in from the dirt road a well-hidden small trench that had been previously dug by someone and left covered with loose scrub and tea tree branches. He did not think anything more about the trench until 20 April 1979, nearly a year later on, when he was again out exercising his dog. His curiosity was aroused when he observed that the concealed trench on lot 59 had recently been both widened, deepened and had fresh, loose scrub and tea tree branches placed over it. He would later tell police investigators that he became apprehensive when looking at the enlarged trench, as it looked suspiciously like a newly prepared grave. It was not until Friday 18 May, however, that Dennis Brown with his dog would come through lot 59 on Danny Street again. His suspicions of foul play were instantly aroused when he saw that the well-hidden trench had recently been filled in with dirt and more loose scrub and tea tree branches placed over it. At the same time as he was observing this suspicious new development, his dog became very agitated and started digging into the earth that now covered the once empty trench. What was worrying his dog? he wondered. What was buried there? It was obvious to him from the disturbed earth that other animals, possibly wild dogs or foxes, had been digging in the earth as well. A less curious or observant man may have just ignored the newly filled-in hole and carried on walking his dog, but not Dennis Brown. After putting his dog in his vehicle, he drove the four kilometres to the Rye police station to report his suspicions.

After listening to Dennis Brown's apprehension about the abnormal, grave-like trench, the local police initially thought it might only be a case of thieves hiding stolen property. Nevertheless, they dutifully went out to lot 59 on Danny Street with a couple of probes to have a look for themselves. A cursory insertion of one of the probes into the earth soon uncovered the unmistakable stench of death. Homicide detectives were quickly called in and a full murder inquiry was soon underway. When the site was excavated, the bodies of Douglas and Isabel Wilson were uncovered.

It would only take Victorian police officers two days to formally identify them. Three days after they were found, at a hastily called meeting in his office at Park Street, I was shocked when a clearly agitated Brian Alexander told me about the gruesome discovery of the Wilsons' bodies in Victoria. At that meeting, Alexander also told me he had rung Terry Clark in London to inform him about the recent developments. I was told to come back the next day and he would let me know what was happening as far as the police were concerned. I must admit, I left Alexander's office with a heavy heart that day. It was clearly obvious to me what the ramifications of this gruesome development would mean for all of us: trouble with a capital T. Corrupt police can only protect you up to a certain point, when bodies start turning up all over the countryside, that protection can soon evaporate. And that is what happened with us. Like rats deserting a sinking ship, the corrupt police involved with Alexander started scuttling for cover. It obviously worked, because not one police officer involved with us through Alexander was ever convicted of corruption. A few were tried along with Alexander on corruption charges, but after a magistrate described Allison Dine as a witness 'unworthy of belief,' all the charges against them were dismissed.

By the time the Wilsons' bodies were discovered, Clark was already ensconced in the Hyde Park Hilton hotel in London. On 26 April 1979, using one of his many false passports, Clark had flown out of Melbourne en route to London. During a two-week stopover in Singapore, he met up with Martin Johnstone whom he had not seen for a while, and Chinese Jack Choo. Although Chinese Jack had been hoping for a confrontation with Johnstone about moneys owed by him to both Clark and himself, he was badly disappointed. Being the persuasive talker he was, Martin Johnstone mistakenly thought he had managed to allay Clark's concern about all their money he had lost in foolish investments. It has been my experience that, when you are dealing with psychopathic killers, you do not make empty promises to them that you cannot keep. If you do, there is a big chance you will end up dead. No doubt while he was talking and socialising with him in Singapore, Clark was already planning Martin Johnstone's murder.

Over the last 30 years I have read and heard a lot about how the Wilsons were murdered. During that time I have also managed to glean bits of information from here and there as to what actually occurred. In his book *Greed*, Richard Hall put forward the hypothesis that the hole on lot 59 in Danny Street, Rye, had been dug for someone else first. He was correct with that supposition. Evidently, the trench was dug in 1977 to accommodate someone else who had fallen out with the wrong people in Melbourne. It was obviously not used at that time, but the man later convicted of killing the Wilsons, an ex-Painter and Docker named James Frederick Bazley, must have remembered the unused site and unfortunately for him, Clark and Trimbole, decided to reactivate it as a suitable grave site. For someone reputed to be as meticulous as James Bazley was, it was a grievous and disastrous error. I should point out that although there was a very strong case against him, James Bazley has always strongly maintained his innocence, despite being convicted of killing both the Wilsons and Donald Mackay. Over the years I have met a few criminals from Melbourne who know Jimmy Bazley, and to a man, they all speak highly of him. I know it might be difficult for a hardworking, honest person to comprehend how anyone could like a man who is a contract hit man, but in the criminal underworld, tough and violent men who live by the unwritten criminal code of never giving anyone up, even at the cost of not saving themselves, are admired and respected. Although nothing is certain in this life, I expect James Frederick Bazley will take all his many secrets to the grave with him.

A close associate of Bob Trimbole's named Franco Tizzoni was the man who later confessed to police – to save himself from serious drug charges – that he was the person who contracted James Bazley to murder the Wilsons and also Donald Mackay in Griffith on 17 July 1977. He arranged the murders, he attested, through a well-connected Melbourne gun dealer named George Josephs. According to Tizzoni, he paid Bazley – through Josephs – $20,000 to kill the Wilsons. Franco Tizzoni maintained in court that at all times he was acting on Trimbole's orders and instructions. It has never ceased to amaze me how indemnified witnesses like Tizzoni are always acting on someone else's orders when they commit very serious crimes. In evidence he gave in the Supreme Court in Melbourne at James Bazley's murder trial, Tizzoni said the Wilsons originally headed off to Melbourne on 8 April 1979, but due to an arm injury he had suffered, James Bazley could not make the arranged rendezvous with them, so the Wilsons returned to Sydney. On 13 April, five days later, the Wilsons again set off for Melbourne in their green Toyota Celica. This time their killer was waiting for them, as was that shallow grave in vacant lot 59 Danny Street, Rye.

Before the Wilsons were murdered, I remember asking Clark in early April 1979 what he was intending to do about Doug Wilson. The guy looked me straight in the eye and said he was sending Doug down to Melbourne, to be out of the way. I must admit I felt relieved as I told Clark that was the sensible thing to do. I guess Clark did not mind lying to me, as he never thought their bodies would turn up to disprove what he had told me. When questioned by Australian police in England, while serving his life imprisonment sentence, about where he was on the night of 13 April 1979 – the night the Wilsons were suspected of being murdered – Clark replied: 'I was having dinner at the Wentworth Hotel in Sydney with four other people.' He did not afford me the courtesy of telling me to make sure I had an alibi for that night. On the night in question, I had dinner at a friend's house in Dover Heights, but was home early and spent the rest of the night alone in my apartment at Sutherland Crescent, Darling Point.

Although I never met or knew Franco Tizzoni, if he is to be believed, then Clark got Bob Trimbole to organise the murders of Doug and Isabel Wilson. Looking back on it now, it is obvious to me that Clark must have had other surreptitious meetings with Bob Trimbole in March 1979 that I was unaware of. There is a saying that has been spoken in many memorable gangster movies that 'it's only business'. These words are usually said when a gangster in the movie has done something unpleasant to a friend. That is how I now see Bob Trimbole's relationship with Clark back in 1979. Bob Trimbole was under no obligation to tell me what he was doing for Clark, or whether he was going to go into business with him. At the end of the day, we all do what is best for ourselves; friends are friends, but business is business. When it counted though, Bob Trimbole's friendship with me helped keep me alive.

The day after getting the disastrous news about the Wilsons' bodies being discovered, I received a telephone call from Brian Alexander to come into his office at around 4pm that afternoon. He ended his call by telling me to bring $20,000 with me when I came: 'The money was needed and a priority.' Despite the fact that I knew he was a hopeless and inveterate gambler, I put the money in a briefcase and went down to his office that afternoon. The first thing Alexander said to me after I walked into his office was: 'Have you got the fucking money?'

I tapped my briefcase and said: 'The money's here. What do you need it for?'

'This is becoming a fucking unmitigated disaster, we are still dealing with the Joyce Allez arrest, now this,' he complained. 'This is bad, real fucking bad.'

As he said those words, I could see he was close to a nervous breakdown. He was highly agitated and anxious while I was in his office, constantly waving his hands around and shuffling about in his seat. No doubt he was already getting the message from those corrupt police who gave him a copy of the Wilsons' tapes that they were not happy and he was the man responsible for their unhappiness. Having spent the previous twenty years dealing with violent criminals and corrupt police, Alexander would have realised only too well how precarious his situation was, because he appeared terrified to me. 'The twenty thousand,' he told me, 'was required to keep the boys downtown pacified, as they were fucking angry at what had happened with the Wilsons.' At the moment, he informed me, I was just a person of interest to police. But as I was now one of the people being discussed by senior members of the drug squad as connected to the Wilsons, it was his strong recommendation that I disappear for a while. His contacts would let me know when it was safe to return. Obviously with the passage of time, my memory of what was said in Alexander's office may not be word for word accurate, but what I have written is not far off what was said. The gist of our meeting was simply this. The police were pissed, the situation was real bad, my name was being mentioned downtown, I should disappear for a while, I would be told when to return, he was fucking terrified. Although I hated doing it, I realised it was 'just business', so I handed over the $20,000 for the warning and information he had passed on to me. For once, I considered it money well spent.

As I got up to leave his office, I did not realise as I shook his hand that I would never see him alive again. I spoke by phone to him a few times during 1979, inquiring as to my current status in Australia as far as the police were concerned, but I was never to physically meet him again. On 1 January 1982, a cousin of Alexander's walked into the Chatswood police station on Sydney's north shore and reported him missing. The missing report stated that he had not been seen since 21 December 1981. The last people to see him alive would have been the police officers who tied him to a chair with heavy weights attached to it and then threw him off the back of a police launch to a watery grave.

Sometimes there can be a heavy price to pay for anyone involved in serious criminality. Just look at those involved in the Mr Asia syndicate who were murdered: Greg Ollard, Julie Theilman, Harry Lewis, Doug and Isabel Wilson, Martin Johnstone, Brian Alexander. And these are just the people we know about. There were more than likely four or five others who are still missing and unaccounted for. All these people were either seeking easy money or drugs when they became involved with the syndicate. They all found out in the most brutal way, how treacherous and deadly dealing in drugs can be. There is a salutary lesson to be learnt from their deaths for anyone contemplating becoming a drug dealer. It may look like easy money, but it never is. Death and prison will be your constant companions; never forget that.

The discovery of the Wilsons' bodies was a turning point for me. As I left Brian Alexander's office after paying him $20,000 to appease the boys downtown, as he put it, for the first time I really started to question my involvement with Clark and dealing drugs. Since I was sixteen years old, I had fought many battles and done a lot of hard prison time to forge a reputation for myself in the criminal underworld. I had committed daring crimes over the years that hurt no one, gave me a lot of personal satisfaction and also made me a lot of money. Now here I was, a low-life heroin dealer, involved with a psychopathic killer who had no compunction in either killing his friends or getting someone else to do it for him. I felt my hard-fought reputation was in tatters and, despite the money, clothes and women, my self-esteem was at an all-time low and my future in Australia was looking decidedly bleak. The edifice that was the Mr Asia syndicate was starting to crumple from the top. Although I would not tell him until I saw him in London a few months later, I decided there and then that I was done with the Mr Asia syndicate. When people start killing their friends and lying to you about it, then it is time to move on.

The three guys I had working with me were all tough, street-smart, trustworthy men who were no strangers to prison or the police. When I decided to get out of the business and leave the country, I sat down with my crew and explained to them why I was leaving. Before he left for London, Clark had brought around a huge cache of heroin that he had dug up from one of his many hidden stashes. Despite wearing medical masks, it took three of us two days of constantly being stoned on heroin fumes before we finished weighing and bagging the lot. Even though we were moving the product in increasing numbers, we figured we had enough to last another four months. This was all before my 21 May meeting with Brian Alexander.

As all the guys I had working with me were friends of mine, they were understandably concerned about me as well as themselves. They were relieved when I explained to them that I was the only one known to the police. If they wanted to carry on the business without me, I would consult Clark and get his blessing. As Clark had no one else in Australia capable of moving the amounts we were doing, I did not anticipate any problems getting the go-ahead from him. It took the three of them all of ten seconds to decide that despite the risks, they were more than willing to carry on the business. Just like me two years previously, the lure of so much money was irresistible to them. I designated John as the new team leader, as he was a man used to handling large amounts of money and someone I trusted implicitly.

As strange as it may seem, there are many criminals who cannot handle huge sums of money. If you are running a large operation where millions are involved, you have to have criminals working with you or for you who are accustomed to handling huge sums of money. It takes a certain mind-set to carry around suitcases full of money. Unlike Clark who allegedly paid those working for him minimum wages – both Steven Muhary and Allison Dine said while giving evidence that they were paid a retainer of $300 a week – the guys working for me regularly made over $5000 a week. That is why I've always found it hard to swallow that two of Clark's key workers were, in their words: 'only paid $300 a week.' I guess they must have equated smaller wages with less direct involvement in what was happening around them. Today, you regularly read in the papers about criminals getting caught with millions of dollars in their possession. The drug trade has grown so big that it is a billion-dollar business. But back in the 1970s, the only criminals making millions from the drug trade were the Italians from Griffith and us.

It was agreed with John and the other two guys in my tight crew that until the current supplies ran out, I would get $50 per bag sold. As I knew how much product was available, I knew to the cent what my share of sales would be. Once the current supplies ran out, then I was out of the loop and it would be up to them whether they continued on. In anticipation of something like this happening, I had been quietly schooling John in all the different methods we used to move money offshore. I have to say, John took to moving money like a duck to water; he was a natural. It was just as well I had schooled him, because three days after getting the warning from Brian Alexander, I was dusting off a false passport and packing my bags.

As I boarded a Qantas flight in Melbourne, destination London, I could not help but reflect on the irony of me travelling under the same name as my old enemy from Mt Eden Prison, Richard McDonald – Maori Mac. Life can be full of meaningful coincidences. So for me, it was goodbye James Shepherd, hello Richard McDonald, and London here I come.

29

THE KIWIS HIT LONDON

When I was in the security block in Mt Eden Prison, on many a long, lonely night in my sparse prison cell, I used to dream of visiting the great cities of the world. The four cities and one destination I daydreamed about the most were London with all its history; Paris and the Eiffel Tower; New York and the Empire State Building; San Francisco and the Golden Gate Bridge; and every gambler's mecca, Las Vegas. I would eventually go to all those places I dreamt about, but London was the first city on my list that I actually made it to.

When I stepped off the plane at Heathrow Airport in late May 1979, Margaret Thatcher was about to become the first woman elected Prime Minister of England, and the IRA were in the middle of a deadly bombing campaign in London. To underline just how deadly the IRA's campaign was, a conservative politician named Airey Neave was killed by an IRA bomb planted under his car in the House of Commons car park, and a much loved member of the royal family,

Lord Mountbatten, was killed later in the year by a bomb planted near his fishing boat. Despite the IRA terror campaign, life in the great city of London went on. In 1979 disco was king. Donna Summer was singing about 'Bad Girls'; the Bee Gees were wailing about 'Tragedy'; Meat Loaf was screaming about 'A Bat Out of Hell'; and Gloria Gaynor was pounding out 'I Will Survive.' The swinging sixties and seventies were coming to an end, the Beatles had gone their separate ways, the English climate was real bad, but for a 38-year-old Kiwi with plenty of money in his pockets all that did not matter. Just being in a city I had dreamt about so many times while lying on my prison bed was good enough for me. I was determined to enjoy myself – and I did.

The first call I made after booking into the London Hilton hotel was to Terry Clark, to let him know I had landed in London. As he had no one in London with him at that time except his de facto wife Maria Muhary and his baby son Jarrod, Clark was delighted to hear from me. We made arrangements to meet the next day and have lunch together at a pub in Knightsbridge. I cannot recall the name of the pub, but I remember we had one of those ploughman's lunches they like to serve in their pubs over there. It's a mixture of breads, cuts of meat, pickles and cheese. The food was washed down with the warm maiden's piss they pass off as beer. Getting a cold beer, or ice for your alcoholic drinks in a London pub back then was a very difficult proposition indeed. I also found their quaint method of shutting their pubs for a few hours in the afternoons a nuisance. I guess even great cities like London can have their shortcomings.

Over our less than salubrious lunch, I brought Clark up to date on the latest developments concerning the discovery of the Wilsons' bodies in Victoria. After I had finished recounting everything Brian Alexander had told me about what an unmitigated disaster this was for all of us, I finished by telling Clark that I was personally disappointed he had not heeded my advice to send the Wilsons somewhere out of sight. At least Clark had the good grace to appear embarrassed when he apologised to me for not heeding my advice and also for not telling me about it. I told Clark that fortunately for me, I was in Sydney on the suspected date they were murdered but I had travelled down to Melbourne directly after their disappearance to see Darryl Sorby about some business we were involved in together. Had I been aware of what was going down, I would not have gone within 100 kilometres of Melbourne. With the benefit of hindsight it has occurred to me that now knowing how treacherous he was, Clark may have tried to put me in the frame, because he knew I was going down to see Darryl Sorby around that time. There were a couple of other things that happened while I was in Melbourne that seemed to be so coincidental that I now realise they could have been done with me in mind. Because he was so devious, I have often wondered if Clark ever read any books on Machiavelli while he was in prison. It would not surprise me if he had.

For Clark, all my misgivings were like water off a duck's back. I can still see him sitting opposite me in that pub gesturing with his hands and saying: 'The world is opening up, Jim. There's millions waiting to be made. First the UK then the US.' I now realise that those grandiose statements were a direct result of all the cocaine he was then using heavily. He was genuinely surprised when I told him I was pulling out of the syndicate. 'But why, Jim? There's still millions to be made,' he implored. I then told him in a matter of fact way that I realised my time in Australia had come to an end. Drug squad police were openly discussing my activities as a high-level drug dealer and I was a person of interest to police officials investigating the murders of Doug and Isabel Wilson. That was enough for me. I told Clark that the money I had made with him, plus the money I already had, meant I was in a very comfortable position financially. Besides the money stashed away, I also had a lot of legitimate business ventures in Australia that I was confident would give me a good return on my investments.

'But what about all the product we still have in Australia?' he asked me in a concerned voice. It was business as usual, I told him. My crew with John – whom he knew – were in charge, and handling everything back in Sydney, I explained to him. I also went on to tell him that all moneys owing to him and Chinese Jack Choo would be sent out through the usual banking channels. As an added insurance and to allay any doubts he and Chinese Jack might have, I would stay on in London until all the current product was sold.

My statement that I would hang about in London until all the current product had been sold seemed to mollify Clark and he agreed without any argument to let John and the rest of my crew carry on the business in Sydney. Despite having heard a lot of garbage from different quarters about when Bob Trimbole was supposed to have hooked up with Clark, I firmly believe that it was at that lunch with me in a London pub in late May 1979 that he first started thinking about working with Bob. To carry on the business in Australia without me being present, he needed someone with the same drive, abilities and ruthlessness as me. My friend Bob Trimbole fitted those capabilities to a tee. I would be willing to wager that as soon as he started thinking about Trimbole taking over the Australian operations from me, he also began planning, right there and then, to either try to kill me himself or have someone else take me out.

There is one particular story about Bob Trimbole's involvement with Clark that has been repeated so often that people actually think it is true. I am talking about the fallacy that Trimbole was going to pay Clark $30 million for his business. Who are they kidding? Thirty million dollars for what? All Clark had to sell was access to the markets I had established. It was my crew who knew all the customers we were dealing with, not him. Obviously Clark could have introduced Bob to Chinese Jack Choo so that he could access large supplies of heroin, but that is not worth $30 million. And let us not forget, I knew Chinese Jack Choo as well. Remember, I had been to Chinese Jack's crocodile farm, so if required I could have arranged an introduction for Bob myself. Now let's look at the monetary figures associated with this fallacious story. For Clark to make $1 million when he was operating in Australia he had to sell 10 kilos of heroin. Each kilo sold equating to $100,000. Therefore, for Trimbole to pay Clark this fictitious amount of $30 million for his business, he would have had to sell 300 kilos of heroin just to service the payment. I think not.

Where have all these fanciful stories about the Mr Asia syndicate come from? I'll tell you: from Allison Dine and other indemnified witnesses willing to say or do anything their police interrogators asked them. I can forgive all those indemnified witnesses for trying to save themselves, because that is just human nature. But for lying while they did so, that I cannot forgive so easily. It is the ridiculous and errone-ous stories like this fictional $30 million purchase price for Clark's foundering drug empire that have led me to write this book. Because of continuing public interest in the Mr Asia syndicate, I have simply wanted to set the record straight and let the general public know what really happened during the years the Mr Asia syndicate operated.

As we got up to leave the pub that late May afternoon, Clark invited me to his sister Judith's wedding. The wedding was being held on 3 June at a little village called Three Cups, situated near the town of Battle, near Hastings, some 90 kilometres from London. He told me he and his near were heading down there the next day and he would call me once he was there to give me directions. When I told him I was going to look for a furnished apartment in the city to rent, he asked me to see if I could find one for him also. We parted on good terms and I even managed to find a luxury apartment for him at 550 Carrington House located, in the exclusive Mayfair district, in the West End of London. For myself, I leased a lovely, furnished two-bedroom apart-ment in Devonshire Street, near Regents Park, just around the corner from a street world-famous for doctors, Harley Street. Although I stayed at my address until I left London, Clark did not stay at the Carrington House address long. He found another apartment at Stafford Court in Knightsbridge and stayed there until his arrest in November 1979.

On the Thursday before his sister's wedding, Clark rang me in London to give me directions to the village of Three Cups, where she lived. When he asked me how I intended to get there, I told him I was going to hire a London cab to take me down there. On hearing this, Clark asked me if I could do a favour for him and stop off in the town of Wellington on the way, to pick up one of his financial advisers – Robert Scott – who had flown in from Australia to see him. After assuring Clark that I would do so, I set about finding a London cab driver willing to make the trip down to Hastings. On my second day in London, I had hired one of London's indomitable cabbies to drive me around all the city's historical sites, Buckingham Palace, London Bridge, Parliament House etc., and his name was Don. Like most London cabbies, Don was a knowledgeable, cheerful and outgoing chap and he left a contact number with me in case I required his services again. When I rang him and asked whether he would be interested in driving me down to Hastings, he thought about it for ten seconds, then said: 'It will cost you!' When I asked how much, he jovially replied: 'Three hundred quid but I'll buy the petrol.' I did not quibble over the price, I just asked him to pick me up at the London Hilton at 8am the next morning and we would be on our way. I have to say Don was great company and I enjoyed talking to him as we wound our way through the lush, green English countryside, en route to Wellington, where I picked up Bob Scott. On arrival at Three Cups we bade farewell to our genial cab driver Don, made a phone call to Clark and waited at the local pub for him to come and pick us up, which he did ten minutes later.

After Bob and I had settled in at Clark's sister's farm that afternoon, the three of us headed up to the local pub. Standing at the bar that evening with a pile of £20 notes on the bar in front of us, were Clark, Bob Scott, the groom, all his friends and myself. It was one helluva raucous, drunken night. We all had a great time, drinking, singing and telling tall tales. I vaguely remember climbing into bed in the early hours of the morning with the groom's sister. As I was in an extremely drunken state, I'm sure that sexual escapade would not have been one of that lady's more memorable experiences. I was told by Clark's sister a few weeks later that the locals were still talking about those crazy rich Aussies and Kiwis who had shouted the bar all night. I guess after reading about Clark's arrest six months later in London, all those villagers who were in the bar with us enjoying our hospitality would have realised that all our money came from crime and drugs.

The wedding went off the following day without a hitch. Although severely hungover, we all managed to party on again at the reception afterwards. As I was feeling embarrassed by my drunken, sexual encounter the previous evening, I went to bed alone that night.

On the Sunday morning following the wedding, if I had not been so hungover from the previous two days' festivities, the alarm bells would have been going off instantly when Clark invited me to go out rabbit shooting with him. Without giving his invitation any thought, I agreed to go out hunting with him. I thought some exercise and fresh air would do me good, and that thought was nearly a fatal mistake. As everyone staying at his sister's farm were still asleep when we left, I firmly believe that I would not be alive today had the groom's sister – the one I slept with – not walked downstairs to make a pot of tea and said hello to us as we left together. Looking back on that morning all those years ago, I now realise how significant her seeing us leave was. Without her there would have been absolutely no witnesses to us leaving the farmhouse together.

Although we were only carrying light calibre hunting rifles, as most professional criminals know, the weapon of choice for many contract killers is a light calibre .22 pistol with silencer attached because those weapons make hardly any noise when fired. On this day, however, as Clark and I made our way through the surrounding countryside of empty paddocks, wooded glens and winding country lanes, the cobwebs in my head started to clear and my innate sense of imminent danger kicked in. As we walked quietly along the deserted country lanes it slowly dawned on me that I was deep in the English countryside with a man whom I knew had killed at least six people and there was not a living soul in sight. The uneasy feeling that I could be in danger heightened my senses and I slipped the safety catch off my rifle and carried it ready for instant use. I also reminded myself that, under no circumstances, was I to walk in front of Clark. But as that old saying goes, 'The best laid plans of mice and men.'

As we came around a bend of the country lane, about ten metres in front of us, grazing on grass near the side of the lane, were three rabbits. Before they could dart off into the surrounding scrub, I quickly fired at them, killing one instantly. After letting out a little whoop of triumph, without thinking, I moved forward to get the dead rabbit. It was only after I had taken four paces towards the dead rabbit that I suddenly realised Clark was standing behind me with a loaded weapon and in a great position to shoot me in the back. I do not mind saying that, at that particular moment, the hairs on the back of my neck stood up. On my mother's side of the family there are reputed to have been a few members of the family who had strong psychic abilities. Some of their psychic abilities must have filtered through to me, because all my life I have always been able to sense – when sober – if someone was going to attack me. And right at that moment, that is how I felt. I believe to this very day that the only reason he did not shoot me in the back when the opportunity presented itself was because someone saw us go out together. When I belatedly looked back at Clark, he had a sickly grin on his face but, much to my relief, his rifle was pointing at the ground. Shortly after this incident we stopped hunting rabbits and returned to the farmhouse.

The next morning, despite Clark's pleas to stay on for a few more days, I went with my gut instincts about his intentions towards me and left the farm. I had called Don as soon as I got back to the farm from our hunting excursion and arranged for him to come down and pick me up the following day. I was much more subdued and contemplative on the trip back to London. Was I being unnecessarily paranoid? Was I imagining things? After years of criminal activity, were my nerves finally getting the better of me? All these thoughts and many more kept swirling around my head as I sat in Don's cab on the way back to London. One of my mottos in life is 'forewarned is forearmed,' so just to be on the safe side I decided I had better take a few precautions when I got back to London.

The first thing I did as soon as I got back was call Bob Trimbole in Sydney and ask if he knew anyone in London who could get me a weapon. Within 24 hours Bob had rung back and I was given a name – let's call him Luigi – along with an address in Hammersmith to go to. Bob told me over the phone that his distant relative would be expecting me. After getting a cab out to the Hammersmith address and knocking on cousin Luigi's dilapidated apartment door, I was greeted by a big fat Italian with a strong English accent. Within five minutes of my meeting him, Luigi excused himself, left the room and returned a few minutes later carrying a well-maintained and well-oiled Browning .32 automatic pistol wrapped in a white towel. Despite thinking he was more than likely ripping me off when he said he wanted £750 for the gun, I did not haggle about the price. I figured that as I was a long way from home and my life was worth a lot more than £750, I'd gladly paid the price. Before I left, as a parting gesture of goodwill for his long lost cousin in Australia Luigi gave me two full clips of ammo for free. As I walked away from cousin Luigi's apartment, I was comforted not for the first time by the sense of security a loaded gun can give you. That gun would be with me at all times for the rest of my stay in London.

The second thing I did on returning to London was to become a member at a casino called Ladbrokes, located in the exclusive Mayfair area of London's West End. I have read in different publications over the years that Ladbrokes was a sleazy gambling casino. That is simply not true. When I joined Ladbrokes, I would have to say that, despite being a small casino, because of the huge money I saw bet there, it would have had to rate as one of the biggest betting casinos in the world at that time. Oil sheiks, Greek shipping tycoons, publishing magnates, bankers and the British aristocracy all used to gamble there. I remember standing next to the publishing magnate Robert Maxwell one night as he was gambling on the roulette tables. On two roulette tables that were situated side by side, he was placing £20,000 ($AU50,000) on each spin of the wheel, on each table. I have gambled at casinos in Las Vegas, Lake Tahoe, Atlantic City and Reno in the States; at gambling tables in Monte Carlo, casinos in Macau, Greek casinos, other European casinos and many casinos here in

Australia; and I can state that Ladbrokes in London matched them all for massive, high-stakes gambling.

If you were regarded as a high roller, which I was, then even the Dom Perignon was free at Ladbrokes. At that time, Ladbrokes had one of the best restaurants in London and I enjoyed many fine, free meals there. Being a valued high roller, I was also given invites to many prestigious London sporting events. That year I was given tickets to the Wimbledon tennis final when Björn Borg defeated Roscoe Tanner over five sets. That evening I was taken as a guest along with fifteen others to the Wimbledon Ball, where the casino had two tables reserved. One of the celebrity guests that evening was Muhammad Ali. For an old fighter like me – old being the operative word – his presence at the ball was a huge thrill, as he was a personal sporting hero of mine – still is for that matter. Besides the tennis I was given tickets – which I did not use – to the enclosure at Royal Ascot to see one of the blue ribbon derbies being run there. I think it was in the month of July that I was given an invitation by the casino to Prince Charles's annual charity ball in Berkeley Square, where Ladbrokes had their own marquee set up. As an interesting footnote to my attendance at this ball, I took Allison Dine, who was visiting London at that time, along with me to enjoy the occasion.

It was at Ladbrokes that I had the biggest win of my life in a casino. How that win came about was both amusing and embarrassing. There is an old saying in the criminal world: 'No one hollers louder than a thief who has been robbed.' Well I got robbed and I hollered loud and I hollered long. It came about because a friend of mine who was visiting me from Australia ignored my request that he bring no one back to my apartment.

It was in August of that year that my friend came over to London to visit me. As he was married at that time, I will not embarrass him by using his real name; I will just call him Tony. While he was in London, Tony stayed with me. One night while he was out having a few drinks, Tony got lucky, pulled a lady at a club and brought her back to my place for, as he put it, 'a night of unbridled, drunken sex.'

Being totally unaware that Tony had someone in the spare bedroom with him, the following morning I got up at about 7.30am and went for a run in nearby Regent's Park. After returning to my apartment some 40 minutes later, imagine my shock when, as I was taking off my sweaty running gear, when I discovered my prized gold Patek-Philippe watch and my diamond ring were not sitting on top of the bedside drawers where I had left them. A quick check under my bed revealed that my briefcase containing £10,000, which I had withdrawn from a bank the day before, was also gone. 'I've been fucking robbed!' I screamed out. I was absolutely stunned and extremely angry. At that moment I could have shot someone very easily. I ran into the spare bedroom to wake my still half-drunk friend Tony to ask him if he had brought anyone home with him, and I was given the news I did not want to hear. Still in an alcoholic stupor, Tony apologised profusely for disregarding my instructions and bringing a lady back to the flat with him. If disregarding my wishes was not bad enough, worse was to follow. Tony could not remember where he picked the lady up – I say lady advisedly – and he did not know where she lived, in fact, he could not even remember her name. To say I was mightily pissed with my friend would have been putting it mildly. I gave him a helluva blast and unreservedly blamed him for my loss. As my watch was valued at $10,000 Australian, my diamond ring about $8000 and £10,000 equated at that time to $25,000 Aussie dollars, all up my losses were just over $40,000. That opportunistic female thief must be still chuckling today over her unexpected score from my bedroom that morning while her lover snored blissfully unaware in the other bedroom. The only positive for me was the fact she didn't steal my gun, which was in my bedside drawer at the time.

Although it galled me to do so, I had to ring Terry Clark, explain to him what had happened and ask him for a loan of £15,000 until I could get some money sent over from my accountant in Hong Kong. I was aware that Clark always had bags full of money in his apartment so I knew getting £15,000 off him would not be a problem. After picking up the money from Clark at his Stafford Court address that evening, instead of going straight back to my apartment, on the spur of the moment I decided to go to Ladbrokes and have a bet. When you are angry or upset that is usually not a good time to have a bet, but for some inexplicable reason that night I decided to do just that. As I walked up the steps to the casino entrance, I told myself, I'll have one £10,000 bet on a red colour turning up on the roulette table, then leave.

For people who are not conversant with casinos or gambling, at the roulette table there is an even amount of red and black numbers. Most people choose a number and bet on it. If their number came up, they used to get odds of 35 to 1. My preferred way of betting at the roulette table was to bet on either a red or black number turning up, nearly a 50–50 outcome. When you bet like that, the only small advantage the house has is the zero number. Today, most roulette wheels around the world have two zeros, but back then European casinos only had one zero on their roulette wheels. So to give myself that small advantage, whenever I had a large bet on red or black, I would also put a bet on the zero number.

On this particular evening, that is exactly what I did. I placed £10,000 on a red number turning up and, as a saver, I put £1000 on zero. I thought, If I win, I'm out of here. Well there was sheer joy in my voice as I yelled out, 'You beauty!' when the zero number turned up. I was now £35,000 in front. As was customary back then, if zero turned up, all bets on red or black would be halved. So as the wheel spun again, I had £5000 on red, and my £1000 bet on zero – because zero had won the previous spin – went around again. When the wheel stopped spinning, I went into my version of a Maori haka as zero turned up again. It was fist pump and yahoos; I was beside myself with excitement. Now I was £70,000 in front. Before the wheel spun again, I decided to increase my bet on red. My original £10,000 bet on red had been reduced because of two zeros turning up, down to £2500. So using some of my winning chips, I put another £7500 on red, thus giving me what I originally started with, £10,000 on red and £1000 on zero. The Maori haka was brought out again as a red number duly turned up. Another £20,000 had just jumped in my kick. For once in my life, common sense prevailed and I made sure the casino was not going to get its money back by cashing in my chips and walking out the door a big winner. I walked in with £15,000, I walked out – after freely tipping staff – with just on £86,000. Not a bad night's work! After repaying Clark the £15,000 I had borrowed from him I was still £71,000 in front, about $176,000 Aussie dollars back then. Even after taking away the $40,000 I had lost in the robbery, I was still miles in front. Although my unexpected win could not take away the deep embarrassment and humiliation I felt over being robbed, it certainly helped put a smile back on my face. From that night to this present day, I have never been able to emulate that fantastic winning run I had at Ladbrokes in August 1979. I guess the gambling gods only ever smile on you once.

After dropping by Clark's apartment the next day to repay the money, I went straight down to Bond Street – a street famous for exclusive jewellery stores – to look for a new watch. At one of those stores, I purchased another gold Patek-Philippe watch for £8000. Even though it was much more expensive than my original watch, I liked my first watch better. At another jewellery store, I brought a 2.5 carat diamond ring for £17,000. After buying the ring, I took it to another jeweller and had him take the stone out and put it into a ring designed to my specifications to look exactly like the one I had stolen. If only our lives could always be made up of such great wins and happy outcomes.

Now that I had a new watch, a new diamond ring and plenty of money in my pockets, I was ready to paint good old London town red. The only problem was, I could not get into any of the really exclusive, private nightclubs like Annabel's, Regine's or Tramp to have a good time. Unlike today, where Australian and NZ expatriates are respected for their business acumen, academic qualifications and strong work ethic, back in 1979 it was a totally different situation. Although there were a few Australians like Clive James, Germaine Greer, Barry Humphries and an idealistic young lawyer named Geoffrey

Robertson making names for themselves in England, any fair-minded person would tell you that snobbery was alive and well in that country back then. Rightly or wrongly, 30 years ago, the average English person regarded Aussies and Kiwis as drunken, good for nothing louts, only interested in finding the nearest party or pub. I'm afraid we were not welcome in any of the better class London establishments. Despite always wearing a suit and being presentable, I could not get into any of the exclusive private clubs until I was introduced to an attractive, aspiring actress named Vivian. The fortuitous introduction came about through the only woman I knew in London, a white South African lady named Sonia. As Vivian was a member at Annabel's, Tramp and Regine's, when she heard about my difficulties in getting into those establishments she agreed to sponsor me in all three clubs. After paying hefty membership fees to all three establishments, I suddenly found that the quality of the women I was buying drinks for improved dramatically. Although my success rate with the ladies did not improve after becoming a member at these establishments, I still had a helluva good time trying.

30

A MISTRESS CALLED COCAINE

Why was I out drinking, gambling and clubbing instead of get-ting involved with Terry Clark and his English associates selling drugs in London? Well, my reasons were manifold. One, I was slowly cutting all my ties with the Mr Asia syndicate; two, I did not want to deal in heroin any more; three, apart from Andy Maher who I had met when he was in Australia in May 1978, I did not know any of the peo-ple Clark was working with; and four, I could see that Clark's cocaine addiction was starting to affect his judgement. Rather prophetically, my observation to Clark that he did not really know the people he was working with was proven correct in a devastating fashion six months later after he was arrested. Every one of the English guys Clark was working with made statements to the police, incriminating themselves and him in everything from drug dealing to murder.

I really began to notice Clark's increasing cocaine use after I returned to London from a holiday on the Greek island of Corfu. As a matter of fact, Clark and Maria Muhary and their son Jarrod were supposed to join me at the villa I had leased in a little village called Nissáki, about 20 kilometres up the coast from the main township of Corfu. The villa came complete with a competent cook and I really enjoyed the two weeks I spent there. Crystal-clear ocean waters, blue skies, a blazing sun you could actually see, a lovely villa on a cliff top, attractive women, friendly people and fresh local seafood: what more do you need for a holiday? After the depressing, overcast weather that seemed to pass for summer in England, Corfu was paradise. For me, the two weeks in Corfu was a wonderful release from all the stress I had been feeling since the Wilsons' bodies had been found in a shallow grave in Victoria. My problems did not go away, but the sun, the sea and the clean air of Corfu helped me forget, albeit just for two weeks, the bleak future that lay ahead of me.

As Clark had just taken delivery of a new Mercedes-Benz in Stuttgart, Germany, the plan was for him and his family to drive down through Italy and catch the car ferry from Brindisi across to Corfu. As Jarrod took ill while they were travelling through Italy, however, they left the car there and flew straight back to England so that he could have better medical treatment in London. I was not sorry to hear about their change of plans as I still had a nagging suspicion in the back of my mind about Clark's intentions towards me that just would not go away. The thought of spending a week in close proximity to him without my gun was tempered by the fact that with his family in attendance, I did not think I had anything to worry about.

At first Clark had been circumspect about his cocaine use. Like most cocaine addicts are prone to do, he would make numerous visits to the toilet, where he would surreptitiously snort cocaine. After a few months, however, he gave up any pretence about his habitual cocaine use and started to openly use the drug. At night after the maid had left there would usually be a small mound of cocaine on the table in the dining room, for him and his guests to use. On more than one occasion, I can remember stopping by Clark's apartment at Stafford Court in the evening to find him and a group of friends sitting around the dining room table with a huge pile of cocaine in front of them babbling away to each other. Cocaine can make even quiet people loquacious.

I did not know much about cocaine in those days, as it was not as widely available as it is now, but I have since learned that cocaine is not a harmless 'party' drug, that can be used with impunity. It is a highly addictive insidious drug that can do irreparable damage to your health. Constant use of cocaine can affect your nervous system and make you paranoid, delusional, fearful and depressed. The reason there are so many skinny cocaine addicts is simply because it acts as an appetite suppressant. The drug also acts in a similar way to the amphetamine speed, and prolific users of cocaine can go days without sleep. Lack of food, lack of sleep, paranoia, delusions, fear and depression – any sensible person's body and mind deserves to be treated better than that. No temporary high, no matter how good you think it makes you feel, is worth those side effects.

When I moved to the United States in late 1979, the cocaine epidemic was just hitting full stride. During the six years I lived there, I did not go to one private party or even one business function – I am talking about the top end of town here – where cocaine was not used. It was everywhere. Because cocaine was so freely available when I lived in the States, I saw first hand the dangers of this addictive party drug. The sudden deaths of three friends of mine in San Francisco, who were only in their mid-forties but whom I knew to be heavy cocaine users, reinforced for me that besides being bad for your health, using cocaine on a regular basis could kill you very easily.

For someone who has been heavily involved in drugs since the 1970s, my comments about the dangers of using cocaine may appear hypocritical. But I take the view that what I have written in this book are just my observations of the effects that drugs have had on people I know. At the end of the day it is up to the individual to decide whether they use drugs or not. Besides Clark, I witnessed first hand while living in San Francisco the ease with which cocaine can destroy even a healthy, hardworking, decent person.

In 1980 in San Francisco, I was introduced through mutual friends to a quiet, conservative accountant named Jeff. At the time I met him, Jeff was working for a prestigious San Francisco accounting firm, drove a luxury Porsche, owned his own apartment in downtown San Francisco, had a wide circle of friends and was in excellent health. A keen tennis player, for over a year we would get together every Saturday morning for a game of tennis, playing either singles or doubles. In early 1982 Jeff started using cocaine. Who got him started, or why he started, I do not know. All I know is that by the end of 1982 he was badly addicted to cocaine. By mid-1983 he was no longer playing tennis with me, had lost his job, his car, his apartment, his friends and his self-respect. After I was arrested in March 1984 in San Francisco, I was held, pending extradition to Australia, in San Francisco County Jail. About a year after my arrest, the jail chaplain came to my cell one day to pass on a message to me from a prisoner being held a few floors below, on drink driving and drug possession charges. Even though he had just been beaten up and had his shoes taken off him by other inmates, the barefooted prisoner wanted the chaplain to pass on his regards and good wishes to me. The prison inmate was my old tennis partner Jeff. Despite my own uncertain future at that time, I felt a strong sense of sadness at my friend's dramatic fall from grace. The sobering story of what happened to my friend Jeff only highlights how deceptively easy it is for anyone to become addicted to cocaine.

Terry Clark's slow disintegration from prolonged cocaine use was a real lesson to me. From being an entrepreneurial, street-smart, switched-on and fit criminal, he had become a loose and talkative cocaine addict surrounded by like-minded individuals. Even if you are a criminal who is not using drugs and a teetotaller, it is extremely difficult to stay one step ahead of the law. You can count on one hand the criminals I have known over the last 50 years who have managed to do so. But any active criminals who use drugs or are heavy drinkers may as well book their jail cells now, because sure as I'm typing this, that is where they will end up.

I can still remember the night when I really observed for myself how Clark's cocaine use was affecting him. It was about ten days before my birthday that Martin Johnstone flew in from Singapore with his latest love interest, an English girl named Julie Hue. When Clark called me on the afternoon of Martin's arrival to tell me he was in town for a brief visit, I said I would drop over to say hello that evening. Since acquiring my .32 automatic from cousin Luigi, I did not have any concerns for my safety whenever I had to meet Clark. The comforting feel of a gun nestling against the small of my back gave me all the confidence I needed. That evening as I arrived at Clark's Stafford Court apartment, I was sober, alert and armed. When I walked into the apartment, it was all, 'Jim's here,' from both of them. 'How are you mate?' All handshakes and backslaps, just like we three were one, big, happy family. But as they say, appearances can be deceiving, because I now know that even then Clark was already plotting to kill Martin Johnstone and me.

Although it was only 9pm, the two of them were already well and truly stoned. On the dining room table in front of them was a small mound of cocaine. While I was there, they each made lines of cocaine on the table, then used rolled-up £20 notes to snort the cocaine up their noses. A quote later made famous by the American comedian and actor Robin Williams would not have been out of place here: 'Cocaine is God's way of saying you have too much money.' I later learnt that the reason Clark had such an abundant supply of cocaine was because he had been swapping a pound of heroin for a pound of cocaine with English drug dealers. The conversation when I arrived was about the Wilsons. As I sat opposite them at the dining room table sipping on a cold beer, I heard all the chilling details about how Clark lured the Wilsons to their deaths.

The cocaine he was snorting had caused Clark to become very talkative and loose. The thing that really struck me as I listened to Clark complain to Johnstone about the Wilsons' murders was that he was depicting himself as the aggrieved party. Despite knowing I had counselled him against killing the Wilsons, Clark spoke to

Johnstone as if I was not in the room. I could have been a concrete post sitting there for all the notice they took of me. From what Clark told Johnstone, I ascertained that before the Wilsons set off on their first trip to Victoria, he had given them one-half of a torn $5 note. The trip was ostensibly to set up a heroin sale for Clark. So they would know they were meeting the right person, the Wilsons were told the contact of Clark's they were going to meet down there would have the other half of the torn banknote. Evidently, if Franco Tizzoni is to be believed, the shooter – James Bazley – hurt his arm in an accident the same day they left Sydney and could not make the arranged rendezvous, so the Wilsons returned to Sydney. Five days later, the Wilsons set off again in their green Toyota Celica for the long trip to Victoria. This time, the shooter with his half of the torn banknote was waiting for them, as was a shallow grave in lot 59 Danny Street, Rye. To prove the Wilsons had been executed, Clark said before he left Australia he was given back the two halves of the $5 note.

As Clark was recounting his litany of complaints to Johnstone, Marty would interject after every sentence with either, 'It's a fucking shambles' or 'It's a fucking disaster.' His responses seemed to make Clark even more upset about what had happened.

'They were supposed to be put through a fucking meat grinder,' he lamented to Johnstone. 'You know I gave specific instructions for the shooter to kill their dog. When I made inquiries as to why the dog had not been shot. You know what I was told?' a clearly indignant Clark complained to Johnstone. When Johnstone just shook his head and looked at him, Clark continued, his voice full of contempt: 'The motherfucker would not shoot the dog because, as he put it, the dog had not given anybody up. Can you believe that, a fucking moral hit-man, he kills two people but will not shoot a dog?' I remember Clark kept shaking his head in disgust as he sat there.

Unlike the two of them, I was stone cold sober as I sat there listening to both of them, between snorts of cocaine, raving on about what they had done in the past, and what they intended to do in the future.

As they dissected the murder of their late friend Doug Wilson and his wife, I could not help but reflect again on the saying: 'With friends like these, who needs enemies?' That thought was running around my head when Clark suddenly laughed and said to Johnstone: 'Well at least the shooter did one thing I asked for.' When Martin asked him: 'What was that?' a no longer morose Clark said: 'On the tapes I listened to, you could hear the Queensland jacks reassuring Doug that no one outside the room would ever find out what he had told them.' He was chuckling in a sadistic manner as he told Johnstone: 'I specifically asked that the shooter tell Doug before he shot him that someone did find out.' The sick bastard was actually smirking as he said: 'I was assured that at least that request was carried out.'

That was enough for me, I got up from my chair and said I was heading home. The bile I had from listening to Clark ranting about how he had helped facilitate the Wilsons' murders was too much. I was a tough man back in those days, I had seen and done many terrible things in my life up until then, but having friends killed in a sadistic way was not among them. It wasn't as if I got suddenly moral, it was just the way Clark had chuckled as he recounted the last words Doug Wilson had heard before being shot dead that really sickened me. All of a sudden, I was bitterly regretting giving Clark my word that I would stay on in London until all his heroin in Australia was sold. For those people wondering why I did not just pack my bags and leave on the first available flight instead of hanging around until all Clark's heroin had been sold in Australia, at that time in my life that simple solution wasn't available to me. Up until then I had lived by my own crooked code of ethics. Despite being a convicted criminal within the confines of the criminal underworld, I regarded myself as an honourable man. I had never given anyone up, I had never ripped off anyone who worked with me, and my word was my bond. Once it was given, for better or worse, that was it. Stupid, I know, but that is how I lived my life back then. As I walked out of the apartment I told them I would call back the next day, but they were both oblivious to what I was saying and even that I was going.

They were too busy snorting more lines of cocaine through their rolled up £20 notes.

The following morning after a good night's sleep, I went for a brisk 40-minute jog around Regent's Park. After getting cleaned up and having a breakfast of bacon and eggs – cholesterol levels were not as important back then – I got dressed and called a cab to take me over to Knightsbridge. Before the cab arrived, I made sure my gun was tucked snugly against my back, inside the waistband of my trousers, under the jacket I was wearing that day. Even though it was already summer in England, I still required a jacket. It was around 10.30am when I arrived back at Clark's apartment. The main reason for me going over to his place that morning was so that I could talk to Johnstone. I was giving some serious thought to putting together a large shipment of buddha sticks for both the Australian and NZ markets. I thought Martin might be someone I could work with, or at the very least, someone I could use as a conduit to acquiring such a large quantity of buddha sticks in Thailand. What I saw when I arrived at Clark's apartment immediately cancelled out that plan.

When I walked back into Clark's apartment, it was as if I had not left: the two of them were still sitting in their exact same seats at the dining room table. The only difference was that the mound of cocaine was nearly gone. They both looked dishevelled, were unshaven, had bloodshot eyes and were nearly incoherent when they spoke. Oh how the mighty have fallen, I thought. I remembered Martin Johnstone as he was when I first met him in Auckland five years previously. He was tall, handsome, well dressed, spoke well and had a confidence about him that only money can give. The Terry Clark I introduced to Bob Trimbole in 1977 was sober, street smart, well dressed, fit and healthy and did not use drugs. Now here they both were, hardly able to put a sentence together. Any thoughts I may have had of working with Johnstone in Thailand were shelved immediately. Any doubts I may have had about cutting my ties with Clark were also set aside that morning. Looking at the two of them sitting there after their cocaine-fuelled night, I could not help but think to myself, this is a disaster waiting to happen. It would take only three months for that thought to become a reality.

For Martin Johnstone, that cocaine binge with Terry Clark at his apartment would be the last time they ever partied together as friends. As he sat with Clark that night, most of his money gone on foolish business ventures, it must have been extremely humiliating for Marty. Here, sitting alongside him, was a man whom he had delegated to sell on his behalf the 450,000 buddha sticks that he, Martin Johnstone, had successfully smuggled into New Zealand aboard the yacht *Brigadoon*. Now, three years later, their roles were completely reversed. A man who once worked for him was now calling the shots, and there was absolutely nothing he could do about it.

Those sun-filled days just fifteen months earlier at the Hyatt hotel in Fiji, when the three of us got together with Chinese Jack Choo to plan our future moves, must have seemed a lifetime ago for Martin. Although he did not know it, when I saw him that morning, Martin Johnstone's brief career as a drug dealer–drug importer–businessman was nearly over. Life can indeed be cruel sometimes, because my last memories of Martin Johnstone are of him as incoherent, dishevelled, bleary-eyed and drug affected.

31

AN ITALIAN,
A LAWYER AND
A PIMP

It must have been a few weeks before my birthday in July 1979 that Bob Trimbole came over to London to see Terry Clark and myself. His visit was ostensibly to discuss with us whether we still wanted to invest in his casino project in Sydney. According to Bob, the news about the casino was positive – as long as George Freeman got a piece of the action, he would not stand in the way. The police were onside Bob told us, so it was all systems go. Although Clark was still keen on being involved in Bob's casino project, I had gone cold on the concept. I guess Clark saw Bob's casino project as a natural fit for any future drug deals they might do. Money earned by either of them through selling drugs could then quite easily be channelled into the casino. That is how I would have viewed the casino project, and I'm sure Clark would have done likewise.

As I was in the process of severing all my ties with Clark, the thought of being involved with him in a business venture, no matter

how lucrative, was not an option for me. As I did not want to antagonise Bob who had been real helpful to me since I first met him on a
racetrack some two and a half years previously, however, I tactfully
declined his offer to participate in the project. I told Bob in a non-
judgemental way that since the Wilsons' bodies had been discovered
in Victoria, the landscape in Australia had fundamentally changed
for me and I was having reservations about investing in any further
projects back there. I explained to Bob that a few real estate projects I
was currently involved with in Australia were all being done through
companies controlled by me in Hong Kong. Those business interests
did not require my presence in Australia I told him, therefore, I was
just going to maintain the status quo with no more business investments until the current situation settled down.

I should point out that not all my dealings with Bob Trimbole
since I first met him had the proverbial happy ending. In April 1978
Bob approached me about a project he was starting and asked if I
wanted to become involved in it. After he ran the projected profit esti-
mates by me, that little green man called greed kicked in and I readily
handed over $100,000 as my share of start-up costs. By the end of
the year, that project would cost me a further $100,000. By February
1979, my $200,000 investment was like yesterday, history. I never got
a cent back. At the time, however, I figured that all the money I had
made with Bob at the races, not to mention all the fun I had winning
that money, more than compensated for my losses in our failed land
project. I fell back on a mantra that criminals know only too well:
'Easy come, easy go.'

Besides wanting to talk to Bob about the casino project, I'm sure
Clark would have been extremely anxious to find out personally from
him what had gone wrong with disposing of the Wilsons' bodies.
Because I have read many trial transcripts over the years relating to
the Wilsons' murders, as well as numerous transcripts from different
inquiries into their murders, including the Stewart Royal Commission, I
cannot defend my old friend Bob Trimbole from all the accusations that
have been made against him about his involvement in arranging their

murders. Although there was only ever one witness – Franco Tizzoni – who actually said Bob Trimbole was involved in arranging the deaths of Donald Mackay and Doug and Isabel Wilson, the circumstantial evidence against Bob was fairly strong and I have no doubt he would have had a hard time proving his innocence in a court of law.

As far as me not being aware of what was going on around me – I refer of course to Bob Trimbole getting involved with Clark's drug dealing operations as well as his assumed involvement in the Wilsons' murders – that was not an unusual circumstance for me back then. It was not as if I was making like an ostrich with my head in the sand, far from it, but it may be hard for some people to understand my reasons and explanations for not being aware of Bob Trimbole's business dealings with Clark. I was just following rules instilled in me since I was a boy of sixteen, locked up in Invercargill Borstal. Not questioning what other people did was simply the way I lived my life back then. I had been educated – both inside and outside prison – by older and more experienced criminals, who I respected, into some of the hard and fast rules they lived by. Rule number one: You never give anyone up or make a statement. Rule number two: You never rob or rip off any other crims. Rule number three: You never cooperate with the authorities, inside or outside prison. Rule number four: You must always operate on a need to know only basis. If you were not involved in something that had happened, then it was no business of yours to ask any questions. Rule number five: Never work with people you have not known for five years or more. Rule number six: Even if you know someone has committed a crime, you do not ask them about it. Rule number seven: Remember, loose lips sink ships, so never, ever, discuss your crimes with anyone. Rule number eight: If someone tries to tell you about a crime they have committed, tell them to shut up, you do not want to know what they have done because it is no business of yours. Rule number nine: Never call someone a 'dog informer' unless you are absolutely 100 per cent sure of your facts. Rule number ten and perhaps one of the most important: Always mind your own business. What Clark and Trimbole did or did not do together was their business, not mine.

I could quite easily go on, as there are many other lessons I was taught, but I think you get the picture. All I have tried to do, is give you some understanding, as to why I never questioned Bob Trimbole or Terry Clark about any criminal activity they may have been involved in. I came along in an era when there were many other criminals exactly like me. It is different today, of course. It seems to me that there is no respect, no honour and no loyalty among criminals today. I do not see any young versions of myself anywhere. In all the years I was in the NSW prison system, I never had one aspiring young criminal come up to me and ask me questions (like I did with Skip Gardiner), about how to try and stay one step ahead of the law; about banking systems; about educating yourself; about my contacts in the underworld. No one even asked me about the old rules I used to live by. Youngsters running around today seem to think they know it all, so now that I am officially retired, I will take all my hard-earned knowledge to the grave with me. I guess in the long run that is a good thing, because all my hard-earned knowledge never did me any good and I would not wish the life I have led on anyone.

While Bob Trimbole was in London, I took him to Ladbrokes casino and nominated him for a membership there. That nomination by the way, actually came back to haunt me seven years later when it was produced as evidence at my trial in 1986. You do not think about things that might incriminate you several years later, however, when you are out having a good time. I remember that night well because of the fact that the extremely popular NZ entertainer of that era, named Ricky May, was headlining the floor show at Aphrodite's Cabaret, located in Piccadilly Circus. Although a proud New Zealander, Ricky May lived and worked most of his life in Australia. I first met Ricky when he was sixteen years old singing in an Auckland nightclub owned by a friend of mine. For the life of me, I cannot remember the name of the club, but I certainly remember Ricky as being a brilliant entertainer even at that young age. My half-brother, Ron Cooper, who was also a musician and singer back then, was a good friend of Ricky's and that is how I stayed in touch with him while I was in Sydney. On a whim, Trimbole, Clark and myself decided we would catch Ricky's late show at Aphrodite's Cabaret. After handing out some largesse at the door, we managed to get a table right at the front of the stage. It was quite funny what happened after we sat down, because as Ricky started his show he looked down and saw me sitting there. After giving me a 'is that really you?' look, he acknowledged me with a surprised wave and a lovely smile. Whoever thought up the descriptive phrase 'a million dollar smile' certainly had Ricky May in mind. After his show, Ricky came and joined us. A few years later when Ricky would have learnt through the media about the life and crimes of the three men sitting drinking champagne with him that night at Aphrodite's Cabaret, I'm sure he would have had a quiet laugh to himself. When you are a well-known entertainer like Ricky May was, you meet a lot of real gangsters and would-be gangsters along the way at different entertainment venues. Meeting us would not have fazed Ricky. When Clark invited him back to Stafford Court for a late night drink, however, I discreetly shook my head towards Ricky and he got the message. 'Sorry guys, but I have to be on the golf course early,' was his tactful reply. Sadly, that night was the last time I ever saw Ricky May. He died of a heart attack before I got out of prison. There have been many entertainers come out of New Zealand who might have been better than Ricky May was, but there have certainly not been any who were more loved than he was.

I think it was only a day or two after our night out that Bob Trimbole headed back to Australia. As we shook hands before he left, I could sense there was something he wanted to say to me. There was a concern in his eyes as he looked at me before we parted. As he was walking away, Bob stopped, turned towards me and said in a cryptic voice: 'Watch your back, Jim.' I now know that Clark had raised with Bob while he was in London, his desire to get rid of me permanently. You can bet your bottom dollar that had Bob Trimbole, (as he wanted to do before he left London), made me aware of Clark's intent to have me killed, I would have killed him first. It was not my style to run around shooting people back then (I carried a gun strictly for my own protection), but if it came down to a matter of life or death and it was my life on the line, I did not have any qualms with killing the person who was trying to kill me. As I have said on previous occasions in this book; in the dog-eat-dog mentality that exists at the top in the drug world, it is kill or be killed. One thing's for damn sure, had I been aware of Clark's evil intentions towards me, I would not have accepted his invitation to travel to Los Angeles with him a month later.

When I told Clark in late August that I was thinking of flying over to the States to make a pilgrimage to Las Vegas, he told me that he and his family were travelling over to Los Angeles around the same time for a holiday. He suggested we travel together and stay as a group at the Beverly Hilton. As I had nothing concrete to go on at that stage except my own vague feelings of unease about Clark's intentions towards me, I decided to travel over to the States with him and his family. The trip over was uneventful, although what happened after we arrived was anything but.

For Clark, the trip to Los Angeles was both a personal and business disaster. Oh what a wicked web we weave! All the cocaine he had been constantly using up until then started to seriously affect his thinking. That is the only logical explanation to his bizarre behaviour at the Beverly Hilton that I can come up with. I do not know what he was thinking at the time, but he had four different women staying on different floors at the hotel. In his suite on the ground floor he had Maria and his son Jarrod staying with him. On the first floor he had his first wife and his two children from that marriage visiting him from New Zealand. That visit was purely so that he could see his kids. On another floor he had Karen Soich, who had given up her blossoming law career and flown in from New Zealand – unbeknown to Clark's de facto wife – to ostensibly start a new life with him and, in her eyes, live happily ever after. The fourth woman he had staying at the hotel was an aspiring actress from London named Jane or Janice, who had visions of making it in Hollywood. I believe she left the hotel after a couple of days so I never got to meet her. Where and how he met this lady I do not know.

What a fucking shambles that hotel stay was. On the ground floor Clark and Maria were constantly bickering and arguing; on the first floor Clark's first wife was complaining about his lack of attention towards his two children; and on another floor – unbeknown to me – Karen Soich wanted to know when he was going to end his relationship with Maria! The aspiring actress, having got a free airline ticket to La La land, did not stay around to argue with anyone but she simply said adios amigo, packed her bags and left.

While all this mayhem and madness was going on in Clark's life, I was enjoying myself in Los Angeles. A friend of mine from New Zealand had given me the phone number of his sister – who used to be an international model – who was then living in Los Angeles. As she and her son lived only a short distance from the hotel, I was able to hook up with her fairly easily. She turned out to be a wonderful lady. While I was in LA she took me all over the city, showed me some lovely out of the way spots that tourists never get to see and took me out to some fabulous restaurants. Besides being tall, tanned, curvaceous and very attractive, my friend's sister had smarts and a great personality. Although we had a great time together while I was in LA, she just treated me as a friend of her brother's and nothing more.

The reason I didn't head off to Las Vegas as soon as I arrived in the States was money. I had to wait for a money transfer through a Swiss bank located in the city. When the money finally arrived, (four days later), I told Clark I would be back in three or four days, checked out of the Beverly Hilton and headed off to the glittering neon lights of Sin City, Las Vegas. As a cab took me from the airport to the MGM Grand hotel and casino, located in the heart of the Las Vegas gambling strip, I silently ticked off another one of the destinations I used to dream about in my prison cell. I was on such a high about making it to Las Vegas, that I did not even mind the fact that I lost all my money while I was there on that first trip. Crazy I know, but for someone who had walked to school in his bare feet, just being in Las Vegas, the mecca for all serious gamblers, was my version of heaven.

Because Ladbrokes in London had notified the MGM Grand casino management that one of their high rollers was heading over to Las Vegas, they welcomed me with open arms. Whoever created the phrase 'a fool and his money are soon parted' surely had me and the millions more like me – who think they can win money in Las Vegas – in mind when they coined those words! Within two days I had lost all my hard-earned cash and was on the phone to my accountant in Hong Kong to send more money to me via another bank in Los Angeles. I had so much difficulty getting my money out of the Swiss bank I first used that I decided to go to another more accommodating bank.

My first foray to Las Vegas had been a losing one. It would take two more losing gambling trips to Las Vegas after I moved to the States before the penny finally dropped. At that point of time in my life I considered myself a lucky gambler, so for me to do my money cold on three separate occasions, signalled to me very clearly that the boys in Las Vegas were too hard to beat. Once I came to that conclusion, I decided to never gamble seriously in Las Vegas again. I notified the casino of my decision and they took me off their free comp list. That calculated decision meant that whenever I ventured to Las Vegas during the six years I lived in the States, I had to pay for my accommodation and meals like normal punters do. As many people would be aware, the entertainers and entertainment available in Las Vegas casinos is second to none in the world. So what I learnt to do while I was living in the States, was to read the *Variety* show-business newspaper to see what acts were headlining the different casinos on any given week. When I noted in the *Variety* that there were four or five great acts appearing in Las Vegas at the same time, I would simply jump on a plane – usually with a lady – and fly there for a week of fun. No gambling, just sunbathing, drinking, you know what else and catching all the shows.

Although my first trip to that fabled city ended with me leaving broke, I still left with a smile on my face. I had finally made it to Las Vegas; another dream realised. But before I got the complimentary bus to the airport on the morning of my departure, I had to ring my friend's sister in Los Angeles to come and pick me up on arrival at Los

Angeles airport, because I did not have enough money in my pocket to pay for a cab to the bank in Century City where I had some money waiting for me.

To get away from Clark and his complicated domestic life, I checked into the Beverly Wilshire hotel, which is just across the road from Rodeo Drive in the heart of Beverly Hills. When I went over to the Beverly Hilton to see Clark, I got the shock of my life when Karen Soich answered the door to his suite. With a big smile on her face she invited me into the suite with a cheerful: 'Hello Jim, how are you?' To say she looked like the cat that had just swallowed the cream would have been an apt way to describe her that day. I hid my astonishment well, but I have to say, I was completely gobsmacked by her unexpected appearance. What had happened to my friend Maria Muhary? Evidently, while I was away in Las Vegas, Maria had decided that enough was enough, she was sick of competing with other women and she was taking their son Jarrod and returning to New Zealand. That is the gist of what Clark told me anyway. Although he later told friends that he would never have hurt Maria, even after she told him she was leaving him, I am inclined to doubt that statement. I believe it was only the fact that Clark was in an unfamiliar country that saved her from being murdered. In the United States Clark had no access to weapons, no support systems if he wanted to kill someone and no familiarity with Los Angeles at all. I am sure all these factors would have influenced Clark's decision not to kill Maria and to agree, albeit reluctantly, to let her return to New Zealand with his beloved son.

If I needed any more convincing that Clark was losing the plot, a LA pimp named Benjamin 'Benji' Bennet, supplied it for me. Not satisfied with all the women he was currently involved with, Clark went out and picked up an unattractive black hooker named Roxy. As a further indication of how erratic his behaviour had become, after taking this scrubber back to his hotel suite at the Beverly Hilton, he sent her out to buy some cocaine for him. Being a street-smart whore, Roxy immediately rang her pimp, Benji Bennet, to notify him about this rich client from New Zealand staying at the Beverly Hilton hotel, who had more money than sense. After acquiring some poor-quality coke for Clark, the helpful Roxy offered to introduce him to her source, a man capable of accessing and purchasing large quantities of cocaine if required: Benji Bennet. The mere fact that Clark was even talking to a prostitute he had just picked up on the street about buying large amounts of cocaine emphasises very clearly how irrational his thinking had become. The Clark I first met in 1975 would not even have spoken with this woman, let alone slept with her. As for Benji Bennet, Clark would have immediately picked him for what he was, a cheap pimp and a fraud.

Those two, particularly Benji Bennet, played Clark beautifully for three days, treating him like the unsuspecting mug he had become. The first time I became aware of Benji Bennet was after I returned from Las Vegas and Clark asked me if I would accompany him to a meeting with a high-level drug dealer. No more details were forthcoming about this meeting when he asked me, but I nevertheless agreed to do so. The convoluted reasoning behind my presence was the fact that Clark wanted to let this so-called drug dealer see that he was not alone in Los Angeles. For some reason we had to meet the guy out at LA airport. When Benji Bennet arrived in his car to pick Clark up, I was to just stand there looking like a pseudo bodyguard. Now if you knew me back then and were aware of my criminal background and reputation, despite my lack of size and height you would have considered me as someone to be reckoned with. However if, like Benji Bennet, you were seeing me for the first time, standing on the footpath outside one of the airline terminals there, I doubt very much that I would have invoked any fear in him, or anyone else for that matter. Nevertheless, I went through with Clark's charade. After Clark shook hands with Benji the pimp on the sidewalk, just 20 metres from where I was standing, he gave me a little wave to indicate all was well, then climbed into Benji's pimpmobile and they drove off.

There were two things that struck me about the guy straight away. The first was his car. Although Benji the pimp was driving a brown Rolls Royce – more than likely borrowed – it was a very old model that looked like it had seen better days and not the type of car an affluent drug dealer would own or drive. The second was his clothes. He was wearing a garish red suit and yellow shoes. I can be accused of many things, but doing drug deals with someone dressed in a red suit and wearing yellow shoes is not one of them. The guy, to me, looked exactly like what he was, a two-bit pimp. As I stood at a cab rank waiting for a cab to take me back to my hotel, I could only shake my head in complete bewilderment at Clark's decision to go off with someone he had just met to buy drugs. His behaviour went against everything I had been taught over the years, particularly rule number five; the rule about only doing business with people you have known for five years or more.

When I saw Clark the following afternoon, he definitely looked the worse for wear. Despite the fact he was suffering from lack of sleep and was in a bad mood, I decided to raise the subject of Benji the pimp with him. I started by telling him it was utter madness to be dealing with someone he had just met and did not know. Furthermore, I told him, the guy did not look like a prosperous drug dealer to me. When Clark told me he had already parted with $10,000 to get Benji the pimp on side during their supposed negotiations, I could only look at him in utter disbelief at his foolishness. Although I did not know much about cocaine at that time, a friend of mine familiar with the drug had told me while we were chatting about drugs one day about a cheap way to test the purity of any cocaine I might be interested in buying. The quickest and easiest test, he explained to me, was to simply get a glass of water, drop a small amount of cocaine into the water and watch it dissolve. If the cocaine left a trail of oil in the water as it sank to the bottom of the glass and dissolved completely, then you could be assured that was good cocaine. If the cocaine you were testing had been cut with something else, then you would see after the cocaine had dissolved small sediment lying on the bottom of the glass. As Clark still had some of Benji the pimp's cocaine sample left, I applied my friend's water test to a small amount. Before dropping the cocaine into the glass of water, I explained to Clark how the process worked. I cannot say I was surprised when I saw a lot of white sediment at the bottom of the glass after the cocaine had dissolved. 'I'll be damned,' was all Clark could say. If this guy wanted to sell him any more samples, I suggested to Clark that he go to one of the drug paraphernalia shops located around Los Angeles and buy himself a 'hot box' – a drug-testing kit that uses heat to measure the purity of drugs – so that he could use a heat test himself to measure the purity of any cocaine the guy might give him in the future. My simple water test on the cocaine sample he had acquired from Benji the pimp, spurred Clark into action and he went out and brought himself a 'hot box'.

Interestingly, he had Benji with him when he bought the gadget from a shop in the seedy run-down area of Hollywood. The presence of a hot box did not slow slippery, smooth-talking Benji the pimp down for one minute, however. Although unable to buy or produce even one kilo of cocaine for Clark, the pimp never stopped trying to con him. After going out and acquiring with Clark's money another ounce of cocaine from his supposed connections, Benji the pimp was not fazed when a heat test on his latest sample showed it was only 50 per cent pure. 'The bastards are trying to rip me off,' he told Clark in an indignant voice. I have to give the guy an A for effort, because he then told Clark he had another more reliable source he could rely on. This source had access to large amounts of cocaine and if Clark gave him the money required, he would go and get another ounce sample immediately. When Clark repeated Benji the pimp's comments back to me a few hours later I did not comment on what he said, I just thought to myself, The sooner I'm out of here, the better. The man standing before me was a mere shadow of the clearheaded, calculating, and street-smart individual I had met four years previously. That man would not have pissed on Benji the pimp, even if he saw him lying in the street on fire. Now here he was trying to do deals with him!

It took Clark another two days before his drug-addled brain finally realised that Benji the pimp had played him for a fool. As soon as he reached that conclusion, he changed hotels and had no further contact with Benji Bennet. Unfortunately for Clark, that would not be the last time he saw Benji the pimp. The next time they saw each other, one would be in the dock and the other in the witness box. As for myself, as soon as I got back to my hotel on the evening Clark told me about the 50 per cent purity heat test, I booked myself a first class flight back to London, leaving the next day.

The true extent of Benji the pimp's dealings with Clark while he was in LA were revealed at his trial, when Bennet was flown in from the United States to give evidence against him at his murder and drugs trial in Lancashire in England. At one time early in his criminal career, Clark had been a police informer, so I guess that old saying 'what goes around, comes around,' would have been apt here. Besides being a two-bit hustler and pimp, when it suited him Bennet was also a part-time police informer. His handler was a Los Angeles detective named Roger Fiderio, who had known Bennet since 1974 when he investigated a series of burglaries that a drug dependent Bennet had been involved in. Through Detective Fiderio's intervention on his behalf, Bennet was given a reduced sentence and allowed to serve his two year prison sentence at the California Drug Rehabilitation Centre. After his release in 1976, Bennet would meet with Fiderio at least once a month for coffee and a chat. Over a period of time, Fiderio became both a father figure and a police confessor to Bennet. How many men Bennet put away through his work as an informant I do not know, but I would hazard a guess and say it was many.

On 2 October, a few weeks after Clark had returned to England, Bennet met Fiderio at Loves Steak restaurant situated on La Cienega Boulevard, in the Venice district, for lunch. Over lunch, Benji the pimp casually mentioned to his handler his recent dealings with a wealthy NZ drug dealer. Although investigating international drug dealers was outside his area of expertise or his immediate department's operations, Fiderio was aware that his new divisional captain, Charles Dahlberg, had recently come from the Administrative Narcotics Division. This elite investigative drug division of the LAPD operated outside normal department protocols and only dealt with major drug dealers. Sensing an opportunity for himself, Fiderio called his divisional captain, Charles Dahlberg, to pass on the information that Bennet had just told him. On hearing what Fiderio had to say about this wealthy NZ drug dealer, Dahlberg rang a detective named Fea who had worked under him at the Administrative Narcotics Division to pass on the information he had just received. The phone call from his old boss so intrigued Fea that before Fiderio and Bennet had finished their lunch, he had raced from downtown Los Angeles out to the restaurant in Venice to join them. He wanted to hear for himself about this big-spending NZ drug dealer going by the name of Peter Heyfron.

To further illustrate how rash and careless Clark had become, he had even given Benji the pimp his London telephone number! Now that is a real no-no. If you are an active criminal, you simply do not hand out your phone number to people you have just met. Rather than hand out your number, you get theirs and tell them that you will give them a call very soon. Now that he had a London telephone number to corroborate Bennet's information, Fea asked him to call the London number. Using his police badge to get the restaurant management's assistance, he was able to listen in on another phone as Bennet rang Clark's London number. The first call went unanswered because there was no one at the apartment, however, Detective Fea, using Fiderio's influence, got Benji the pimp to call the London number again that evening. This time Karen Soich answered the phone. When Benji the pimp asked for Peter Heyfron, she replied that no one by that name lived there. Despite Soich's denial of a Peter Heyfron living at that London address, sensing he was onto something, the persistent Fea rang Scotland Yard in London to see if any of their police officers knew anything about a NZ drug dealer named Peter Heyfron. After being assured by a police officer in the criminal intelligence section at Scotland Yard that they had never heard of a NZ drug dealer named Peter Heyfron, Fea let the matter drop.

The murder and subsequent discovery of Martin Johnstone's body a short time after Detective Fea's phone call to London brought Clark back into the picture. After Clark was arrested and the English police were compiling a case against him, an alert officer from Scotland Yard remembered the strange call he had from a LA drug squad detective inquiring about a NZ drug dealer named Peter Heyfron. When the name Peter Heyfron was identified as one of Clark's many aliases, Fea was contacted in Los Angeles and asked what their informant might know about a certain Clark/Heyfron. For the price of a plane ticket to London, a new conservative suit, shirt and tie, plus a shitload of brownie points with the LA police, their informant was ready to tell the English police all he knew. There would be no red suit and yellow shoes when Bennet got in the witness box against Clark, because that would not do for an English courtroom.

The evidence the new, improved Bennet gave at his trial once again highlighted how Clark's addiction to cocaine had seriously affected his thinking and judgement. In the witness box, Bennet told the jury how Clark, in order to impress him, had shown him copies of bank balances from Singapore and Hong Kong that had millions of dollars in them. He was also shown bank drafts worth tens of thousands. While snorting cocaine together, Clark had told him all about his drug activities in Australia, how he used couriers, how he bribed police, how big he was, how much heroin he had sold and all the millions he had made. He told the jury how Clark had offered him $5000 a week to work for him. After a little haggling he also told the jury with a smirk on his face, he had even managed to con an advance of a week's wages out of Clark. In the cold light of day and the austere surroundings of an English courtroom, particularly a packed English courtroom, hearing your drug-induced boasting being repeated back to you by a two-bit pimp informer must have acutely embarrassed Clark. I know without any shadow of a doubt that had that happened to me, I would have been so embarrassed, I would have just asked someone to go and get me a rusty razor blade or a length of rope, because that's what I deserved.

All that embarrassment, however, was still ahead of Clark when he arrived back in London from his disastrous holiday trip to Los Angeles. The fallout from that LA trip must have affected Clark both psychologically and personally. He had left London for LA with his long term de facto wife Maria Muhary and his beloved son Jarrod and returned without them. His first wife had flown back to New Zealand, extremely disappointed with his lack of attention to his first family. Losing his son Jarrod would have hurt him the most, but allowing himself to be conned out of a lot of money by a two-bit pimp like Benji Bennet would have run a close second. The only positive for the trip was the fact that his latest love, Karen Soich, had now joined him for the last leg of his journey.

Although neither of them knew it at that time, they would only have a few months together before their world would suddenly come crashing down. For Clark, his last few months of freedom would be spent in a continuous haze of drugs, booze and gambling. The Terry Clark I met in 1975 may have been able to elude the police net that was slowly but surely closing in on him in late 1979, however, the drug-addled man I shook hands with for the last time in September 1979 stood no chance. I heard a London police officer who was involved in Clark's arrest in November 1979 reveal on a television program that they could not question Clark for two days after his arrest, because he was that badly affected by the drugs he had been using. I can say from personal experience that there is not a more sobering, cold or depressing feeling than waking up in a police cell and realising you are not dreaming.

32

LAST DRINKS FOR THE MR ASIA SYNDICATE

When I arrived back in London from my pilgrimage to Las Vegas, I received the phone call from my man John in Sydney that I had been waiting three months for. All Clark's product had been sold and, thankfully, my obligations to him and Chinese Jack Choo were now ended. As soon as Clark got back from the States I called around to see him and gave him the news. I told him the boys back in Australia had successfully moved all his product and were ready, if he wanted, to continue working with him. His noncommittal reply to my offer on John's behalf led me to speculate that Clark was already looking at moving in another direction. During our meeting he made a half-hearted appeal for me to stay on and work with him in London, an appeal I prudently declined. I have made many mistakes and bad decisions in my life, but turning down Clark's offer to stay in London and work with him was one of the best decisions I ever made.

It was not a difficult decision for me to make. Over the four years I had known him, it had become increasingly clear to me that Clark not only had a taste for killing people but he actually thought murder was the best way to solve his problems. Having been around a few homicidal psychopaths in my life, both inside and outside prison, I knew from personal experience how unstable, unpredictable and dangerous such men can be. The thought of constantly having to watch my back while I was around Clark was also a factor. The simple truth of the matter though was the fact that I did not like the man anymore, and no amount of money was going to change the way I felt.

One story highlights what I have just stated. Around the middle of 1979, I had a meeting with Clark and Martin Johnstone at Clark's apartment in Knightsbridge. The main topic of the meeting was Allison Dine. Both Clark and Johnstone were of the opinion she knew too much and could pose a danger to all of us. Although Allison Dine had been Clark's lover for over a year in 1978, she was discussed at this meeting like a used car they wanted to get rid of. I was surprised that Johnstone was also of the opinion she might have to go to safeguard the rest of us, because he never struck me as a man inclined towards violence. Because of his romantic involvement with her in 1978, Allison Dine clearly posed a dilemma for Clark and he was hesitant to act against her. Sensing Clark's reluctance, I made my position crystal clear; Allison had been a loyal member of the group, she had stood up to two police interrogations without breaking, therefore she did not deserve to die just because she knew too much. My argument was very simple: if we followed their line of thinking about people who knew too much then we would have to kill a lot of people.

The debate about whether Allison Dine should live or die went on for another ten minutes or so. Somewhat reluctantly, the other two rescinded any thoughts of having her killed. My argument about loyalty won the day. The irony of my impassioned plea on her behalf was this. After becoming an indemnified witness in 1980, Allison Dine was the main prosecution witness against me and was instrumental in me getting 25 years' hard labour. Despite that fact, I still do not regret standing up for her. The premise behind my argument still remains today. You do not kill someone just because you think they know too much. After that particular meeting though, I must admit the thought did cross my mind that if they were prepared to act against Allison Dine because of their belief that she knew too much, would not the same reasons apply to me also?

Because of that meeting and his subsequent erratic, cocaine-fuelled behaviour, leaving was not a difficult decision for me. One thing I really noticed about his behaviour before I left, was his newfound enthusiasm for gambling. I have to accept some culpability for introducing Clark to both the vagaries and excitement of gambling for high stakes. After my big win at Ladbrokes, Clark was intrigued as to how I had done it, so I invited him and Maria to have dinner with me at Ladbrokes to see the place for themselves. They were both suitably impressed by the meal we had in the casino's restaurant and totally amazed at the huge amounts of money being bet on the gambling tables in the casino itself. I think the glitz, the glamour, the huge amounts of money being wagered at the tables, plus the well-dressed people gambling at the tables, all made an indelible impression on Clark. He was captivated by all the colour and excitement inside the casino. Being a natural-born risk taker like most criminals are, he took to gambling like the proverbial duck to water. His first few bets that night were tentative; on the roulette table he was just betting £50 or £100 on a red or black number turning up. Like millions of other first-time gamblers before him who have been sucked in and gone on to become inveterate and hopeless punters, Clark had beginner's luck. If my memory serves me correctly, Clark won £700 that night just quietly gambling on the colours. He was that chuffed after winning, you would have thought he had won a million. I remember him standing there in the bar at Ladbrokes, his winnings in his pocket, a drink in one hand, a celebratory cigar in his other hand and saying to me with a smile on his face: 'How long has this been going on, Jim?'

Before we left the casino that evening, Clark nominated himself for a membership. As we both walked out the door of the casino that night, I should have said to Clark: 'Welcome to the mug punter's club mate,' because for the rest of his time in London, Ladbrokes casino would become his preferred option for a night out.

By the time I decided to leave London and slip quietly back into Australia, Clark and his cohorts were all out of control. The cocaine parties were becoming more regular and no one was taking care of business, and if you are a criminal that is a sure-fire recipe for disaster. The foundering ship called the Mr Asia syndicate was slowly going down, with all hands on board; I was about the only survivor who managed to get off that sinking ship! Because I was not using drugs like Clark and the rest of his crew, I was able to observe from the sidelines with a clear mind and eye just how dissolute and reckless he and his associates had become. When I told him in September that I was leaving England and intending to slip back into Australia for business and personal reasons, he did not object. The only questions he asked me about my trip were when would I be back and would I be seeing Bob Trimbole when I got there? On the first question, although I had no intention of returning to London, I said I would be back in about three weeks. To add some credibility to my story about returning, I left a false passport and some gold jewellery of mine with Clark for safe-keeping until I returned.

I solved the problem of what to do with my trusty Browning automatic pistol that had given me so much security and comfort while I was in London by returning it to cousin Luigi. The evening before I flew out of London, I caught a cab out to Hammersmith and knocked once again on cousin Luigi's dilapidated door. After his initial surprise at my proposal, he agreed to go along with it. I simply asked him to hold the gun for me until 25 December and if I had not returned by then, the gun was his. When I told cousin Luigi there was a strong possibility I would not be back, he was more than happy to accept my proposal. I would learn a week later from his distant relative in

Australia, Bob Trimbole, why Clark had been so keen to know if I was going to catch up with him in Sydney.

Although Terry Clark was only 35 years old when I shook his hand for the last time at his apartment in London, he looked at least ten years older. I guess the stress and the constant cocaine use, perhaps even his conscience, had worn him down. He looked tired, haggard and old. That is the lasting impression I have of the guy, a man old before his time. A life of crime is not the bed of roses some young people seem to think it is. The Clark I left behind in London was the perfect illustration of this fact. When I think back to our final farewell, I still shake my head in disbelief at his treachery and bare-faced duplicity as he said goodbye to me. I can say that now, because I have since learnt that before I left London, Clark had already made a call to Australia to try and arrange to have somebody kill me while I was back there. I remember that last goodbye like it was just yesterday. It is now obvious that he was only simulating concern as he shook my hand in a firm grip and said: 'Be very careful while you're there, Jim. I'll see you in three weeks when you get back.' Those were the last words he spoke to me and that was the last time I saw him. Since I had met Terry Clark, my life had irrevocably changed and not for the better. As I flew out of London I closed a chapter of my life that I still deeply regret.

Travelling under a passport bearing the assumed name of Richard Allen McDonald – a name I would travel under for the next six years – I had no trouble re-entering Australia through Perth. Once I cleared Customs, I caught a domestic flight to Adelaide and stayed there for a day while waiting for my friend John to arrive from Sydney in his car to pick me up. As I was keen to avoid Sydney airport at that time, I thought it would be more prudent to opt for the long drive back to Sydney by car rather than flying. After the miserable summer I had just spent in London, the warm September sunshine of an Australian spring day in Adelaide was a real joy. Although I was a long way from my usual haunts around Sydney, it felt great to be back in Australia. On the long drive across to

Sydney with my friend John, I told him of my decision to withdraw completely from any further involvement with Terry Clark and the Mr Asia syndicate. After hearing what I had to say about Clark's wild cocaine-fuelled parties in London and my considered assessment that the whole situation over there was a disaster waiting to happen, John agreed to cut all ties with the syndicate as well. And just like that, my old crew and I dissociated ourselves completely from Clark's foundering drug empire. My decision in September 1979 to finally stop working with Clark was both a personal and necessary one, but it was made two years too late. That belated decision did not stop the forces of law and order from pursuing me for five years, before finally arresting me in the United States. That old adage about the 'long arm of the law' was certainly very applicable in my case.

Although I had told Clark that I was returning to Australia for both business and personal reasons, the main reason for my risky trip back to Australia was a purely personal one. That personal reason was waiting for me in a Sydney hotel. For affluent criminals, along with the crime and big money come the attractive women, and plenty of them. Regrettably, my active criminal lifestyle did not make for long-term or meaningful relationships. My lifestyle meant that I could not, nor did not want to have ties with any women wanting a more settled and permanent relationship. When you live your life on the edge, that is just the way it has to be most of the time. So the relationships you forge are based on an unspoken understanding that you are there when you can be, the bills get paid, and clothing, expensive jewellery and holidays are all part of the package. The only stipulation you place on your arrangements is that the women you are involved with do not ask any probing or compromising questions about where your money comes from. Often the relationships are very superficial but that is the currency and everyone understands the trade-off. As a consequence, it is not surprising that when the going gets tough these women soon depart. Once the money disappears, it is very rare to see one of these relationships survive. Having seen this scenario played out many times, I knew how it worked and had no illusions about some of the women I saw regularly.

One of the supposedly long-term relationships I had – according to the Stewart Royal Commission – was with a woman I will call Tara. At the time it would have been described as an intermittent relationship of around three years. A very attractive and younger woman, I met Tara in an Auckland nightclub in 1976 and enjoyed her company whenever I was in New Zealand. For an unemployed office worker, I would have had 'Mr Opportunity' written all over me. For me, she was the required accessory for any successful criminal: an attractive woman. With her long dark hair, flashing brown eyes, olive complexion, sensual figure and good looks, she got my attention, off and on, for over three years.

Unfortunately for her or any women involved with me back then, I was incapable of sustaining a meaningful relationship or even remaining faithful to her. Despite the strong attraction I felt towards Tara I was, nevertheless, chasing after and sleeping with many other women, both in Australia and New Zealand. It took me many years to realise that no matter how hard I tried, or how many women I slept with, I could never catch up for all those barren lonely years wasted behind bars. Nevertheless, during the 1970s, like the proverbial dog trying to catch its tail, that's what I continually tried to do.

My cosy relationship with Tara was interrupted around August 1978, however, when I learnt that she had developed a bad drug habit. I did not know when I first met her in 1976 that she had been in a previous relationship with a man who had died of a drug overdose. It is not unusual to find that when one partner has a drug habit, so does the other one. Although she was clean when I first met her, a combination of factors – including the death of her sister in 1978 – precipitated her slide back into using heroin again. It shows how ignorant I was about drug addiction back then that I did not even know what tell-tale symptoms to look for – the nodding off while they spoke to you, the constant scratching, the slurred speech – when around a drug addict.

It was during a trip to Auckland in September 1978 that a criminal friend of mine who I respected, pulled me aside and informed me about Tara's heavy drug use. I do not mind revealing that I was shocked. Although we had grown apart and were not close at that stage, I still felt deeply concerned at hearing this disturbing information about her and more than a little guilty because of the fact that I was personally involved in selling the drug she was hooked on. When all you are doing is literally counting money, you are not personally affected, or do not see all the human misery that is caused by your involvement in selling heroin. So it was very confronting for me to suddenly find that someone I had been close to had developed a serious drug problem.

When I returned home to New Zealand for the last time in December 1978, Tara spent some time with me at my hotel in Auckland. While she was with me, it became obvious that she had a serious drug problem. Her once glistening hair had no sheen, her brown eyes were dull, her skin sallow and her speech slurred. The 23-year-old woman with a drug problem sitting at a table in my hotel room in December 1978 was a mere shadow of the vibrant, healthy, attractive young woman I had met in 1976. When I learnt that she had spent all her savings plus any money I had given her on drugs, I was able to hear and see for myself how being addicted to a drug you cannot control can leave you broke, destitute and desperate. My offer of assistance to enable her to enter a drug rehabilitation program was met with the mantra most heroin addicts use at one stage or another: 'I am going to beat this problem myself.' Before I left Auckland to return to Sydney, I sat Tara down and said if she ever needed help in getting clean, I was just a phone call away. A mealy-mouthed offer, I know, but the only excuses I can offer for my less than understanding behaviour are these facts.

I had never knowingly been involved before with a woman who had a drug problem, mainly because I have found that such women can end up being a liability. Therefore I was at a complete loss about how best to handle Tara's problem. Also, at that point in my life I had other extremely dangerous criminals to deal with. Unless you were an underworld figure or an active criminal in the 1970s, you would not have been aware of Linus Driscoll and his toe-cutter gang. These boys used to specialise in grabbing other criminals who had carried out successful crimes – armoured car robberies and so on – and then torturing them by cutting off their toes one by one with bolt cutters until the hapless crim revealed where his stolen money was hidden. Criminal folklore has it that a couple of criminals who successfully carried out a half million dollar armoured truck robbery in the early 1970s, were tortured in this manner until they each handed up their share of the take. After doing so, they were then murdered. One of them lies under the tarmac at Sydney airport to this very day. It is a measure of how tough Linus Driscoll – a man born in Liverpool, England, and later deported there – was that no one, inside or outside prison, was able to kill him. The guy was super violent and super tough. These were the types of criminals I was up against in the 1970s. In April 1978 I was extremely lucky to escape the botched attempt on my life. To add to that, while I was operating in Sydney, I also had other drug dealers looking to kill me if they could. And last but not least, I had honest police both in New Zealand and Australia to contend with. Because of all these factors, plus the fact that I was working with a confessed serial killer, my main focus at that time was simply protecting myself and staying alive. When you have to watch your back every day of the week, you just do not have the energy or motivation to worry about someone else's drug problem, even if that someone is a person who has been close to you. It's a terrible way to look at your priorities in life, I know, but self-preservation guided a lot of my decisions back then. Until I cut all my ties with the Mr Asia syndicate, I could not devote the time needed to effectively help Tara overcome her drug problems.

I think it was late in July 1979 that I made a phone call to Tara in New Zealand to find how she was. The despair in her voice was palpable as she asked for my assistance. I asked her if she was prepared to go through an extensive rehabilitation program then available in a well-known Sydney drug clinic that specialised in drug addiction. Her answer was a resounding 'yes'. After hearing her say that, I promised her I would pay for her airfare to Sydney and all her hospital expenses while she was undergoing treatment. As an added incentive for her, I also promised Tara that if she successfully completed the rehab program, I would travel back to Sydney to meet her and then take her with me on an extended holiday overseas as part of her recovery plan. Her treatment, coincidentally, was undertaken at the same private clinic the Wilsons had unsuccessfully used to try and cure their addictions. I forget how much her treatment cost me at the time but it was not cheap, however, it was money well spent as she came through the program with flying colours. She completed the program in late August and it was incumbent on me to honour my promises to her, hence my risky trip back to Australia. No doubt one of the few decent things I did back then.

I would later realise that doing the right thing by Tara had a totally unexpected but beneficial result for me. In fact, I still thank my lucky stars that I left London when I did, because the English police were able to ascertain that I left the country before Clark and Andy Maher actually started planning to kill Martin Johnstone. Because of this important fact, I could not be connected in any way with a personal involvement in the murder of Johnstone, like many of Clark's English associates were. I shudder to think what would have happened to me if I had accepted either of Clark's requests to work with him in the UK. There is no doubt that, had I stayed, I would have been arrested and charged along with the eleven other people who stood trial with Clark. And, more than likely, one of those charges would have been conspiracy to murder Martin Johnstone. Before being extradited back to Australia to face the charges I ultimately served a 25 year sentence for, I would have had to serve a twenty year sentence in one of those filthy, run-down, archaic English prisons. Bizarre as it may seem, for me, 25 years in an Australian prison was the lesser of two evils. I guess my good luck in returning to Australia when I did goes to show that even villains get rewarded for good deeds sometimes.

About a week after arriving back in Australia, I arranged through an intermediary to meet Bob Trimbole at a mutual friend's house in the Sydney suburb of Paddington. Out of respect for Bob I was not carrying a gun when I met him, but my friend John and another member of our crew – Earl – who were with me, were both armed. As I was not concerned about my safety with Bob, I asked my two friends to wait outside while I went into the house to talk with him. The first thing I noticed about Bob was his demeanour. He was not his usual jovial self, his lips were tightly pursed and he had the look of a deeply worried man. After warmly shaking his hand and telling him how pleased I was to see him, we went outside and sat down in a small pergola that had been erected in the middle of the lawn at the rear of our friend's house.

After sitting down opposite him, I immediately thanked Bob for helping me acquire a weapon in London through cousin Luigi. I was not surprised to learn that cousin Luigi was not a relative of Bob's at all, just the cousin of someone he knew. Whatever he was did not matter, I told Bob, the fact that he helped me meant everything. I was then pleasantly surprised when Bob told me that as yet, there had been no arrest warrants issued for me. Although the police were keen to speak to me, I was just a person of interest to them. Bob was of the opinion, however, that if they got their hot little hands on me I would not be seeing daylight for a long time. He suggested that I disappear overseas for a lengthy holiday. If and when the situation improved, he would let me know. I can clearly recall him then telling me in a concerned voice: 'Jim, the word I am getting from my police contacts is not good. There is a very strong push going on at the highest levels for a Royal Commission into drugs and the Wilsons' murders. If that eventuates then we will all have some serious problems to deal with.' When I told Bob that I was no longer involved with Terry Clark and I was seriously contemplating moving to the United States, I was surprised by Bob's reaction. He looked relieved as he said to me: 'That's a good move Jim, because there is something I have been wanting to tell you since I was in London.'

What Bob then proceeded to tell me at first sent a cold shiver through my body, closely followed by a searing bolt of anger. Terry Clark wanted me dead. My gut instincts about his intentions towards me while out hunting with him in the English countryside had been correct. As he leaned towards me, Bob put his hand on my forearm and said to me in a quiet voice: 'I was brought up to always honour a confidence. To never talk about anything told to me in secret. That is why it has been so difficult for me. While I was in London, Clark asked me if I knew anybody over there who could take you out. When I asked him why, he said you knew too much and could not be trusted.' While Bob was telling me this, I was seething with uncontrolled anger. Here I was, a man who had made millions for Clark, never robbed him of one gram of heroin or one dollar, yet he wanted me dead because I could not be trusted! I was still shaking my head in disbelief when Bob said in a disgusted voice: 'That is not all he wanted, Jim. Last week he called me and said if I was interested in working with him, I would have to show him how serious I was by arranging to have you killed and chopped up while you were down here.' I cannot remember the number of times I said, 'That motherfucker!' when Bob told me that additional information.

I thanked Bob profusely for his loyalty and friendship towards me. I told him I understood how hard it was for him to betray a confidence, but where friends are concerned I reiterated that was a different ball game. Anyone asking me to do damage to a personal friend better have a real damn good reason for wanting me to do so. What Bob said to me next is one of the reasons why, despite all his negative press, I will never say a bad word about Bob Trimbole: 'Jim, you were introduced to me by a personal friend of mine, as a close friend of his and someone to be trusted. Since I met you we have done some business together, made some money together, and I have come to like you. My friendship cannot be bought. Not by Terry or anyone else. I will never be involved in having a friend killed.'

I should point out again that with the passing of time I cannot remember word for word what was said between Bob and I that evening, but what I am relating here is not far off the mark. We spoke of other matters that evening, it is just that the information about Clark wanting me dead has remained etched in my memory. When I related to Bob what Clark had been doing since he visited us in London – in particular the LA trip and Benji the pimp, plus the drug-fuelled cocaine parties with his English cohorts in London – he ruefully shook his head. As I got up to leave, I shook Bob's hand and said to him: 'You have been a good friend to me, Bob. I will never forget that and I thank you. Now let me be a friend to you. I do not know what your arrangements with Clark are, it is none of my business. All I can say is this, the guy is a disaster waiting to happen. I would not do any fucking business with the man as he has lost the plot. Think twice before getting involved with this guy. I do not have to tell you how treacherous he is.' After thanking me for my advice, Bob asked me what I was going to do about Clark. I remember saying to him as I walked out: 'I'm going up the coast to relax for a few weeks with a lady friend, and while I am away I will give the matter some serious thought.' The last words Bob said to me as I walked out the door were: 'If Clark calls inquiring about you, I'll tell him you have gone to ground and no one has heard from you.' It was on that informative note that we parted.

When I got into John's car outside and told him and Earl what Bob Trimbole had just told me, they could not believe it. They were both as outraged as me. 'Are you fucking kidding?' was John's immediate response. Like me, both John and Earl were old-school criminals, men who still believed loyalty counted for something. If you did the right thing by them, they would do the right thing by you. Neither man would ever rip you off or try to rob you. Having said that, neither of them, or me for that matter, were the type of men you wanted to have as an enemy. I have no doubt that had it been possible that night, the three of us would have gone around to wherever Clark was and shot him. When John said to me in an indignant voice: 'You cannot let the arsehole get away with this, Jim!' I just repeated to him what I had told Bob Trimbole: 'I am going away up the coast for a few weeks, when I get back I'll let you know what I intend to do.'

The next two weeks were a mixture of sunshine, surf, sand and relaxation with Tara and her elder sister who had come over from New Zealand to help with her sister's rehab and was travelling with us. We travelled down the south coast of New South Wales and then on to Melbourne where we visited my friend Darryl Sorby. Although we enjoyed ourselves at each destination, I could not stop thinking about the threat posed to me by Terry Clark. As Tara did not know anything about my business – I never once divulged anything about my criminal activities to her – she was totally unaware of the emotional turmoil I was going through at that time.

What should I do? was the recurring thought running through my head. My thoughts were based around these four points: one, Clark wanted me dead therefore he was a threat to me; two, I had the distinct tactical advantage of knowing what his intentions were; three, now that I knew Clark wanted me dead I could simply walk away and disappear to the States; or four, I could take direct action against him myself. After a week of quiet reflection about what I should or should not do, I finally decided on option four.

I came to this decision because I did not like the thought of constantly having to look over my shoulder, no matter where I was. Another important factor in my decision was my anger at being marked for death by someone I had never done the wrong thing by. The man's treachery towards me was unforgivable in my eyes. As I have stated elsewhere in this book, if it came down to a matter of life or death and it was my life on the line, then I did not have a problem with killing the person who was trying to have me killed. When you are a hardened criminal, you cannot – like a normal person would – go to the police for help or protection. You have to solve your own problems, usually by violent means. Once I made up my mind on what course of action to take, I was able to enjoy the rest of my holiday with Tara and her sister.

On returning to Sydney in late October 1979, I met with Bob Trimbole for the last time. I did not know it at the time of our last meeting, but Bob had already been diagnosed with prostate cancer. He hid his illness well, because I had absolutely no idea he was suffering from a cancer that would eventually kill him. Rather than compromise Bob, I did not tell him of my real intentions as regards to Terry Clark. I just told him I was first heading off to Hong Kong to finalise some business, then travelling on to Hawaii for a long vacation. It was on a Sydney street corner just down the road from the old Arthur's nightclub in lower Crown Street that I said my final farewell to Bob Trimbole. I could not know then as I watched Bob walk briskly away into the warm Sydney night, a short-brimmed hat on his head and wearing his familiar three-quarter length fawn raincoat, that I would never see him again.

The arrest of Clark a few weeks after our last meeting, plus the setting up of the Stewart Royal Commission a few years later, changed both our lives dramatically. After that last meeting we would both travel in different directions and our lives would have different outcomes. In May 1981, just before Justice Stewart's Royal Commission into Drug Trafficking was to commence, Bob Trimbole quietly slipped out of Australia. For the next six years he would lead the life of a fugitive. His travels would take him to the United States and Europe, in particular France, where he lived in Nice on the French Riviera, then Ireland where he lived in the small coastal resort town of Westport, and finally Spain, where in a backwater town called Alicante, in May 1987, he finally succumbed to persistent ill health and died.

By the time of Bob's death, my journey through life had taken me first to the Far East and then on to the United States. After my arrest there in March 1984 and subsequent extradition to Australia in July 1985, in June 1986 I was sentenced to 25 years' imprisonment for drug importation. In late May 1987, I was sitting in the main prison yard at Parklea Prison, on the western outskirts of Sydney, when Nick Paltos, who before he was sentenced to ten years' imprisonment for smuggling hashish used to be Bob Trimbole's personal physician, walked over to me and gave me the sad news about Bob's death. As Nick and I reminisced about our mutual friend, I turned to him and said: 'He was a long way from home Nick, but at least Bob died a free man.' I can still remember Dr Nick smiling wistfully at me as he replied: 'Amen to that, Jim.' I did not shed a tear when I heard about Bob Trimbole's death, but in my cell that evening I said a silent farewell to a man I had come to like and respect.

I see from some old Customs records that I still have from my trial in April 1986, that using the name Richard McDonald I flew out of Perth on 25 October 1979. From the records I can ascertain that I arrived in Singapore the same day and stayed there, with Tara, until 30 October when we both flew on to Hong Kong. Apart from a brief visit to Macao, we spent the next week in Hong Kong. The main reason for my trip to Hong Kong was to enable me to set up through my accountant money transfer systems whereby money held by me in trust accounts in Hong Kong could be telexed to me whenever needed.

Once my business matters had been taken care of, I turned all my thoughts towards my decision to go after Clark in London. A plan of action had been slowly taking shape in my mind. Although very basic at that stage, my plan was predicated along these lines. I had a target, Clark; I had a weapon (with cousin Luigi); I knew where Clark lived and his movements; I needed to find accommodation and acquire some transport; I had to ensure that once the job was completed I could slip out of the country quietly and quickly; before leaving, my gun would have to be dismantled and the parts thrown away. Despite being a work in progress, I was very confident that whatever plan I came up with would succeed. My confidence was based around the simple fact that I had the huge tactical advantage of surprise. My one-time business associate did not know where I was; nor did he suspect I might come after him. I was also emboldened by a statistical fact that is irrefutable: gangland killings are rarely solved.

I have found that recalling my feelings and writing about my thought processes back then has been an interesting exercise for me. By revisiting my past, it has made me realise just how distorted my reasoning was at that time. I guess it would be fair comment to say that at that point in time, because of what I was prepared to do, I was not much better than Clark. Fortuitously for me, fate intervened before I could carry out my plan.

On 4 November I was ready to leave Hong Kong for London. Before leaving I rang my friend John in Sydney to notify him of my imminent departure for London. Being the solid, staunch, stand-up guy he was, when I told John before leaving Sydney what I intended to do about Clark, he immediately offered to fly over to London so that he could help me carry out my plan. Although it was my problem not his, I gratefully accepted his offer of assistance. By phone we had already made bookings at the same hotel in London for 6 November, so finding each other over there was not going to be a problem. As Tara was not aware of my intentions to fly to London, she was oblivious of the fact that I was not travelling to Hawaii with her. All I intended to do was give her enough money to live comfortably in Honolulu for ten days while I took care of my business in London. Once that had been successfully concluded, I planned to rejoin her in Hawaii.

As I was getting ready to go out to the airport to board a flight to London, I picked up a local English newspaper to browse through while drinking a cup of coffee. The caption at the bottom of the front page caught my attention immediately: 'Gang of New Zealand Drug Dealers Arrested in London'! There were no names mentioned in the article, but drugs and murder were quoted. The likelihood of another gang of Kiwi drug dealers operating in London at the same time as Clark was, in my estimation, extremely remote. Therefore I thought it prudent to immediately cancel my flight to London and remain in Hong Kong until I could find out the names of the drug dealers arrested in London. I did not have to wait long. The following day the same local English newspaper carried all the lurid details and names: Terry Clark, Errol Hincksman, Karen Soich, Andrew Maher, Freddy Russell, Leila Barclay, Sy Pigeon were all named. What a fucking unmitigated disaster!

I must confess that at the time I felt a huge sense of relief as I rang my friend John in Sydney to tell him about Clark's arrest. Although he never said so, I'm sure he was as relieved as me that Clark's arrest meant neither of us had to travel to London to carry out my plan. After spending a few more days in Hong Kong gathering additional information about Clark's arrest, I decided to head, with Tara, for the beautiful islands of Hawaii. On 8 November 1979 I flew out of Hong Kong, having changed my first class airline ticket to London for a first class airline ticket to Honolulu. Tara stayed with me another month before flying home to New Zealand for Christmas. Apart from a brief meeting in Fiji in 1980 and a visit she made to me at Long Bay Prison in 1985, I have not seen or heard from her since. Although she had some problems herself in the early eighties in New Zealand, a friend told me about ten years ago that she eventually got married and made a success of her life. I was really pleased to learn that.

I now know that while I had been in Australia with Tara and Bob Trimbole, in England Terry Clark and his hapless cohorts had played out the final acts of the Mr Asia syndicate. Like everything else associated with the Mr Asia syndicate from its inception, the end was violent, brutal and deadly.

33

ANATOMY OF A MURDER

If you are a big-game fisherman, often when you are trawling the waters for big-game fish like blue striped marlin or sharks, you throw what is called burley – bloody bait – into the water to attract these predators of the deep into the vicinity of your boat so that you can attempt to catch them. If you are a big-game hunter trying to shoot a tiger or leopard, one method of attracting the animals close enough so that the hunter can shoot them is to tether a goat to a stake then wait for a tiger or leopard to attack it. The bait used to lure Martin Johnstone to England from his Singapore base were two supposed Scottish drug dealers eager to buy large amounts of buddha sticks. According to Johnstone's best friend of several years, Andrew Maher, the only problem standing in the way of them all making a lot of money was the fact that the two Scottish drug dealers he had recently met wanted a face-to-face meeting with Johnstone. Like a hungry mouse eyeing off a tempting piece of cheese Martin Johnstone smelled money – big money – and in what proved a fatal decision for him, walked unwittingly into a baited trap.

Unfortunately for Maher, neither he nor his father's cousin, James Smith, who was with him the night he murdered Johnstone, were experienced big-game fishermen, or expert big-game hunters. Both of them were simply rank amateurs when it came to murder. Despite having served two tours of duty in Belfast with the Scots Guards, James Smith was no professional killer. Patrolling the dangerous streets of strife-torn Belfast in the 1970s was a far cry from killing someone in cold blood in the sedate and quiet, English county of Lancashire.

What was the motive that drove Andrew Maher to murder his friend of several years on 9 October 1979? Was Martin Johnstone trying to sleep with his de facto wife? No. Was Martin Johnstone trying to rob him? No. Did Martin Johnstone owe him money? No. Was Martin Johnstone trying to kill him? No. Had Martin Johnstone ever hurt him? No. Did his new boss Terry Clark want Martin Johnstone dead? Yes! That is the cold, unarguable truth about the whole treacherous decision to murder Martin Johnstone. Clark wanted Johnstone dead and Maher was the pliant and obedient henchman he used to carry out his wishes. How did Clark manage to turn Maher – a one-time best friend of Johnstone's – into a cowardly assassin, ready to shoot his old friend in the back of the head?

I mentioned earlier that the first time I met Andy Maher was in May 1978. That meeting was at Allison Dine's flat in Manly, Sydney, where I observed him, Clark and Dine crushing and bagging heroin. No doubt over the next eighteen months after I met him, Maher would have been able to observe who had the power, who had the money and who really controlled the Mr Asia syndicate. He would have realised that Johnstone was not the big boss; that person was Clark. It is a common human trait that subservient people tend to gravitate towards the person with the most power, the person with the most money. Maher was no different in that respect to many others of a similar ilk. Since he first met Johnstone in 1972 at a men's clothing store in Auckland, where they worked together, Maher had always been subordinate to Johnstone. No doubt since they first met and started working together selling cannabis in Auckland, Maher would have done a huge amount of Johnstone's dirty work. That factor alone can inspire resentment in a person. When you also factor in the disillusionment Maher would have felt at seeing his one-time friend squander money through bad investments and drug deals gone bad, then you have the fertile ground needed to plant the seeds for murder.

The final disillusionment for Maher would have come in late July 1979 during a trip to Thailand with Johnstone, ostensibly to source a new drug supplier for the organisation. A falling out between Chinese Jack Choo and Terry Clark seems to have been the catalyst for this decision to source a new supplier. The money to pay for the trip and the drugs – approximately $300,000 – had been given to Johnstone by Clark. Also in Thailand with Maher and Johnstone was Monique van Putten, Martin's married lady friend from Singapore. What she was doing there has got me beat as she was not part of the crew and, despite her saying otherwise, had no contacts in Thailand whatsoever. I guess she was there for moral support. According to her version of events which she later gave to police, shortly after arriving in Thailand the group moved on to Pattaya, a beach resort town, located on the coast a few hours' drive from Bangkok. If you are a foreign drug dealer looking to source drugs in Thailand for the first time, the sleazy, seedy resort town of Pattaya is one of the areas you are usually directed to.

While in Pattaya, Johnstone hooked up with some very nasty-looking, supposed Thai drug suppliers who absolutely terrified Monique van Putten. After sitting around Pattaya for a week with Maher – waiting for Johnstone to return from a quick trip to London to see Clark and obtain the money required to buy a large amount of heroin – van Putten told police she became very frustrated as Johnstone's absence meant she missed her wedding anniversary party which was being held in Singapore on 29 July. Van Putten told police that after a false start on 1 August, at around 8pm on 3 August, both she and Johnstone were taken to a house in Chonburi, some 15 kilometres from Pattaya, where they negotiated to buy a large amount of heroin from a group of Thai drug dealers. Those Thai drug dealers must have been salivating as they negotiated with Johnstone and van Putten, at the thought of robbing these two naive, trusting foreigners. As van Putten told police, on returning to the same house the following evening they were introduced to 'Uncle', the drug gang's boss. Unlike most Thais who are slimly built, this drug boss, she recalled, was short and very obese, somewhat like a Japanese Sumo wrestler. She also recalled the other three men in the room at the time had guns stuck in their belts. To my way of thinking, seeing three armed men in a room with you, especially while you were doing a drug deal, should have been cause to sprint for the nearest exit as fast as you could. Although van Putten says Johnstone was carrying a .45 automatic gun himself, he would have had, in my opinion, neither the expertise nor the willingness to use it. A gunman, Johnstone was not. Besides the armed men in the room, as soon as the Thai drug dealers insisted on seeing all Johnstone's money first, that should have set off alarm bells as well. To her credit, van Putten told police that she argued vehemently with Johnstone in front of the drug dealers against doing so. When you are as desperate as Johnstone was at that stage of his life, however, desperation can overrule common sense. That seems to have been the case with Johnstone, because according to van Putten, he told her to return to their hotel and bring the money required to do the deal back with her. As she recounted to police later, after dropping the money off to Johnstone, she became so fearful of the men driving her back to her hotel that when the car stopped at a set of lights on the outskirts of town, she jumped out and fled on foot, fully expecting to be shot as she ran for her life.

Her fears, she told the police later, were well founded, because around 4am the following morning, Johnstone stumbled into the room where she and Maher were waiting for him to tell them in a barely coherent voice how he had been ripped off. Evidently the Thai drug dealers had driven Johnstone around through deserted jungle roads until, on a particularly dark stretch of road, they had stopped.

According to Johnstone, their vehicle was then approached by a small van carrying three armed men. After opening the back door of the van to show Johnstone some packages sitting there, the men asked him to hand over his cash on the pretext of counting it. Like the proverbial dill, that is what a fearful Martin Johnstone did; he handed over his money to the Thai drug dealers. The heavily armed Thais then simply climbed back in their van, said 'Sayonara mug,' and drove off with his money, leaving a bewildered Johnstone standing on a deserted road in the middle of the jungle holding nothing but his dick in his hands.

From what van Putten then told police, after his arrival back at the hotel, Johnstone complained of a severe migraine, took a blanket off the bed and curled up on the floor in a foetal position and pulled the blanket over his head. She said she could see his body shaking under the blanket as he lay there. If he appeared terrified, he had good reason to be. In the ruthless world that drug dealers live in, losing large amounts of money that does not belong to you can get you killed very easily. Losing large amounts of money belonging to a merciless, psychopathic killer can not only get you killed very easily but also very quickly. That is what happened to Johnstone. Within two months of being ripped off in Thailand, his handless, mutilated body would be lying on a ledge 25 metres under water, in a abandoned stone quarry in Lancashire.

It is widely believed that after being ripped off in Pattaya, Johnstone, in desperation, cut the 700 gram sample of pure heroin he had been given by the Thai drug dealers before they robbed him and sent the cut heroin back to London with a drug courier they had on standby in Bangkok. The drug courier was a West Indian named Christopher Blackman who had been recruited by his two main drug dealers in London, an Englishman named Freddy Russell and his de facto wife Leila Barclay, to bring back what they expected would be a large amount of heroin. According to statements made by some of the accused before Clark's trial, Russell went ballistic when he realised the heroin sent back by Johnstone had been heavily cut with caster sugar. I have been led to believe that there were two lots of adulterated heroin passed on to Russell, causing him to complain long and loud about being ripped off to his new best friend, Terry Clark. My own inquiries have led me to the belief that Clark had a hand in passing on that adulterated heroin to Russell. Despite what many witnesses have said about Johnstone not contacting Clark after being ripped off in Pattaya, I have been told otherwise. For what it is worth, this is what I was told transpired.

In early August before we headed off together to Los Angeles, Clark received a call from Johnstone requesting his assistance. He told Clark that his main man in London – Freddy Russell – needed supplies urgently and could he help out by giving Freddy a kilo of heroin until he had some more money transferred over from Singapore? No doubt seeing an opportunity, Clark agreed. Although he owed Clark money, Johnstone had no reason to suspect his old business partner would not do the right thing by him. That was another bad mistake by Johnstone. I have been told the kilo of heroin given to Russell on Johnstone's behalf was not only severely cut by Clark, but also handed over to him as if it had come directly from Johnstone himself. When the predictable outburst from Russell about being ripped off came, an understanding Clark said that if required, he was ready to step into the breach and supply Freddy and his boys with all the A-grade heroin they needed. 'People who rip their friends off, do not deserve to live.' I have been told that those were Clark's exact words. I guess Johnstone's fate was sealed right there, even before we left for our trip to Los Angeles.

It just shows how far out of the loop I was back then, that it has taken me all these years to find out for myself what actually transpired before Johnstone was murdered in October 1979. Evidently, after Clark's return to London in late August 1979, a penitent Maher flew in from the Far East and confessed to Clark about Johnstone being ripped off in Thailand. A forgiving Clark absolved Maher from any blame for the debacle in Thailand. I have been told by someone who was close to Clark in London at that time that after Maher came clean about Johnstone being ripped off, Clark offered him a senior position working with him, the sole proviso being that he would have to cut all ties with Johnstone. Apparently Clark told Maher there was always room in his crew for a loyal person like him. I'm sure if he was still alive, Johnstone would have had something to say about that. Nevertheless, from the moment he accepted Clark's offer to join his team, the die was cast. Maher was now one of Clark's team and his old friend Johnstone was conveniently abandoned. With both Maher and Russell pledging their allegiance to Clark, Johnstone's fate was sealed.

In a very meaningful indication of how much Maher meant to Johnstone, his girlfriend Julie Hue later told police that the night before he was murdered, she walked into their bedroom and found him crying. When she asked him what he was crying about, he tearfully told her that Andy had just told him he was not going to work with him anymore, he was getting out of the business. The absolute fucking irony of those words still staggers me all these years later. Within 24 hours of saying those tearful words to his girlfriend, the man he was shedding tears over, Andrew Maher, would shoot him in the back of the head. The murder of Martin Johnstone by a man he believed was his best friend truly portrays how treacherous criminals can be. Those famous words written by Shakespeare in his play *Julius Caesar* are very apt here: 'Et tu, Brutus.'

On 9 October, the night he was murdered, Johnstone would have been excited. Visions of a successful comeback would have been running through his head. Despite having lost millions in bad investments – not to mention getting ripped off in Thailand for $300,000 – as well as owing a lot of money, redemption would have appeared close at hand to him. All he needed to do was meet two Scottish drug dealers face-to-face and he would be on the road to fame and fortune again. New drug markets in Scotland would have meant big money to him. Not far from where Andy Maher rented a Housing Corporation place on the Robin Hey estate in Leyland, in Lancashire, Martin Johnstone dropped off Julie Hue at her mother's house. After kissing her goodbye, he had told Julie that Barbara Pilkington, his old friend's de facto wife, would be around later to pick her up and take her back to Andy's place to spend the night. According to Julie Hue's later testimony, Johnstone's last words to her were: 'I will call you as soon as the business meeting in Scotland is over.' She never received that call and she never saw him alive again.

The trip north to Scotland that Tuesday evening on 9 October 1979 had earlier been delayed as the three men waited until a spare tyre for the car – an old Jaguar XJ6 – could be delivered from a local garage. While waiting for the spare tyre, Maher, James Smith and the doomed Johnstone, remained at Maher's house watching television and drinking red wine. Once the spare tyre arrived and after they dropped Julie Hue off, Maher, Smith and Johnstone headed off along the old A6 highway which runs through Lancaster and many other towns and villages, supposedly heading for Scotland. As he sat in the front seat of Maher's old Jaguar, Johnstone was casually dressed. According to police transcripts, he was wearing a beige pullover with stripes down the sleeves, blue cord pants, navy socks and tan sandals. In a brown zip-up suitcase he was carrying, he had packed a navy blue double-breasted pin-stripe suit, a blue silk shirt, another pair of white cord pants, a red cashmere polo neck sweater, shorts, a pair of black shoes as well as a pair of joggers and, finally, a squash racquet. On his left hand were a couple of rings – neither very expensive – around his neck was a Chinese medallion bearing the characters for good luck (obviously the medallion and the words inscribed on it, did not help Martin Johnstone); and around his wrist he was wearing the last indication of his once wealthy self, a gold Patek-Philippe watch valued at over £3000. In his pockets he had about £200. It was not much to show for a man who since 1973 had made millions through his drug dealing activities.

What happened next on that evening I have been able to ascertain from reading court transcripts, newspaper accounts from reporters who covered Clark's trial and a well-written and documented book called *Greed*, by the late Australian author Richard Hall. It is obvious from reading Richard Hall's book that he was given access to a lot of sensitive case files from police officers covering the case because he quotes directly from confidential interviews conducted by them. Util-ising research from Richard Hall's book and the police statements of Andrew Maher and James Smith, I have been able to gather a lot of information about Martin Johnstone's gruesome murder.

And gruesome it was. According to James Smith's statement of events on the evening of Tuesday 9 October 1979, it unfolded like this. About seven miles out of Lancaster, after passing through the village of Carnforth, they stopped at a lay-by not far past the village. Both Maher and Smith would later say they were unsure where the lay-by was but they remembered that it was not far past the village of Carnforth. As Smith would tell police, although he knew what his distant cousin was going to do – he did not actually think he would do it – he was absolutely shocked and horrified when he did. After pulling into the lay-by, Maher asked Johnstone if he wanted to drive. As soon as Martin agreed and started to get out of the car, Andy leant over from the driver's seat and shot him in the back of the head with a .38 calibre revolver. Although he was sitting in the back seat, Smith said he nearly shit himself as Johnstone fell onto the ground outside the car. He told police he could hear gurgling sounds coming from Johnstone as he lay on the ground. The gurgling sounds so unnerved Maher that after getting out of the car, he walked around and shot him again in the head. Smith told police he was in a state of shock as he helped his panic-stricken cousin pick up Johnstone's lifeless body and place it in the front passenger seat, which they laid back. 'It was fucking horrible,' he told police. 'Andy was screaming: "Shut the cunt up. Shut the cunt up." Even after I told Andy he was dead, he would not stop screaming.' The noises emanating from Johnstone's body so panicked him, Smith said, that he grabbed a knife from the car's dashboard and stabbed Johnstone in the stomach. After leaving the lay-by Smith said, they headed off back to Andy's house in Leyland, with Johnstone's blood-covered dead body lying on the front passen-ger seat. 'Before we could transfer the body to the boot of the car,' Smith later recounted: 'We actually saw two police cars while Martin's bloody body was still lying in the front seat.' Eventually, they found a quiet lane and transferred Johnstone's dead body into the car's boot.

'After we arrived back at Andy's house,' Smith later told police, 'we could see the lights were still on, so after dumping Martin's body in the garage, we drove around until we could be sure Julie had gone to sleep. Around 12.30am,' Smith said, 'Andy called the house to see if Julie had gone to bed yet.' After being told by Barbara Pilkington that Julie was still awake and waiting for a call from Martin, Andy suggested she tell her that Martin was unavailable and get her to go to bed. Smith told police that after calling the house again at 1am, they got the all-clear that Julie had gone to bed. What happened next would have sickened even someone like myself who was used to gratuitous violence.

According to James Smith, after stripping Johnstone's body of his clothes and jewellery in the garage, he could only watch in horror as his cousin, Andrew Maher, with great difficulty, chopped and hacked off both of Johnstone's hands with an axe and then placed them in a large envelope. As he freely confessed to police later, despite his two tours of army duty in strife-torn Belfast, he was not much use in helping his cousin with his gruesome, gory work. When his cousin asked him to smash in Johnstone's face with a hammer, he could not bring himself to do it and could only watch with revulsion as Andy – despite continually retching as he did so – put a jumper over Johnstone's face and using a large hammer, proceeded to smash his face beyond recognition. Before lashing over 150 pounds of lead weight to Johnstone's body, Smith said his cousin first wanted to empty the body of any gases that might allow it to float to the surface. After an initial unsuccessful attempt to open Johnstone's stomach with a spade, he was eventually able to do so using the axe. While all this grisly chopping, hacking, smashing and gutting of Martin Johnstone's body was going on in Andrew Maher's garage, his girlfriend Julie Hue was peacefully sleeping in the front room upstairs, blissfully unaware of the bloody carnage going on below.

The village of Eccleston is several miles from Andrew Maher's house. According to James Smith, after driving to the abandoned stone quarry called the Eccleston Delph, just outside Eccleston, they parked on the eastern bank and, after pulling Johnstone's weighted body out of the boot, managed to roll it into the water. As they both watched his weighted body disappear into the murky depths of Eccleston Delph, Smith later recalled to police that they both felt a huge sense of relief. After dumping the body, Smith said, they went back to Andy's garage, changed their bloodstained clothing, and set off for Scotland. On the way north to Scotland they stopped at an all-night garage to clean themselves up. Then, a little later, they stopped by a fast-flowing river and threw Johnstone's hands into it. The reason for the trip north to Scotland, Smith said, was to try and give themselves an alibi. That was the plan anyway.

Sometimes killing someone is the easy part, however, getting away with it is the hard part. Within two weeks, Johnstone's mutilated body would be discovered by two amateur divers; a 23-year-old motor mechanic named Jeffrey Ashcroft and his friend Ian Redding. While diving in the Delph in mid-October, the two friends had come upon what they thought was a dummy resting on a ledge 25 metres below the surface. On grabbing the legs of what they thought was a dummy, they were horrified when they realised the tubes trailing out of the dummy's stomach were in fact the insides from a dead person's stomach. On surfacing, they immediately called the Lancashire police. Martin Johnstone was about to reach out from his watery grave and claim all those responsible for his horrific death.

From the outset, Johnstone's murder had been poorly planned – and pardon the pun – poorly executed. To give some indication as to how amateurish they were, consider these facts. Before setting out on the evening of Tuesday, 9 October 1979 – the night they murdered Martin Johnstone – the witless distant cousins dropped his girlfriend Julie Hue off at her mother's house before continuing on with Johnstone on their murderous road trip. What did they think Julie Hue was going to tell the police when she realised he was missing? She would have told the police that the last time she saw Martin, he was heading to Glasgow with Andrew Maher and his cousin James Smith, in Andrew's car. This is an example of how constant drug use can affect your thinking and reasoning. Martin used to ring Julie religiously, three times a day, every day. By Wednesday evening, the next day, she would have been extremely worried about not receiving a single phone call from her beloved Martin. The murder was committed using Andrew Maher's own car, which is a definite no-no. After Maher shot and killed Johnstone, the bumbling duo had no idea what to do with the bloodstained car, the weapon used to shoot Johnstone, their bloodstained clothes or the other implements used in the murder. Although they chopped off Johnstone's hands after they murdered him so the police could not get fingerprints if the body was found, and smashed his face to make facial recognition difficult, they still left a very distinctive large Chinese good luck medallion hanging around his neck when they dumped his body. These two would-be killers left so many clues that even the hapless television character Mr Bean would have been able to track them down.

For me the most amazing aspect of Martin Johnstone's murder was that the police didn't find out about it before it was actually committed. I guess it is also a telling reflection on Johnstone's character that not one person who was aware he was about to be murdered thought enough of the man to warn him. The treachery shown by Johnstone's long-time friends towards him before he was murdered was sickening. The man he got started selling buddha sticks for him in New Zealand, Terry Clark, organised his murder. His one-time best friend and a man he shed tears over, Andrew Maher, carried out the murder. Andrew Maher's de facto wife, Barbara Pilkington, who had named her daughter Marti after Martin Johnstone and had enjoyed many shared holidays with him, knew he was about to be murdered yet did nothing. Freddy Russell, who supplied the gun used to shoot Martin Johnstone, had done business with and knew him very well, as did Russell's de facto wife Leila Barclay. Billy Kirby, who used to make suitcases for Johnstone and also knew him, brought an axe, rope and some weights used in the murder, as well as showing Maher where the Eccleston Delph was and suggesting it as the ideal place to dump a body. Sy Pigeon, Clark's chauffeur, who knew Johnstone, got his daughter to deliver a package containing the gun that was used to shoot him to Andrew Maher at his house on the Robin Hey estate in Leyland. James Smith, the ex-Scot's Guardsman who was with Andrew Maher when he murdered Martin Johnstone, had met Johnstone but did not know him that well. By my reckoning that is eight people who not only knew Johnstone, but were aware at the time that he was about to be murdered. That is why it is a wonder the police never got wind of his imminent murder. If even two people know you have committed a murder, you have a serious problem. If eight people know you have committed such a crime, you may as well go down to the police station now and hand yourself in, because as sure as I'm typing this sentence, the forces of law and order will nail you.

As if eight people knowing about Johnstone's death were not enough, after his murder Maher and Smith decided to add a few more people to the list. The more the merrier, seemed to be their motto. A friend of Smith, another ex-Scots Guardsman named Kingsley Fagan, who had been recruited by Smith as a potential drug courier prior to Johnstone's murder, was delegated to help him get rid of Maher's bloodstained car. Instead of dumping the car as he had been instructed to do by his cousin, Smith and his friend Fagan drove around in it for two weeks so that Smith could impress his local neighbourhood with his new-found prosperity. The discovery of Johnstone's body in mid-October forced Smith to act. For the measly sum of £200, Fagan was given the job to dump the car. Showing a distinct lack of imagination about where to abandon the car, Fagan drove a short distance to the local railway station at Airdrie and left the car there. After seeing the abandoned car sitting at the railway station for two days, alert local police patrolling the area checked the numberplates of the car and up came Maher's name, thus proving another old adage true: 'If you want something done properly, you had better do it yourself.'

The only two items from the murder that Smith did follow instructions and get rid of were the car's bloodstained seat covers and the revolver. He threw the seat covers and the revolver into the water at an abandoned quarry in Blackrigg a few days after the murder.

His friend Fagan had showed this particular quarry to him. Instead of throwing away Johnstone's gold Patek-Philippe watch, Smith and Fagan contacted an antique dealer named Alexander McAuley at his home in Airdrie on the Sunday following Johnstone's murder with the aim of selling the watch to him. After first offering to sell him the watch for £400, they accepted £200 from McAuley and promptly went off to celebrate their windfall with a slap-up dinner for both of them and Fagan's father. The pair also gifted Fagan's father with Johnstone's expensive burgundy leather attache case. The spoils of treachery.

On the Friday after the murder, Bill Kirby told police he received a call from Maher asking him to come down and meet him in Leyland. After meeting Maher, Kirby said he accompanied him out to his house on the Robin Hey estate. According to Kirby, it was the first time that Maher had revisited the murder site. He was a mess, Kirby later recounted to police. The guy was shaking and fearful about the blood still splattered all around the garage. In his statement to police, Kirby said that when he saw all the blood in the garage, he nearly panicked and shit himself as well. Despite his revulsion, however, he managed to maintain control of himself and cleaned up the garage. After cleaning the garage, Kirby and Maher packed all the bloodstained clothing into a box. Along with the clothing they placed a bloodstained coil of rope, a sheet of polythene, an axe and a lump hammer – both implements still stained with blood – into the box as well. From Maher's house, Kirby told police, they travelled over to his father's house in nearby Preston. Kirby's father, an unemployed painter, agreed to burn all the rubbish for them at his house. Before burning the rubbish, however, Bill Kirby senior told police he could not help himself and looked inside the box. He said that he panicked when he saw all the bloodstained clothes as he thought his son might have killed his wife. Although his son later assured him the dead person was someone else and not his wife, he had remained extremely concerned because his son's friend, Maher, had come around a few days after he burnt the bloodstained clothes to give him a veiled warning. Bill Kirby senior told police that Maher had said to him in a threatening voice: 'If you know what's good for you, you will not say anything about what you have done for us.' The implied threat did not have much affect because Bill Kirby senior, being a frugal man, had decided the axe and lump hammer were useful tools and had not destroyed them as instructed. I'm sure the police who later questioned Bill Kirby senior were also delighted that he had not destroyed that axe and lump hammer because both implements were later used as vital evidence in Clark's murder trial!

From all the information I have read about her, Julie Hue, Martin Johnstone's girlfriend at the time he was murdered, was not particularly bright. I cannot remember meeting the lady while I was in London, so I can only go on what others have said about her. That Maher and Barbara Pilkington were able to keep her quiet for two weeks with lie after lie whenever she asked where Martin was, definitely gives credence to the assumption that she was very gullible. To keep her preoccupied, Maher sent Julie and his de facto wife over to Benidorm in Spain where his father had a small bar. The trip was ostensibly to help Maher's father run the bar. The real purpose of the trip, however, was to get Julie Hue away from reading any of the English newspapers that were giving extensive coverage to the mutilated body found in an abandoned quarry in Lancashire. Like most half-arsed plans, this one failed miserably, because on her 23rd birthday on 21 October, Julie Hue did something she rarely did back in England; she picked up an English newspaper and read it. Featured prominently in the paper was a story about the mutilated body found in an abandoned quarry at Eccleston Delph in Lancashire. The disturbing and most distressing part of the newspaper story for Julie Hue, was the description of the Chinese good luck medallion found around the corpse's neck. When she voiced her fears to Barbara Pilkington that the unidentified body found in a Lancashire quarry might be her beloved Martin whom she had not heard from in two weeks, she was shocked at the response she got.

As she told police later, after confronting Barbara Pilkington with the newspaper article, Barbara broke down in tears and proceeded to tell her what had happened to Martin. According to Julie Hue, Pilkington was insistent that her de facto husband had been coerced into killing his best friend by his fear of Terry Clark. Pilkington was adamant, Julie Hue said, that Clark had threatened to kill Andrew's family if he did not murder Martin. From what Julie Hue told police, it seems the women spent the next two days discussing what to do before irrationally deciding to commit suicide together. Fortunately for them, but unfortunately for Clark and all the others who later stood trial with him, the sleeping pills Julie Hue and Barbara Pilkington took were not overly strong. As a consequence of this significant oversight, all the delusional pair got for their inept suicide attempts was a deep sleep followed by two days of walking around in an incoherent state.

While all this drama was being played out in Benidorm, Terry Clark and Errol Hincksman were going through their own form of madness back in London. A week prior to Julie Hue's birthday, Clark won £16,000 gambling at Ladbrokes casino. On 18 October, Clark celebrated his gambling win by buying a XJS Jaguar, which he registered in the name of Aaron Stevens, the false name Hincksman was travelling under at that time. In an eerie sequence of events, on the same day that Julie Hue discovered Martin Johnstone had been murdered – 21 October – Hincksman was pulled over in the south coast town of Bexhill-on-Sea, driving Clark's second London car, a late model dark blue Mercedes. Because of his appearance – a sinister-looking bearded man driving a flash Mercedes – purely on suspicion, local police pulled him over. A search of the car revealed a small amount of marijuana in the glove compartment, a passport in the name of Aaron Stevens and inside a suitcase located on the back seat, a passport bearing the name Choo Cheng Kui. Evidently Chinese Jack had been visiting Clark in London to try and sort out their differences and Hincksman had been on his way to meet him. From what Chinese Jack later told me while we were in prison together at Sydney's Long Bay Remand Centre, he was not a happy camper after having to go to the local police station at Bexhill-on-Sea to retrieve his passport. An interesting footnote to my conversations with Chinese Jack back then was his confirming the stories about Clark and all his cohorts running out of control in London. It was barely a week after Chinese Jack Choo left London for Singapore that Clark was arrested.

After Errol Hincksman's brush with the law at Bexhill-on-Sea, you would have thought that incident would have caused Clark to be extra careful himself. But that did not prove to be the case. A few days after Hincksman was released on bail, Clark was arrested himself on drink-driving charges after crashing his new Jaguar in the London suburb of Kentish Town. While driving back to London after spending a few days together at his sister's farm, Clark and Karen Soich stopped at several pubs on the return trip and had a few drinks. Evidently Clark's erratic driving after the drinks got so bad that Soich argued with him continuously most of the way back to London. While travelling through south London, she became so alarmed and angry that when they stopped at a traffic light, she jumped out of the car and started walking. Not knowing the streets of London that well, Clark got lost and ended up crashing his car in Kentish Town. When police from the Kentish Town police station detained and searched Clark, they found a passport on him bearing the name Alexander Sinclair and several thousand pounds in his pockets. A drunken, unshaven man with limited identification, driving an XJS Jaguar and with several thousand pounds in his pockets would be enough to make even Constable Plod suspicious. The Kentish Town police officers were no different. They were so suspicious of Clark that they accompanied him back to his Stafford Court address, where he was able to allay their suspicions a little by producing more documentation in the name of Sinclair. Despite letting Clark go, the Kentish Town police impounded his car while further inquiries were carried out.

If Clark's thought processes hadn't been so affected by his constant cocaine use, he would have packed up and left London immediately after the police released him. The mere fact that he did not do so proves conclusively that he was incapable of making rational decisions at the time of his arrest. The discovery of Martin Johnstone's body in Lancashire, Errol Hincksman's arrest in Bexhill-on-Sea, plus his own arrest in Kentish Town should have been clear warning signs to him that it was time to move on. He did not move on, however, and the rest, as they say, is history. His last few days of freedom were spent in a constant whirl of cocaine, drinking and gambling. The sinking ship called the Mr Asia syndicate was nearly under the waves; it would take a Jehovah's Witness to finally sink it.

On Sunday 28 October, a penitent Barbara Pilkington and a grieving Julie Hue flew back to London, where they stayed overnight at Pilkington's mother's house. While in London, a remorseful Barbara Pilkington rang Andrew Maher, who was back in Singapore, to tell him she did not love him anymore. According to Pilkington, during the course of the phone call, Monique van Putten got on the phone and admonished her by saying how much it had hurt Andrew to have to kill his best friend. I guess the obvious retort to that ridiculous statement would have been, not as much as it hurt Martin Johnstone, dear lady. From the comments van Putten made during the phone call, we can confidently assume that Andrew Maher had told her while he was in Singapore about what had happened to Martin Johnstone. By my reckoning, van Putten made twelve people who were aware that Andrew Maher had killed Martin Johnstone. For Terry Clark, Andrew Maher and the ten others who would later stand in the dock with them, it would be the thirteenth person – unlucky for some – who would finally notify the police about what she had been told concerning Martin Johnstone's murder.

The day after arriving back in London, Julie Hue and Barbara Pilkington travelled back to Leyland, Lancashire, where they stayed the night at Julie Hue's mother's house. A devout Jehovah's Witness, Julie Hue's mother, Claire Hatch, was a deeply religious, law-abiding woman. During the course of the evening, both her daughter and Barbara Pilkington unburdened themselves to her about the details of Martin Johnstone's gruesome murder. It did not take long for this moralistic woman to act. In the early hours of the morning, she rang the Lancashire police to inform them of what her daughter and Barbara Pilkington had told her. By 6am of that morning, local detectives were listening as both women gave them all the grisly details about Johnstone's murder, including the identity of the man who murdered him, why he murdered him and the names of all those they suspected of being involved with him.

As soon as the Lancashire police were given this vital information about who had been involved in Martin Johnstone's murder, they took immediate and decisive action. Sometimes the forces of law and order are accused of being too slow in arresting suspects, but that was certainly not the case with the Lancashire police investigating Johnstone's murder. At 8.15am that morning, Maher was the first person arrested as he stepped off a flight from Singapore at Heathrow Airport. By 11am, Bill Kirby had been arrested. Ex-Scot's Guardsman James Smith was arrested late that afternoon. A senior Lancashire police officer – Detective Chief Inspector Peter Newhouse – travelled up to London that same afternoon to consult with his Scotland Yard colleagues about arresting Terry Clark. After putting Clark's Stafford Court address under surveillance overnight; rather than trying to smash in the steel-reinforced front door, the police instead smashed in the weaker rear back door the following morning. A drug affected Clark was then arrested in his bedroom at his Stafford Court address, along with a shocked Karen Soich.

I did not know Martin Johnstone well enough to comment on his personal life, but there is one aspect about what happened to Martin that I feel very strongly about. Despite his shortcomings, despite the money he owed, Martin Johnstone did not deserve to die like he did.

34

TIME TO PAY

By 5 November, at the Chorley Magistrates' Court, police had enough evidence to charge Terry Clark – who was still using the Alexander Sinclair name – Andrew Maher, James Smith, Bill Kirby and Freddy Russell with murder, conspiracy to murder, and conspiracy to contravene the provisions of the *Misuse of Drugs Act 1971*. Errol Hincksman, Karen Soich, Leila Barclay and her son Jack Barclay were charged with conspiracy to contravene the provisions of the *Misuse of Drugs Act 1971*. The last three men charged – Kingsley Fagan, Charles Blackman and Sy Pigeon – all faced different conspiracy charges. None were granted bail.

After a heavily guarded committal hearing which began on 19 May 1980 at the Chorley Magistrates' Court before Manchester City Stipendiary Magistrate Mr John Coffee, QC, all the accused were committed for trial. The only three accused granted bail at the completion of the committal hearing were Jack Barclay, Sy Pigeon and

Karen Soich. It would take Karen Soich's parents three weeks before they could finally arrange her £75,000 bail surety. The judge who would preside over their trial, Justice Heilbron, in early July set down 5 January 1981 as the trial date.

On that day, in the Gothic surrounds of the Lancaster Crown Court, which had been constructed inside an old castle built there in the 1700s, their trial before Justice Heilbron began. At the time of their trial, Justice Rose Heilbron was one of the most prominent and accomplished female jurists in England. It was the considered opinion of many reporters and interested observers at the time that Justice Heilbron leant over backwards to ensure that all the accused got a fair trial. As strange as it may seem, if you are an accused person, a fair judge can hurt you if perchance you are found guilty. This anomaly occurs because a fair judge usually leaves an accused with no grounds to appeal their guilty verdict. That was certainly the case here.

During the course of the trial, the Crown presented a strong case of direct and circumstantial evidence. Just as damning for many of the accused were their own incriminating statements they made to police while being interviewed. The combination of a strong prosecution case as well as their own culpability, meant after a trial lasting 121 days, the jury came back with unanimous verdicts. Terry Clark was found guilty on three counts of murder and two drug conspiracy charges. Both James Smith and Bill Kirby were convicted of their murder charges. Errol Hincksman was convicted of his drug conspiracy charges as were Sy Pigeon and the West Indian, Charles Blackman. While the trial was in progress, three of the accused – Andrew Maher, Freddy Russell and Leila Barclay – all pleaded guilty to their respective charges. Only Jack Barclay and Karen Soich were found by the jury to be not guilty of all charges against them.

Two days after the guilty verdicts were handed down, Justice Heilbron began the lengthy process of sentencing all the accused. Deeming Terry Clark an evil man, she sentenced him to life imprisonment, with a minimum term of 22 years. Andrew Maher, despite his guilty plea, was given a similar sentence. His accomplice on the night he murdered Martin Johnstone, James Smith, was given a life sentence with no stipulated amount of time to serve. Both Freddy Russell and Bill Kirby received a similar sentence. Leila Barclay was given a particularly harsh sentence of thirteen years on her drug charges. On his drug charges, Errol Hincksman was sentenced to ten years. The hapless West Indian courier, Charles Blackman, and Clark's chauffeur, Sy Pigeon, were each sentenced to five years' imprisonment on their charges.

After Justice Heilbron finished sentencing the last of the accused on 15 July 1981, I think it would be fair comment to say that on that day, the Mr Asia syndicate officially ceased to exist. For law enforcement officers and criminal historians, a bloody and violent part of New Zealand, Australian and English criminal history also ended that day. As I stated earlier, the impact and the irony of Martin Johnstone's murder has never been lost on me. It was his buddha sticks and money that breathed life into the Mr Asia syndicate and it was his brutal murder that ultimately destroyed it. As I have said on more than one occasion in this book . . . life can indeed be stranger than fiction!

What may have happened to Terry Clark after he started serving the sentence imposed on him by Justice Heilbron only highlights that sentiment. It would be remiss of me if I did not address some of the mystery surrounding Clark's sudden death in an English prison in August 1983. I learnt about Clark's death while I was sitting in a diner having breakfast in a small town called Novato, located in Marin County about 50 kilometres out from San Francisco. While perusing a local newspaper, I was intrigued by an article in the paper that had the headline 'Drug Kingpin Dies in Prison'. Although brief, the article was about Clark's death in Parkhurst Prison, on the Isle of Wight. Included in the article was a short summary of Clark's past and the information that he had died of a heart attack. As I read the article that morning, I cannot say that I shed a tear or was saddened by the news. On the contrary, I just felt that the door to a shameful period of my life had finally closed. I could not help but think as I read that article; karma has a way of catching up with you, even in prison. My karma caught up with me in the NSW Supreme Court in Sydney, when on a cold, wet June day in 1986, I was sentenced to 25 years' imprisonment for my involvement with the Mr Asia syndicate.

To satisfy my own curiosity about Clark's death I decided to make a few inquiries both in Australia and England. While making my enquiries I was told by two different sources that Clark's death had resulted from an escape attempt gone wrong. According to my sources, Clark had a drug smuggled into the prison that, when taken, would induce suspected heart attack symptoms. The idea being that a suspected heart attack would see him transferred from escape-proof Parkhurst Prison on the Isle of Wight to a hospital back on mainland England, thus making it much easier to mount an escape attempt. Unfortunately, my sources told me, the drug he took to simulate a heart attack actually induced a real heart attack in Clark that killed him. For many years I believed this is what happened to Clark. I now think differently and comments attributed to retired Justice DG Stewart are the reason why.

It is no secret that Justice Stewart who presided over the Royal Commission into the Mr Asia syndicate has always suspected that Terry Clark was murdered in his prison cell at Parkhurst Prison. From what I have been able to ascertain, Justice Stewart came to this conclusion through access he had to Clark's official autopsy report. Evidently the autopsy report showed that Clark's heart had literally exploded, possibly from enormous pressure being placed on his body. Justice Stewart's belief that Clark was murdered invariably leads us to ask questions. If he was murdered, who did it? And if so, why? After making discreet inquiries overseas, I have come up with a few interesting conclusions.

While Clark was on remand, he is reputed to have made careless statements in a newspaper article about having done business with the IRA involving drugs. The IRA back in those days used to get most of their funds from supporters in the United States and could not be seen – even if it were true – to be doing business with drug dealers. I have been told that members of the IRA took offence at what Clark said and later arranged through criminal associates inside Parkhurst Prison to kill him. I have been led to believe that a group of prisoners – with prison officers on duty turning a blind eye to what was happening – were able to run into Clark's cell and, using mattresses, smother him on his bed. The pressure from all the weight on him is what caused his heart to burst like it did. I ran this scenario past a doctor friend of mine and he told me that theory was very feasible, and that could indeed cause someone's heart to burst like Clark's did. When Clark was found dead in his cell in August 1983 there was only one organisation in the world with the will, the connections and the ability to reach inside a maximum security prison and murder someone if they wanted to. That organisation was the IRA, and that is why I have changed my mind about how I think Clark died. Whether that supposition is right or not, it sure sounds a lot more interesting and intriguing than having someone say he died of a plain, old everyday heart attack.

However Terry Clark died, we can safely say he left a terrible trail of death, violence and drug addiction behind him. There is no doubt in my mind that Terrence John Clark will be remembered by future crime historians as the man who set in motion all the heroin-related crime we see today. Terry Clark's main ambition after he came out of Wi Tako Prison was to be a successful, big-time criminal. For a few years, between 1976 and 1979, he achieved that distorted ambition. But like many, many ambitious criminals before him, his time at the top was brief. A cold and lonely prison cell in Parkhurst Prison on the Isle of Wight is not a glamorous place in which to end your life.

EPILOGUE

So there it is, the plain, unvarnished, unpleasant story about the rise and fall of the Mr Asia syndicate. If you remember, I said at the start of this book that stories about murderous drug dealers are never pleasant. When I wrote that, I should have also added that they never have happy endings. I think you the reader will agree that what happened to all the main players involved in the Mr Asia syndicate is a salutary lesson to anyone contemplating a life of crime. We all paid extremely harsh penalties for our involvement with the syndicate. Some paid with their lives, while many paid with long prison sentences.

The only ones to escape legal retribution were the twenty or more individuals who gave evidence at the Royal Commission presided over by Justice DG Stewart and were granted indemnities from prosecution by him. Those individuals were the only ones involved with the Mr Asia syndicate who managed to slither off into the sunset, unscathed and unpunished. Although I could not bring myself to join them, I do not hold it against any of them for saving themselves. A free ticket on the last train out of Dodge is very hard for anyone to turn down.

Even though all those indemnified witnesses may have escaped unscathed and unpunished from their involvement with the Mr Asia syndicate, for me personally that was not the case. Writing this book has been a cathartic and disturbing exercise for me. It has made me revisit, sometimes painfully, many of the episodes in my life that I am not proud of. Many suppressed memories have been laid bare and that is never a pleasant experience for anyone. I do not mind saying I have had more than a few sleepless nights while writing this book. The ghosts from my past are never far away and they continue to haunt me still. I fear I will have to take them and my many painful memories with me to my grave.

It was not until I started writing this book that I began to fully comprehend for the first time the sheer totality of all the death and violence associated with the Mr Asia syndicate. That may seem like a strange statement coming from someone who was an integral part of all that criminal activity, but writing this book has made me confront and acknowledge for the very first time just how much murder and violence was associated with the Mr Asia syndicate. I guess subconsciously, over the years, I have tried to suppress my memories of just how vicious, nasty and violent we all were. It has not been easy looking back at my past.

When you are personally involved in a group like the Mr Asia syndicate, you do not get a true perspective of all the criminality that is happening around you. The number of people murdered while involved with the group, the number of people who died through being associated with the group, and the number of lengthy prison terms handed out to members of the group has staggered me. By any quantitative measure, I do not think there has ever been, in the history of Australian and New Zealand crime, any group or criminal enterprise that comes even close to the Mr Asia syndicate for the level of violence inflicted on members of a group or the subsequent lengthy prison terms handed out to members of that group.

Although there were far more people murdered during the Melbourne gangland wars that ran through the 1990s until the early 2000s, those murders were all committed by different gangs and different people for differing reasons. The man associated with arranging many of the killings – Carl Williams – was the only person from his team who received a lengthy prison term; and I might add, all that crime happened in Victoria, Australia. By contrast, the Mr Asia syndicate operated in New Zealand, Australia, Fiji, Singapore, Hong Kong, Malaysia, Thailand and the United Kingdom. No doubt one day an aspiring young criminologist will do a case study of the Mr Asia syndicate and will come up with the appalling facts about what befell many of the people associated with the group. Let us take a dispassionate look at those facts.

I will not detail the uncorroborated murders Terry Clark told me about while we were having lunch at Eliza's restaurant in March 1978 but just list what we do know is fact. In September 1977, Terry Clark murdered Greg Ollard and Julie Theilman. In May 1978 Terry Clark murdered Harry Lewis. In April 1979, Doug and Isobel Wilson were murdered in Victoria, on Clark's orders. In October 1979, Andrew Maher murdered Martin Johnstone because Clark wanted him dead. In December 1980, unknown persons murdered Brian Alexander because he knew the corrupt police officers who supplied information to the Mr Asia syndicate. Bob Trimbole died in Spain while on the run for his alleged connections to the Mr Asia syndicate and other crimes. Terry Clark died a few years after entering prison in England to serve his lengthy prison term. By my count that is nine people associated with the Mr Asia syndicate who were either murdered or died from other causes. Now let us look at the living.

In Lancashire, Terry Clark was sentenced to life imprisonment with a recommendation that he serve a minimum 22 years. Andrew Maher received a similar sentence of life imprisonment with a minimum 22 years to be served. James Smith, William Kirby and Freddy Russell all received sentences of life imprisonment. Leila Barclay was sentenced to thirteen years' imprisonment. Errol Hincksman received ten years' imprisonment. Charles Blackman and Sy Pigeon each received five years' imprisonment. In Sydney, on a charge of conspiracy to import heroin, I was sentenced to 25 years' imprisonment. Chinese Jack Kui was sentenced at the same time to twenty years with a non-parole period of fourteen years. An associate of the group in Sydney, Hans Czajkowski, was also sentenced to eight years' imprisonment on supply charges. In Melbourne, Darryl Sorby was sentenced to twenty years with a fourteen year non-parole period. In Auckland, Peter Fulcher was sentenced to fourteen years' imprisonment. After the dust finally settled on all these sentences, fourteen people, in three different countries had been sentenced to lengthy prison terms for their involvement with the Mr Asia syndicate. Nine people dead and fourteen people in prison serving lengthy terms of imprisonment. Now that's what I call an open and shut case for anyone wanting to argue that crime does not pay.

Although there has been more heartache in my life since I was released from prison, this book covers the first 38 years of my life up until my departure for the United States in November 1979. My story has been incidental to the real purpose for writing this book. This book was written to reveal for the first time the true story of how the Mr Asia syndicate came into being and the people involved in the group. I hope I have achieved that objective. It was also written to highlight to any young people aspiring to a life of crime the misery, suffering, anguish, degradation and shame waiting for them and their loved ones if they follow such a path. Take it from someone who reached the top of the mountain, the view from the top is not worth the violence required to get there, or the brutality needed to stay there. There will always be people who think that crime does pay but I am not one of them. Crime does not pay, it never has and never will.

As I have looked back over my life, the one overwhelming realisation I have is what a senseless waste of so many good years. I have spent 50 years of my life either in prison, trying to stay one step ahead of the law, or trying to survive in a world where murder and violence are accepted as a way of life. It has taken me a lifetime of heartache to finally realise that no amount of illicit money is worth the spending of even one day of your life behind bars. I know I deeply regret the grief, distress, unhappiness and shame I have brought on my family and loved ones. Sadly, no matter how hard I try, I cannot undo the past, I can only learn to live with it.

Perhaps the best way for me to end this book is to quote a quatrain from a translated book of poetry written in the twelfth century by a Persian poet and philosopher named Omar Khayyám that I read while in prison. The book was called *The Rubayait of Omar Khayyám* and the quatrain goes like this:

> The moving finger writes
> And having writ moves on.
> Nor all thy piety nor wit,
> Shall lure it back to cancel half a line,
> Nor all thy tears
> Wash away a word of it.